Sensitive to the diversities of comedy in both drama and fiction, Professor Gurewitch not only challenges existing views of comedy, but offers in their place a firm theoretical framework of his own.

MORTON GUREWITCH is Associate Professor of English at State University of New York College at Cortland. He has also taught at Brown University. A graduate of the City College of New York, he received the M.A. and Ph.D. degrees from Columbia University. Professor Gurewitch is now at work on a study of literature and the ironic imagination.

COMEDY

THE IRRATIONAL VISION

COMEDY

THE IRRATIONAL VISION

MORTON GUREWITCH

CORNELL UNIVERSITY PRESS
ITHACA AND LONDON

International Standard Book Number 0–8014–0843–1
Library of Congress Catalog Card Number 74–15186
Printed in the United States of America by Kingsport Press, Inc.

FOR MICHELINE

Contents

Preface

Although comedy is often generated by the forces of civilized sanity and searching criticism, it is also activated, perhaps just as often, by a drive to celebrate irrationalism. In this book, as the subtitle indicates, my aim is to focus on comedy's interest in illogic and irreverence, in disorder and disinhibition. But this stress is not meant to suggest that comedy is especially oriented toward antic anarchy. The energies of comedy are too diverse to permit procrustean interpretations.

One can distinguish as many as four major components of comedy: satire, which can range from demonic mockery to mild castigation; humor, which either copes with disaster or thrives on whimsy and joy; farce, which is balmily innocuous at one extreme and madly outrageous at the other; and irony, which reveals a cluster of attitudes centering on the absurd. Wit, incidentally, is the servant of all four masters, though it is usually associated with satire and irony.

The distinctions among these four elements of comedy may be briefly clarified by noting the manner in which each handles folly. Traditional satire excoriates folly, finding it ridiculous but also corrigible. Humor seeks, not to expunge folly, but to condone and even to bless it, for humor views folly as endearing, humanizing, indispensable. Farce also accepts folly as indispensable, but only because folly promises delightful annihilations of restraint. Finally, irony sees folly as an emblem of

9

eternal irrationality, to be coolly anatomized and toyed with. The present book considers all four powers of comedy, but it is devoted especially to farce.

Because the bond between comedy and irrationality is my primary theme (in fiction as well as in drama), I make a more than casual use of Freud's thinking on this matter. In various sections of this book Freud's ideas provide both a point of departure and a line of continuity. Nevertheless, Freudian relevancies on the subject of wit, humor, nonsense, and farce do not overburden the text.

A word about the organization of the book. I start with an analysis of a number of theories of comedy, in "The Heart of Lightness." I then go on to deal more particularly with Freud's views, in "Cynical Wit" and "Truth, Humor, and Nonsense," with the latter chapter functioning above all as a bridge between the comedy of ideas and the idea of irrationalist comedy. My last two chapters, "The Imagination of Farce" and "From Demonic Laughter to Magic Buffoonery," concentrate on the most invigorating and irresponsible mode of irrationalist comedy.

MORTON GUREWITCH

Skaneateles, New York

COMEDY

THE IRRATIONAL VISION

I

The Heart of Lightness

Comedy is a miscellaneous genre activated by a plurality of impulses: farce, humor, satire, and irony. These four impulses, which may be distinguishable foes or natural allies, are of course unequally represented in specific comedies. Yet their palpable presence in comic literature makes it hazardous to declare that comedy has a single meaning. Nor is it much safer to vouch for a dualistic design in comedy. For example, the suggestion that comedy may be divided into a Latin tradition of ridicule (satire) and an Anglo-Saxon tradition of geniality (humor) simply disregards, or minimizes, the zaniness of farce and the skepticism of the ironic temper.

How have the theorists managed so often to make comedy a unitary entity? Consider, to begin with, two theories that deal with the largest and the smallest (presumptive) evidences of comic dynamism accessible to human experience and imagination. These are the theories of Joseph Campbell, who sees comedy in the farthest reaches of the cosmos, and Suzanne Langer, who sees comedy even in the microscopic dimensions of the amoeba. First, Joseph Campbell. In *The Hero with a Thousand Faces*, Campbell offers the demoralized man of our era the magic of myth, which he defines as "the secret opening through which the inexhaustible energies of the cosmos pour into human cultural manifestation."[1] These energies are also dis-

[1] Joseph Campbell, *The Hero with a Thousand Faces* (New York: Meridian, 1956), p. 3.

coverable in the depths of the human unconscious, which sprouts golden seeds and harbors thaumaturgic genies who can be prevailed upon to expand life's potentialities. This kind of expansion is especially characteristic of the "monomythic" hero, whose career is quintessentially "comic." That is to say, his adventures (his triumphs over the ordeals of life and the defacements of death) are redeemingly and joyously constructive.

As Campbell puts it in his chapter "Tragedy and Comedy," the mythological hero travels "the dark interior way from tragedy to comedy" (from disintegration to resurrection) in order to rediscover "long lost, forgotten powers . . . to be made available for the transfiguration of the world. This deed accomplished, life . . . becomes penetrated by an all-suffering, all-sustaining love. . . . The dreadful mutilations [of time] are then seen as shadows, only, of an immanent, imperishable eternity" (p. 29). Tragedy comprises only the first half of the mythological experience; comedy, being a "transcendence of the universal tragedy of man" (p. 28), constitutes the other and more significant half.

But is Campbell's cosmic comedy relevant to literary comedy? Not especially. The positing of a golden, Jungian unconscious is useless, for example, in the analysis of farce, which customarily involves the conflict between instinct and culture (and is therefore best explicable as the comedy of the Freudian id). A Jungian unconscious can support comedies of divine harmony, to be sure, but these are infrequent literary commodities. In any event, Campbell mentions no literary comedies at all, whether secular or divine. He does, however, touch on the question of literary values. He is perfectly aware that the happy ending of myth, fairy tale, and redemptive religion seems to be an inappropriate paradigm for modern literary reality, which, he admits, has rightly refused to gloss over life's disfiguring ugliness. But though its repudiation of fraudulent optimism is valuable, and its facing-up to democratized (that is, sordid) tragedy and ironic unfulfillment is courageous, Campbell believes that modern literature has become sick, owing to its drastic denial of myth—of the ultimate reality that a universal happy ending does genuinely underlie the terrors of existence. In Campbell's view, the tragic mystery of dismemberment has evolved into an addiction to disaster, and the banishment of false happy endings has led to a perverse refusal of joy.

Yet one must insist that literary comedy does not particularly thrive on intimations of beatitude; nor does it have much recourse to mythic certitudes. For every comedy that hints at a blissful serenity beyond the grasp of reason and experience, there are hundreds that project not an iota of cosmic blitheness. Such comedies may of course (and often do) give one a final sense of concord or unity; but this feeling is not a surrogate for cosmic blessings. Besides, a comedy may end in an aura of benevolence and solidarity and yet be mainly subversive or even demonic.

If the monomythic concept of comedy is imperfectly commensurable with literary realities, one would imagine that a theory of comedy which emphasizes the vigor of the human body and the power of the human brain would be far more promising for the purposes of literary analysis. Such a biological theory has been developed by Suzanne Langer in "The Comic Rhythm," a chapter in *Feeling and Form*. It is Langer's conviction that the invigoration of organic processes, "the pure sense of life,"[2] is the touchstone of comedy. Whereas the tragic rhythm of life signifies ultimate organic destruction at the hands of Destiny, the comic rhythm of life signalizes equilibrium, resurgence, and episodic continuity amid the hazards of Fortune. The comic protagonist, by virtue of his bodily gusto and "brainy opportunism," is able to squash the threats of imbalance and harm that face him in "an essentially dreadful universe" (p. 331).

The logic of Langer's vitalistic view, based as it is on an unimpeachable urge to life enhancement by means of animal confidence and an all-out dexterity of mind, necessarily divorces comedy from morality. The major drives of Langer's comic protagonist must inevitably promote a forceful, unsaintly an-

[2] Suzanne Langer, *Feeling and Form: A Theory of Art* (New York: Scribner's, 1953), p. 327.

archy of survival and success. Yet Langer tries to establish both a social (and even moral and religious) and antisocial frame of reference for her theory. Comedy, she states, "is at once religious and ribald, knowing [?] and defiant, social and freakishly individual" (p. 331). But since organic movement, as Langer informs us, betrays an aggressive and even murderous streak ("All life feeds on life"), the "deep cruelty" (p. 349) of the comic rhythm compels an acknowledgment of the overwhelmingly antisocial and immoralist nature of the comic protagonist, who will subvert whatever manners and morals threaten to hamstring his rogue's progress. Langer herself best illuminates this point by observing that what counts in comedy is "not moral distinctions and issues, but only the ways of wisdom and folly" (p. 345).

Is the comic protagonist's sexual vitality at the heart of the comic rhythm? Not according to Langer. Though she states at one point that it is in the nature of comedy "to be erotic, risqué . . . impious, and even wicked" (p. 349), and though she concedes that sexuality is the very symbol of organic continuity, she quite consciously steers away from the commonly held anthropological belief that comedy is rooted in the ritual celebration of sexual energy. By adducing an oriental version of the concept of organic continuity—specifically the idea of reincarnation in India—she seeks to rule out any imputation of an equivalence between the comic rhythm and sexual vigor. The trouble with this argument is that both Hinduism and Buddhism (the latter encourages more self-assertiveness, however) illustrate the triumph of theology over vitality. Both religions posit the whole desideratum of effective reincarnation in the gradual erasure, from rebirth to rebirth, of fretful instinct and urgent desire.

As far as literature is concerned, Langer need not have made her brief journey to the Orient. For she finds "the comic" fully exemplified in occidental drama. One must understand, however, that she does not require any display of lightness (laughter, playfulness, blitheness, mockery, and so forth) to identify a literary work as a comedy. Indeed, any kind of drama (for example, the serious heroic plays of Corneille and Racine) that does not end in the protagonist's organic smash-up is hospitably, if rather medievally, accorded the label of comedy. A certain leap of the imagination is needed to grasp the possibility that when Langer accentuates "the comic," she may very well be excluding what she is forced to differentiate as "the comical," that is, whatever is amusing, delightful, funny. To be sure, the "comic rhythm" is not alien to traditional elements of comedy, as is evidenced by Langer's definition of laughter as "the crest of a wave of felt vitality" (p. 340) and by her choice of the buffoon as the very symbol of the comic rhythm's "primitive, savage, if not animalian" energy (p. 342).

Langer also admits at one point that "the natural vein of comedy is humorous" (p. 338). Nevertheless, her final word is that humor "is not the essence of comedy" (p. 346). The comic rhythm—the affirmation of life—need not be informed by the spirit of laughter and need never be familiar with gaiety. Her fundamental argument remains simple: all's "comic" that ends well. "The fairy tale formula ('live happily ever after') is tacitly understood at the close of a comedy" (p. 334). Thus Langer's organic theory embraces Campbell's cosmic theory: comedy is life invincible.

In reality, few notions are more contagious in contemporary comic theory than the idea that comedy involves rebirth or transcendent reconciliation or, on a less exalted plane, social harmony. Northrop Frye, for example, began influentially advancing such views in his brilliant essay "The Argument of Comedy," the gist of which is that comedy makes for "an individual release which is also a social reconciliation."[3] Frye backs up this statement with anthropological insights into ritual patterns of death and rebirth, sterility and fertility. Thus, in much of Shakespearean comedy, Frye observes, one witnesses the triumph of the "green world" over the threat of devastation; one sees "the triumph of life over the waste land" (p. 456).

Frye points the way to Campbell in maintaining that

[3] Northrop Frye, "The Argument of Comedy," in *Theories of Comedy*, ed. Paul Lauter (Garden City, N.Y.: Doubleday, Anchor, 1964), p. 452.

"tragedy is really implicit or uncompleted comedy" (p. 455).
Unlike Campbell, however, Frye converts the message of redemptive joy and life everlasting into literary laws (or at least
laws of comic drama)—a conversion which depends on the
pattern of Greek New Comedy as well as on primitive ritual.
Yet the "laws" of life renewal or even social harmony have only
limited empirical value in furthering an understanding of dramatic and fictional comedy. Petronius' *Satyricon* and Waugh's
The Loved One are brilliant embodiments of farce and satire,
just as Schnitzler's *Reigen* (*La Ronde*) and Proust's *Swann's
Way* (in part) splendidly illustrate the imagination of irony
and the vision of humor, respectively. All four works are comic,
in varying degrees. But none is helpfully explicated by "laws"
that establish comedy as rite-fixated, green-harmonious, and
clairvoyant of ultimate beatitude or reconciliation.

Frye's principal icon in "The Argument of Comedy" is
Shakespeare. In *A Natural Perspective*, a much later work,
Shakespeare remains the commanding exemplar of the universal
comic rhythm, which is "based on the second half of the great
cycle, moving from death to rebirth, decadence to renewal,
winter to spring, darkness to a new dawn."[4] While referring to
Shakespearean comedy as a whole, Frye concentrates in this
book on the Shakespeare of the late romances, which have been
so thoroughly ransacked for transcendental significance. Elsewhere, and specifically in the Penguin edition of *The Tempest*,
Frye comments on "the affinity between the happy endings of
comedy and the rituals marking the great rising rhythms of
life: marriage, springtime, harvest, dawn, and rebirth. In *The
Tempest* there is also an emphasis on moral and spiritual rebirth which suggests rituals of initiation, like baptism or the
ancient mystery dramas, as well as of festivity."[5] This comment
leaves nothing to be desired, alas, as a summation of the uni-

[4] Northrop Frye, *A Natural Perspective: The Development of Shakespearean Comedy and Romance* (New York: Columbia University Press,
1965), p. 121.
[5] William Shakespeare, *The Tempest*, ed. Northrop Frye (Baltimore:
Penguin, 1959), Introduction, p. 29.

tary, ritual, festive, resurrectional, transcendental bias in contemporary comic theory.

Yet one can hardly forget that theorists like Bergson and Meredith are interested only in comedy's worldly affiliation with society and that Molière is their spokesman, not Shakespeare—Molière, whose comedies smack so little of fertility rites or musical immortality. In this connection, Eric Bentley makes some pertinent remarks on culture's transformation of comedy's primal and passionate exuberance: "In the fullness of time comes . . . such a comedy as *Le Misanthrope*. What has been added to the moment of ecstatic identification with the god, the hour of the celebration of sexual energy? In a word, that which separates man from the beasts, and that which it was the glory of Greece to display to the world in all its dignity and power: intellect, mind, reason. *Le Misanthrope* is chiefly words. The old comic rhythms are at work but are given no direct corporeal expression. Comedy has been elevated into the realm of the spirit."[6] Comedy, like culture, unquestionably needs some sort of built-in primitivism to keep its vital juices stirring. But it is misleading to insist above all on comedy's continuing emphasis on blood fervor, spring worship, and fruitful mating, just as it is useless to attempt to hear in the sounds of comedy primarily the orchestrations of eternity.

2

Because contemporary comic theory is crammed with references to fertility celebrations, rebirth, monomythic harmony, the green world, and universal reconciliation, it may be refreshing to consider the nexus between comedy and mundane society. The ideas of Bergson and Meredith must loom large in any such investigation; but we need not start with the nineteenth century if we wish to illuminate the nonritualistic relationship between comedy and culture. Consider, for example, the attitude toward comic modes of expression revealed in that Renais-

[6] Eric Bentley, "What Is Theater?" in *The Theater of Commitment* (New York: Atheneum, 1967), pp. 62–63.

sance guide to gracious living, *The Book of the Courtier*. Expectably, Castiglione's perfect courtier is no lampooning grouch. He is habituated to temper his banter with discretion and his laughter with propriety. This mode of comedy is detailed in the Second Book, where Federico Fregoso and Bernardo Bibbiena, among others, participate in a discussion of the courtier's obligations to the comic spirit. Concentrating on the fine art of wit—the courtier's chief channel for displaying gifted amusement—they mention a number of wit techniques that Freud was to classify under such headings as displacement, condensation, and representation by the opposite. The interlocutors agree that wit springs from nature and genius rather than from art: "A pungent saying must come forth and hit the mark before he who utters it appears to have had time to give it a thought."[7] To put it in Freudian terms, they agree that wit surges up from the unconscious. But the witticisms Bibbiena presents to his urbane audience are devoid of the cynical (i.e., value-destroying) and erotic (i.e., morality-subverting) components that play so large a role, along with personal hostility, in Freud's conception of desirable tendentious wit. Sophisticated hostile witticisms do abound in the illustrations Bibbiena and Fregoso supply; but most of them reveal that social friction has been transformed into playful incongruity. (Bibbiena indicates, doubtless to the satisfaction of later writers like Hazlitt, that incongruity is the source of laughter [p. 145].) Nevertheless, a bite of some kind is inevitable; as Fregoso says, witticisms, or *arguzie*, must sting a little to be well turned (p. 142).

The perfect courtier, then, employs wit in the interests of social delight; his personal sense of triumph in scoring off a superior or a rival is subordinated to the harmony required by an elite. If he were to violate decorous laughter or deviate from polite wit, he would rough up intolerably the courtly ideal of *sprezzatura*, the nonchalance that is the handmaiden of grace. And because bad taste in comic utterances is taboo, an

[7] Baldesar Castiglione, *The Book of the Courtier*, trans. Charles S. Singleton (Garden City, N.Y.: Doubleday, Anchor, 1959), p. 142.

anarchic or sacrilegious twist in a courtier's witticism would be an unthinkable breach of dignity. "We must avoid impiety in our jests," says Bibbiena; "those persons who try to be amusing by showing little reverence for God deserve to be banished from the society of all gentlemen." Also deserving of exile are practitioners of obscene wit, who "seem to have no other amusement than to make [the ladies] blush with shame" (p. 166). In short, the honor of God, of the ladies, and of refined society is not to be encroached upon by the improprieties of a disreputable comic spirit.

The proprieties of the comic spirit preoccupy nineteenth-century middle-class critics as much as they do Castiglione's Renaissance courtiers. Consider the case of Matthew Arnold. In his essay on Heinrich Heine, Arnold speaks for cultural renovation yet is willing to settle only for a measured, Goethean tempo of liberation from the backward condition of Europe. "Dissolvents of the old European system of dominant ideas and facts we must all be," he declares, "all of us, who have any power of working; what we have to study is that we may not be acrid dissolvents of it."[8] Heine has become an acrid dissolvent principally on account of his "incessant mockery" (p. 125), which Arnold views as culturally inadmissible because it flirts with lawlessness instead of mating with Goethean progressivism.

Arnold's animadversion on Heine's comic spirit is symptomatic of the treatment he accords comedy in his major criticism (one recalls especially his notorious toppling of joyous Chaucer from the ranks of the great classics). His effort to give value and tone to a haphazard, utilitarian, partly pathological bourgeois civilization becomes identified in his mind so determinedly with the need for moral responsibility and spiritual seriousness that comedy, whether acrid or not, eventually becomes for him an escape from the pain and perplexity of life. Almost as unambiguously as Hardy, who had more reason to think of

[8] Matthew Arnold, "Heinrich Heine," in *Matthew Arnold's Essays: Literary and Critical*, intro. G. K. Chesterton (New York: Dutton, 1954), p. 104.

tragedy as truth and comedy as a lie,[9] Arnold elevates tragic reality above what he believes to be comedy's misrepresentation of the dark side of life.[10]

In this respect the exact antitype of Arnold is Nietzsche. Few thinkers have credited gaiety (the mordant, not the inoffensive sort) with the superlative value Nietzsche ascribes to it. Indeed he hails astringent comic laughter as the special prerogative of gods and heroic philosophers. And in this select company Heine has a privileged place. When, in *Ecce Homo*, Nietzsche extols two of Heine's chief literary attributes—his "sweet and passionate music" and his "divine sarcasm"—it is the significance of the second trait that is peculiarly noteworthy. For Heinesque comic malice, Nietzsche asserts, is an indispensable element of "the perfect." "I estimate the value of human beings, of races," he continues, "according to the necessity with which they cannot understand the god apart from the satyr"[11]—which is to say that the only gods worth worshiping are those who know how to laugh, resoundingly and recklessly. Nietzsche posits gods who are dancingly un-Arnoldian in their disrespectability (which does not prevent them from being curiously chaste at the same time) and who shine with bright, vivacious mockery, having consigned highminded gravity to oxen.

Their mockery can, however, be emulated by daring, freespirited human beings who have a talent for "objection, evasion, joyous distrust, and love of irony," all of which "are signs of health."[12] The revelations of Zarathustra, for example, make the gift of mockery indispensable to the wonder that is man. In Zarathustra's view, the great soul is the prankish soul, the courageous heart is the laughing heart, and the ironic nihilist

[9] See Mark Van Doren, "The Poems of Thomas Hardy," in *The Happy Critic and Other Essays* (New York: Hill and Wang, 1961), p. 55.

[10] For Arnold's views on tragedy and comedy, see Lionel Trilling, *Matthew Arnold* (New York: Norton, 1939), pp. 375–376.

[11] *Ecce Homo*, in *The Portable Nietzsche*, ed. and trans. Walter Kaufmann (New York: Viking, 1958), p. 680.

[12] Nietzsche, *Beyond Good and Evil*, trans. Helen Zimmern (London: Allen and Unwin, 1923), p. 98.

is the only true creator. "I love the great despisers," avows Nietzsche's prophet, "because they are the great reverers and arrows of longing for the other shore."[13] Clearly, a soberly progressive Arnoldian disloyalty to the decaying shibboleths of civilization does not square with Nietzsche's spirit. On the contrary, he honors a subversive jubilation of mind, a "bold, exuberant spirituality which runs at presto pace."[14] Whereas the Arnoldian principle of culture eschews dangerous gaiety, Nietzschean individuality positively thrives upon the "golden laughter" which energizes life "at the expense of all serious things" (p. 260). Arnold's perfect critic is a Goethean gradualist, a polite Olympian disdainer; Nietzsche's, on the other hand, is a joyous, Heinesque figure who translates mockery into iconoclasm.

In the early 1850's, Heine, who was to be applauded by Nietzsche as a Dionysian ironist par excellence, published *The Gods in Exile*, a little work which traces the disenshrinement and diaspora of the Greek gods, whom Christianity reduced to hardship cases throughout the world. Dionysus was an exception, for he came off fairly well. Heine reports that this pagan promoter of ecstasy entered the very bowels of Christian piety by camouflaging himself in the black robes of a monk. But once a year, in the Tyrolean forests, Dionysus sheds his funereal accoutrements and enjoys an infidel orgy with a "gloriously tipsy crew" risen up from antiquity "to again renew their ancient gay and festive rites, to once more celebrate with games and dance the triumph of the divine liberator, of the savior of sensuality, to revive the joyous dance of heathendom, the cancan of the merry world of yore, without any of the policemen of spiritual morality to hinder [them]."[15] Dionysus, become his old inebriated self once more, redeems the rights of the flesh from the bonds of melancholy Christian spirituality.

Heine's gay, drunken, restraint-disintegrating Dionysus is

[13] *Thus Spake Zarathustra*, in *The Portable Nietzsche*, p. 127.
[14] *Beyond Good and Evil*, p. 155.
[15] *The Gods in Exile*, in *The Sword and the Flame: Selections from Heinrich Heine's Prose*, ed. and intro. Alfred Werner (New York: Yoseloff, 1960), p. 569.

the one god Arnold cannot afford to see let loose in Europe. For Nietzsche, however—at least in the early 1870's—the return of Dionysus is essential to the creative spirit. In *The Birth of Tragedy*, Nietzsche takes over Heine's band of furtive but daringly ecstatic cultists and transforms them into full-fledged representatives of primitive Hellenic man. And in Nietzsche's hands, Dionysus becomes not only Antichrist, the repudiator of the Christian libel on life, but a transcendent source of creative frenzy and mystical jubilation. Indeed, the energy of the god fructifies both tragedy, which Nietzsche defines as the spirit whose sublimity subjugates the terror and nausea of existence, and comedy, which he defines (quite briefly) as the spirit whose joyousness releases man from the tedium of absurdity.[16] Because both tragedy and comedy are based upon irrational exaltation, they are of course profoundly inimical to the inhibitions of Arnoldian liberal culture.

3

Had Arnold been commissioned to respond to Nietzsche with an anti-Dionysian work on the comic spirit, he could hardly have bettered George Meredith's *Essay on Comedy*, which was composed only a few years after Nietzsche's work on tragedy. The un-Nietzschean dispatch of Dionysus in the early pages of Meredith's essay is indicative of the way a rationalist approach to the comic spirit splits off from a divinely reckless one. Meredith acknowledges the ritual Bacchanalianism at the origins of Greek comedy—comedy "rolled in shouting under the divine protection of . . . Dionysus,"[17] he observes—but he does so only for the purpose of banishing Bacchanalianism forevermore from civilized laughter. It is true that Meredith to some extent palliates comedy's obscene and aggressive beginnings by acknowledging the special Greek circumstance of a "festival of the god" held during a regulated "season of licence"

[16] Nietzsche, *"The Birth of Tragedy"* and *"The Genealogy of Morals,"* trans. Francis Golfing (Garden City, N.Y.: Doubleday, Anchor, 1956), p. 52.

[17] George Meredith, *An Essay on Comedy*, in *Comedy*, ed. Wylie Sypher (Garden City, N.Y.: Doubleday, Anchor, 1956), p. 5.

(p. 5). Nevertheless, Meredith brusquely bids Dionysus fare-well.

This dismissal of comedy's irrational genesis is handled in so witty, so dartingly allusive, so intellectually melioristic a manner that one does not immediately grasp the thinness of the alternative to Dionysus that Meredith proposes. That alternative is summed up in the figure of the Comic Spirit, a politely poised, kindly cutting, civilizing deity whom Neitzsche would instantly eject from his private pantheon. Far from being a Dionysian stimulant to creative intoxication, Meredith's Comic Spirit is actually dedicated to the flow of "harmless wine" (p. 50), that is, to spirited sobriety. Why? Because in Meredith's eyes the progress of culture can be verified by its transformation of Dionysian clamor into mental cogency. He is satisfied that the gross guffaws of the satyr have been refined into the "slim feasting smile" (p. 47) of a delicately pouncing Comic Spirit which is part faun and part sage. The faun component of the Comic Spirit may seem promising, but it betokens impishness rather than vestigial barbarism; in any case, the sage fully dominates the faun's potential waywardness.

Yet progress in comedy and culture, Meredith knows, has not been unilinear. Thus the Dionysian impact of Restoration comedy is, in Meredith's opinion, a tremendous relapse in the history of civilization. With the exception of Congreve's *The Way of the World* (which charmingly avoids the usual brand of Restoration sin—though its central idea, Meredith claims, is stale and its brilliant wit superficial), Restoration comedy is a thorn in Meredith's side by reason of its unholy reversion to the early satyr style of Greek comedy. He finds it even more distasteful than primitive Dionysianism, arguing that "cynical licentiousness is more abominable than frank filth" (p. 5). Similarly, he considers Charles II, whom he briefly alludes to as a kind of Dionysus Redivivus, more perverse than his Greek ancestor. The charges are pungent, but Meredith's attack has not worn very well, especially since the Comic Spirit now seems distinctly anemic in comparison with the disinhibitory spirit of the comedy of Etherege and Wycherley.

A century and a half ago, Charles Lamb, in his essay "On the Artificial Comedy of the Last Century," was disposed to treasure Restoration comedy as a refuge from compulsory good conduct. Though Lamb's indulgent attitude is tossed aside by Meredith as part of an outrageously whimsical paradox, we are inclined today to accept Lamb's proto-Freudian argument that in offering an "escape from the pressure of reality" and "the burthen of perpetual moral questioning,"[18] Restoration comedy actually fosters psychic health. Human beings need an occasional airing outside the cage of conscience, Lamb points out; and they need to flee, even if momentarily, from such social restrictions as marriage. This kind of thinking irks Meredith, for he is convinced that the Comic Spirit must support and perfect society's beneficent institutions. Comedy does not jeer at the idea of marriage; it seeks, rather, to improve existing marital conventions. Meredith anathematizes Restoration comedy largely because it desecrates these conventions.

The Restoration comic dramatists are so far from being anathema to Lamb that he considers them to be downright emancipators of those in need of a moral holiday. That is why Lamb at times sounds uncannily like an evangelist of the id, whereas Meredith's moralistic rebuke of Restoration comedy seems to emanate from the cultural superego. Yet there is a catch to Lamb's liberation: the freedom of the id that he cherishes seems to be refrigerated once and for all—mainly within the seventeenth century. That is why he does not extend his unorthodox gospel of release to contemporary drama. "In a modern play," he observes, "I am to judge of the right and the wrong" (p. 211). It is only in the sequestered fairyland world of Restoration comedy that "the painful necessities of shame and blame" (p. 213) may be allowed to evaporate.

For Meredith, the notion of such historical evaporation is preposterous. Morality is no "duenna to be circumscribed,"[19]

---

[18] Charles Lamb, "On the Artificial Comedy of the Last Century," in *"The Essays of Elia" and "The Last Essays of Elia"* (Garden City, N.Y.: Doubleday, n.d.), p. 210.
[19] *An Essay on Comedy*, p. 8.

whatever the epoch. On the contrary, a subtle sense of morality is an indispensable minister to comedy's humanizing graces. Without it, the Comic Spirit could hardly scourge vice exquisitely, or calmly strip "Folly to the skin," or urbanely vindicate the Molièresque virtues of "reason, common sense, rightness, and justice" (p. 17). Meredith's Comic Spirit is in truth eminently well bred. Because it has a "proper esteem for the society we have wrested from brutishness and would carry higher" (p. 16), its laughter is marked by an "impersonal and . . . unrivaled politeness" (p. 47). The Comic Spirit ridicules the patterns of "our conventional life," but it does not make fun of "our unfortunate nature"; for ridicule of human nature would only provoke "derisive laughter, which thwarts the comic idea" (p. 47).

Seen in the best light possible, Meredith's reluctance to have the Comic Spirit excoriate man's naked absurdity is a homage to comedy's refining power. But seen in a harsher light, Meredith's position involves a kind of cheating, or at least a putting-on of exquisite blinders—the same blinders that are applied when Meredith insists that it is "the first condition of sanity" (p. 47) to believe that civilization and common sense (the progenitor of the Comic Spirit) are profoundly akin. This calculated faith in common sense of course clashes with the more candid present-day addiction to the absurd. It is therefore fortunate that Meredith does not make the Comic Spirit a prudential bore. Certainly the Comic Spirit is not straightfaced; it looks "humanely malign" (p. 48), and its sunny malice is matched by a sprightly nature. Describing the critical pleasure the Comic Spirit takes in deflating Folly, that creature "born of Unreason and Sentimentalism" (p. 33), Meredith resorts to the language of hunter and hunted, pursuer and victim: "Folly is the natural prey of the Comic . . . and it is with the springing delight of hawk over heron, hound after fox, that it gives her chase, never fretting, never tiring, sure of having her, allowing her no rest" (p. 33). Meredith's friskily murderous imagery belies the Comic Spirit's "perfectly humane" laughter; but that is not surprising. For however gentle

its bite, however delicate its pursuit, the Comic Spirit is motivated primarily by the aggressions of satire.

Identifying the Comic Spirit as an agent of satire brings up
a special problem. Meredith is wholly disinclined to equate the
Comic Spirit with satire or, for that matter, with humor, farce,
or irony. Farce he deprecates as a fumbling comic vulgarity.
Humor and satire, it is true, are accorded a certain measure of
deference; Meredith grants that they have from time to time
conduced to supreme comic expression, as in the case of
Cervantes and Aristophanes. Yet on the whole Meredith considers these two sources of comic power to be essentially mis-
guided and therefore in need of reshaping by the Comic Spirit.
Humor is objectionable because it is too often prompted by
overgenerous, uncritical impulses that lead to a back-slapping
bonhomie or a viscous tenderness, both of which make sticky
the dry edge of ideal comedy.

The reason Meredith also debars satire from the province
of the Comic Spirit is that its mockery is so ruthless as to
congeal the heart; satire may have a moral animus, but it is
too savage a comic weapon to be utilized in the cultivation of
social intelligence. In his portrait of the satirist, Meredith goes
so far as to exploit a rather unsunny metaphoric extremism.
He calls the satirist a vulture smelling of carrion, a "social
scavenger working on a storage of bile" (p. 44). Yet Meredith's virtually solitary hero of literary comedy, Molière, has
long been recognized as a satirist (as well as a farceur); and
few have ever accused Molière of being a vulture smelling of
social carrion. Meredith's version of the satirist is obviously
more bilious than balanced. Equally limited is his interpretation
of the ironist (the verbal ironist, that is) as a sinister fellow
who destroys good will and even stirs up anguish by delivering
a sting under a "semi-caress" (p. 42). Unlike the satirist's
strategies, furthermore, the ironist's maneuvres lack even the
prestige of a corrective.

Clearly, the Comic Spirit, despite its lively visage and
spirited vocation, is a cloistered entity. Meredith himself confines it to a small circle of intellect within a narrow area of

enlightened society. These boundaries inevitably exclude most of the comic geniuses of the past (whose greatness Meredith does, however, acknowledge). Cervantes and Sterne, for example, transcend the exiguous scope of the Comic Spirit, but even great humorists, unfortunately, are "often wanting in proportion and discretion" (p. 45). Shakespeare himself has created characters who do not measure up to Meredith's standards, because the Comic Spirit is more interested in the witty prose of social laughter than in the whimsical poetry of the forest of Arden. Had Shakespeare's epoch been "less emotional, less heroical," Meredith suggests, "he might have turned to the painting of manners as well as humanity" (p. 12). "Manners" is of course the key word; for humanity without "manners" cannot arouse "thoughtful laughter" (p. 47). The Comic Spirit evidently flourishes best in a cool social world where perceptive affability is the ruling value.

Antisocial comedy is distinctly taboo for Meredith. Aristophanes' plays therefore take on a curiously ambivalent significance: the Greek comedian's robust assaults and priapic merriment make a reincarnation of his type of laughter scarcely feasible in the nineteenth century, Meredith asserts. Nevertheless, he adds, the Greek playwright possessed a sense of civic integrity (however savage) urgently needed in the politically delinquent modern age. The reverse of an Aristophanes—a comic writer who willfully defies commitments to social duty— is easier for Meredith to deal with; such a writer—Byron, for example—must be ostracized from the purlieus of the Comic Spirit. Because Byron is antisocial, he lacks a "strong [i.e., true] comic sense" (p. 44); the matter is made as simple as that. Like Arnold, then, Meredith is convinced that a mocking dissolution of social forms is no solution to the problems of civilization—which is to say that authentic comedy is never an act of subversion. The Comic Spirit propagates "sunlight of the mind" (p. 48), not warfare between gaiety and culture.[20]

[20] In his introduction to the Riverside edition of Meredith's *The Egoist* (Boston: Houghton Mifflin, 1958), Lionel Stevenson points out the parallel between Arnold's "culture" and Meredith's "Comic Spirit."

Like Meredith, Bergson in *Laughter* (conceived in the 1880's) approaches his subject with a deep appreciation of common sense. But though he shares with Meredith the belief that laughter has a critical, corrective, socially purifying aim, Bergson is less apt to blink the several perversities that have long been associated with the comic urge. Basically, Bergson's theme is the need to combat behavioral and mental rigor mortis by exposing to laughter (which will be detonated when the heart is anesthetized) the human tendency to lapse into ridiculous mechanisms of conduct and thought.

Because he focuses on the issue of vitalism versus mechanism, Bergson might superficially be viewed as one of the ancestors of that long line of theorists for whom comedy is essentially the expression of life resurgent. But Bergson makes it clear that his interest lies wholly in the progress of society; he declares categorically that man "must live in society and consequently submit to rules."[21] If this injunction seems to encourage the victory of mechanism over life, Bergson salvages vitalism, according to his own lights, by conceiving of society as a living being, a developing organism. It is a cruel organism, moreover. Bergson does not disguise the ugliness and even the immorality of the laughing chastisement with which society flagellates those aberrant citizens whose fixed notions and obsessive eccentricities make them unfit for social life. Society's laughter is meant precisely to shame, humiliate, and terrorize such psychological separatists. Ideally, the effect of comedy will be to dislodge their stiffened conceptions and compel them

---

Both, Stevenson remarks, have to do with "a disinterested devotion to excellence" in a civilization undermined by "prosperous Philistinism" (p. vii). In his essay "Tragedy, Comedy, and Civilization," Ronald Peacock suggests that Meredith, by implication, adopts Schiller's views on comedy and tragedy as expressed in the latter's essay "Über naïve und sentimentalische Dichtung"; Schiller's main point is that the comic vision serenely sterilizes tragic passion (Peacock, *The Poet in the Theatre* [New York: Hill and Wang, 1946], p. 151). It is Bergson, however, as we shall see, who explicitly underscores the superfluity of tragedy in an ideal society. But Bergson's sense of comedy, it must be added, is less tolerant than Schiller's.

[21] Henri Bergson, *Laughter*, in *Comedy*, ed. Sypher, p. 163.

to resume the "wideawake adaptability and the living pliableness of a human being" (p. 67).

Bergson not only admits that society is often unjustly vindictive in its laughter; he also tracks the source of this laughter to an innate evil in human character. He explains, though somewhat fuzzily, that nature has "implanted . . . even in the best of men, a spark of spitefulness or, at all events, of mischief" (p. 188). This idea seems worth exploring, but Bergson would prefer not to: "Perhaps we had better not investigate this point too closely," he remarks, "for we should not find anything very flattering to ourselves" (pp. 188–189). Still, Bergson is not as chary as Meredith of plumbing the unfortunate human psyche; he candidly admits that we laugh from the depths of a presumptuous egoism and that in the very act of deriding social misfits in real life or on the stage, we turn into unpleasantly superior manipulators relegating the victims we mock to the level of marionettes. The whole enterprise of laughter, Bergson finally avows, is grounded in a "curious pessimism" (p. 189). Yet Bergson by no means allows this insight into the bitterness and vaingloriousness of gaiety to cancel the social gains that spiteful laughter encourages. Nature "here, as elsewhere," he declares, "has utilized evil with a view to good" (p. 189). Satire-loving nature (in speaking of social ridicule Bergson is plainly describing the action of satire, although, like Meredith, he does not adopt the term) has redirected our ingrained malignity toward a useful cultural purpose.

There is a certain knottiness in Bergson's idea of the social good. What society demands of its members, he says, is an "increasingly delicate adjustment of wills which will fit more and more perfectly into one another" (p. 72). Those who, through their unconscious, machine-like behavior (whether commonplace or nobly quixotic), frustrate this need for ever subtler social harmony are by definition comic persons, punishable by laughter. Yet Bergson's assumption that society can be depicted as an increasingly resilient entity is extremely dubious. How far can an ideal sociability—"an increasingly delicate adjustment of wills"—be carried in a world of inhibiting legal and administrative machinery? (Bergson himself writes brilliantly in *Laughter* about professional insensitivity and bureaucratic idiocy.) The idea that society-as-organism can, ever more subtly, laughingly liquidate that part of itself which hardens into society-as-mechanism is a fantasy.

But if, in *Laughter*, people (immobilized into types) seem to be the enemy, while society is the savior, there does come a moment when Bergson appears to be loath to continue celebrating merely enlightened social conformity. In the midst of his analysis of the relation of art to tragedy and comedy, the image of the socially unadjusted man suddenly and powerfully emerges. Bergson has been persuasively pointing out that, whereas comedy must be viewed as a halfway house between art and life—between the quest for individual truth and the pursuit of utilitarianism—tragedy is a true art form that pierces directly through the net of social law to expose the untamed heart of man.

Bergson uses a geological analogy to make this contrast clear: "Just as the life of our planet itself," he writes, "has been one long effort to cover over with a cool and solid crust the fiery mass of seething metals" within, so comedy has acted as a cooling, solidifying force of civilization that has crusted over the fiery, tragic interior of man—in the interests of an "increasingly peaceful social life" (p. 163). Nevertheless, the fiery, tragic turbulence of the individual heart does get conveyed by the grandeur of tragic art, for tragedy is a healing resource the human spirit must positively repair to from time to time. Just as the imprisoned fire of nature seeks an outlet in volcanic eruptions, so the incandescent inner life of man seeks the catharsis of tragic art. Tragedy, then, is nature's revenge against the restrictions of society. ("Nature" is obviously an all-purpose word in Bergson's essay: it foments tragedy yet also guarantees the operation of comedy.) But having said all this, Bergson ends by dismissing tragedy's rebellious individualism as archaic. Neither the aesthetic purity of tragedy nor its power to restore authentic sources of passion can match comedy's ability to pacify man's restiveness and refine his culture. In short, tragedy is primitivism; comedy is progressive adaptability.

One cannot help noting that Bergson's potent metaphor of the solid crust (the cooling surface regulating the disorderly, overheated life beneath it) posits a social salvation which is in essence indistinguishable from creeping rigidity (certainly this is the way the metaphor of the crust functions in his earlier work *Time and Free Will*), and which therefore ought to be repugnant to Bergson. And one could go on to argue that only the sense of tragedy can keep society from freezing into callousness. But Bergson forestalls such a conclusion by insisting that tragedy is "frequently sophistical" in exposing "the inconsistencies of society." Tragic art, he declares, "exaggerates the shams and shibboleths of the social law." (p. 164). Like Meredith, that other defender of the pact between comedy and culture, Bergson profoundly buries the possibility that society may be an organized betrayal of human freedom.

Still, Bergson does have one saving grace not shared by Meredith: he is less disposed than the English critic to see the impress of morality in the lineaments of comedy. When Bergson broaches the question of comedy's relation to virtue and vice, elasticity remains his ideal: flexible vice is less ridiculous than inflexible virtue, for it is chiefly rigidity "that society eyes with suspicion" (p. 150). An indirect admission that morality in comedy may play second fiddle to vitality is, however, potentially dangerous to Bergson's cause. Which is doubtless why he transforms his heretical comment by assuring us, somewhat facilely, that social and moral ideals are possessed of "no essential difference"—much "to the credit of mankind" (p. 150).

Clearly, Bergson remains very much on his guard whenever his thoughts threaten to engender a lack of respect for social cohesiveness. In a symptomatic discussion near the end of his study, Bergson refers to the agreeable human tendency to relax sympathetically and become playful in the presence of childlike, unrestrained attitudes; he refers specifically to the image of a "stern father" (p. 187) warming to his child's prankishness. That particular father, however, is soon rebuked by Bergson for being momentarily self-forgetful—for encouraging an undesirable relief from the strain of living and the pressure of corrective attitudes. (Even a transitory psychic release may be an invitation to cultural treason.) It is an amusing picture: just as Bergson begins to sanction a charming bit of irresponsible buoyancy, he stiffens his jaw and recalls erring spirits (his own and all others) to a sense of discipline. One can only conclude that Bergson is not flexible enough.

4

I have said that if Bergson's theory of comedy is interpreted exclusively (and therefore misleadingly) as a vindication of human vitality, of the energy of life in contrast to the immobility of death, it becomes feasible to mesh Bergson's ideas with the ritual-myth bias of contemporary comic theory, which faithfully follows the ancient worship of the powers of fecundity and regeneration in man and nature. F. M. Conford, in his pioneering study, *The Origin of Attic Comedy* (1914), asserts that comedy is born in ritual or folk drama that is preoccupied with the theme of "the death of the old year and the birth or accession of the new," with "decay and the suspension of life in the frosts of winter and its release and [rebirth] in spring."[22] According to Cornford, the four main types of fertility ritual are (1) the carrying-out of death (and its analogues: hunger, disease, sin), a movement which is complemented by the induction of life (and its analogues: health and wealth); (2) the fight of summer and winter, a seasonal antagonism that must end in the victory of summer over the sterility of winter; (3) the struggle of the young king and the old, ending in the death of the latter (which is the equivalent of the expulsion of

---

[22] Francis Macdonald Cornford, *The Origin of Attic Comedy*, ed. Theodore Gaster (Garden City, N.Y.: Doubleday, Anchor, 1961), p. 9.

winter) and the installation of the former (which is tantamount to the renewal of summer); and (4) death and resurrection, which are often imaged in the dismemberment and rebirth of a god. As for the bridge between ritual and drama, in tragedy the emphasis falls on death; in comedy, on resurrection, especially as exemplified in "the phallic element and the fertility marriage" (p. 23). Hence the erotic tone of comedy and its canonical ending in marriage.

Cornford systematically attempts to relate the heritage of fertility rites to the comedies of Aristophanes, in which he sees a recurrent plot formula featuring an agon, a contest between good and evil forces; a komos, a festal procession linked to a marriage; and, between the agon and the komos, a scene of sacrifice and a feast (this sequence of events is related to the dismemberment and communal eating of a slain god who is brought back to life). Cornford's argument has received mixed reactions from those competent to judge. The layman may be fascinated by Cornford's account of the "curious feature which distinguishes Aristophanes' plays from all other forms of Comedy, that they present a whole series of heroes who are old men and behave as such at the beginning, while at the end they are more or less transfigured into youthful bridegrooms" (p. 45). But the expert, like Sir Arthur Pickard-Cambridge in *Dithyramb, Tragedy, and Comedy* (1927), often has serious reservations about Cornford's ritual plot formula as it is supposedly worked out in Aristophanes' comedies.

T. B. L. Webster, who revised Pickard-Cambridge's text in 1962, and who agrees that the fertility or vegetation ritual theory breaks down when it is applied in detail to Aristophanes' comedies, nevertheless concedes definite value to Cornford's ideas—that is, if they are restated in terms of "ritual refracted into myths";[23] for the spun-off myths are the only primitive material Aristophanes' comedies can possibly preserve. "Even

[23] Sir Arthur Pickard-Cambridge, *Dithyramb, Tragedy, and Comedy*, 2d ed., rev. T. B. L. Webster (London: Oxford University Press, 1962), p. 193.

then," Webster goes on, "the supposed ritual is open to the criticism that it contains much too much; agon followed by marriage is possible, but birth, death, omophagy, and rejuvenation seem to belong to something else" (p. 194). Webster does not deny, however, that vegetation ritual, translated into myth, did have a "potent influence on the shape of comedy" (p. 194).

At about the same time that Webster was revising Pickard-Cambridge, Theodore Gaster was updating Cornford. Gaster, armed with new information about the literary treatment of seasonal festivals in the ancient Near East, reports that while the latest evidence "does not *prove* . . . that the Seasonal Pattern obtained in *ancient Greece* . . . the widespread diffusion of it which is thus attested surely tips the scales of probability in . . . Cornford's favor and places more heavily upon [his] critics the burden of disproof."[24] Gaster does recognize that Cornford has assimilated into his argument certain autonomous, primitive comic energies that correspond to "sheer fun or high jinks" (p. xxiii) rather than to functional ritualism. And he accepts, on the whole, Pickard-Cambridge's analysis of Cornford's inconsistencies. At the end of his editorial foreword, however, Gaster reaffirms the seminal importance of Cornford's theory, an importance which overrides distortions in the interpretation of individual Aristophanic plays.

Suppose we agree, in spite of some shaky evidence, that occidental (dramatic) comedy is in large part the descendant of a sacred, communal participation in the triumph of resurrection over death. We are left, nevertheless, with the problem of how such a genesis can account for comedy's diverse developments. Fortunately, Cornford stresses a dualistic tendency in Old Comedy which is helpful for an understanding of comedy's ultimate variousness: the tendency to exploit both celebration and scorn. The celebration is directed toward fertility, the scorn toward life-deterring influences. This double rhythm, says Cornford, relates to the phallic processions Aristotle mentions

[24] *The Origin of Attic Comedy*, p. xviii.

as the source of comedy, the phallic rites being in all likelihood the germ from which ritual drama sprang. "The element of invective and personal satire which distinguishes the Old Comedy," Cornford states, "is directly descended from the magical abuse of the phallic procession, just as its obscenity is due to the sexual magic." (p. 113). Here the archaizing view of comedy provides an explanation for at least two enduring comic powers: satire and farce. Aristophanic comedy, moreover, may be seen precisely as a merger of satire (deriving from the curse hurled against the forces of sterility and death) and farce (deriving from the obscenity and irrationality of sexual celebration).

Consider *Lysistrata* and *The Birds*. Thematically *Lysistrata* seems to bear out the theory of comedy's primitive rhythms. The enemy of life (the war between Athens and Sparta) is driven out by satire, while the promoter of life (sexuality) is endorsed by farcical pleasure. But in scene after scene, this pleasure turns out to be a very modern phenomenon. Aristophanes' farce inspires so great a release from psychic controls that its original worship of the seeds of life and its actual marital context become largely irrelevant. Thus the Myrrhine-Kinesias episode, which best concretizes the play's presumptive legacy of mandatory bawdiness, offers, in nonritualistic terms, an exhilarating freedom from conventional decency. Given Kinesias' ithyphallic impetuosity and Myrrhine's nymphic tantalizations, the atmosphere created by the provocative wife and the sex-starved husband is necessarily one of outrageous impropriety. The result is that the aroma of zany, excruciating lust in this scene reduces Kinesias' references to domestic, maritally snug reunion to a thin rationalization of voluptuous facts. Kinesias, bulging with love, may look like a fertility symbol and sound off like a husband, but it is not fertility or legality that is on his frantic mind: getting laid is his overwhelming preoccupation. (Lysistrata's and Myrrhine's strategy is to exacerbate the state of his erection to such an extent that he will stumble, groin groaning, straight toward the peace table.) The frustration of the other ithyphallic Athenians and Spartans is funny for the same reason: symbols of priapic potency turn into bludgeons that farcically demolish normal inhibitions.[25]

Aristophanes' satire achieves the same kind of relatively rite-free impact. Men as warmongers and death dealers are amply mocked in *Lysistrata,* but women themselves are hardly exempted from ridicule. The modification of the ritual function of satire becomes especially remarkable when the men and women choruses flay each other; for the battle of the sexes in *Lysistrata* focuses, not on antigenetic threats, but on the follies and frailties of the genders. To be sure, certain of Aristophanes' comedies disclose stronger ritual imprints than others. For example, the banishment of impostors in *The Birds* (Pisthetairos, the expulsion maestro, has a sharp eye for detecting the charlatans of civilization) seems suitably based on ritual satire. Pisthetairos himself, at least initially, is a victim of satire insofar as he is depicted as a seedy opportunist. But he is not a victim for long, since his nerve in dreaming up Cloudcuckooland totally alters his status: the artful old dodger becomes an admirable dislocator of reality, a thaumaturge who can satirize men, gods, birds, and himself with absolute impunity.

But the farcical elements in *The Birds* are even more heterogeneously detachable from ritual than the play's satiric components. Aristophanes' farce, after all, is compounded of sexuality, aggression, scatology, irreverence, nonsense, and fantasticality. Consider the nonsense and irreverence in the scene in which three divine dignitaries descend as a delegation to test Pisthetairos for possible delusions of grandeur. Herakles and the provincial Triballian god, unlike the refined Poseidon, are laughably buffoonish from the beginning. Herakles, who thinks like a moronic, gluttonous gangster, makes no bones about being willing to surrender Basileia (divine power in the shape of a princess) to Pisthetairos just for the sake of a good

[25] For a strong emphasis on the marital significance of the erotic farce in *Lysistrata,* see Cedric Whitman, *Aristophanes and the Comic Hero* (Cambridge, Mass.: Harvard University Press, 1964), pp. 204–205.

roast, for the Olympian menu is not what it used to be; and his abbreviated translation of the Triballian god's gibberish is instrumental in making Pisthetairos the god of gods. But how seriously are we to take this deification? There would seem to be a remarkable abyss between ritual import and Aristophanes' apparently burlesque finale if we accept Dudley Fitts's comment that "the final mockery of this drama, of course, is the apotheosis of the bungling Hero.[26]

Cedric Whitman, on the other hand, in *Aristophanes and the Comic Hero*, considers Pisthetairos' deification not only not risible but "the most astounding victory in Aristophanes, perhaps in all comedy." Moreover, Whitman makes Pisthetairos out to be "the most majestic of Aristophanes' grotesque figures, the comic hero come to fullness."[27] Whitman's idea of the comic hero is embedded in an important conception of Aristophanic comedy: Fantasy, not satire, is the shaping element in Aristophanes' work; and fantasy has affinities with grotesquerie, boundlessness, and world transformation. Aristophanes' comedy, furthermore, is best explained by Baudelaire's theory of the absolutely comic, which, unlike the significantly comic (or satire), is not anchored in the familiar world of utility and morality. (Aristophanes' fantasy does embrace satire and realism; but these ingredients are subordinated to his mythopoeic imagination.) In any case, the absurd, grotesque world that Aristophanes has created is not the symbol of a demonic alienation (this modern, dark view of the grotesque is a leading theme in Wolfgang Kayser's *The Grotesque in Art and Literature*); it is, rather, a fecund, joyously shameless monstrosity wherein animal, human, and divine elements fuse into a magic circle of play (as Huizinga defines play in *Homo Ludens*). Such "play" is essentially nonsense, meaninglessness, nothingness—but in a poetic, not a petty, sense.

Pisthetairos, then, according to Whitman, is a hero of the creative absurd. The driving attribute that allows this magnifi-

[26] *Aristophanes: Four Comedies*, trans. Dudley Fitts (New York: Harcourt, Brace, and World, 1962), p. 250.
[27] *Aristophanes and the Comic Hero*, pp. 196, 182.

cent quack to wield sovereignty over the fantastic world he has invented is "selfmanship," a gay, audacious, devious force that dethrones normality, reason, and even the gods. The "salvation of the self" is, to be sure, fueled in part by impulses secreted in some of "the blacker recesses of the psyche"; but it leads to a vision of absurdity itself, a "divine world of perfect supremacy and freedom" (p. 53). From any rational point of view, this Aristophanic vision is mad; but its madness is a victorious response to the normal world, "which is a case of lunacy too" (p. 57). Pisthetairos' personal liberation from bondage, moreover, becomes part of a universal release from the twisted claims of logic and morality.

Whitman is reluctant to measure this release wholly in Freudian terms, for he is convinced that the delights of Aristophanic comedy transcend a purgative emancipation from conventional pressures. Unfortunately, Whitman gives a narrow interpretation of Freud's conception of comic energies. He sees Freudian comic theory as preoccupied only with the compensatory transgression of taboos and therefore as inaccessible to the "higher slapstick" that offers us "an intuition for the true nature of things" (p. 275), which Whitman defines as absurdity itself. But the fact is that the repressions exerted by logic and banal reality are also evicted in Freudian comic theory (specifically, in Freud's notes on nonsense). Even more misleading is Whitman's complaint that "the cathartic view explains at most some of the content and not the form of Aristophanic comedy" (p. 275). Well, Cornford has tried to explain the form of Aristophanic comedy, from agon to rejuvenation. Freud can be called upon only to account for psychological pleasures. Finally, Whitman believes that therapeutic comedy (together with satire) simply does not have practical results: "There is no evidence for supposing comedy to have reduced the incidence of adultery, violence, or whatever by vicarious satisfaction" (p. 274). But therapeutic comedy can have only a fugitive psychic effect; it has never been heralded as a power that can reduce criminal statistics or make adultery superfluous. Nor is satire, which in Whitman's view is also supposed to prove useful, a generally expeditious means of diminishing folly and corruption.

Whitman offers a number of brilliant observations on the life-stimulating properties of the Aristophanic grotesque. But these observations do not pertain especially to Cornford's theory, the details of which he discounts while granting that "some kind of ritual fertility drama may have played a part in the growth of Attic comedy" (p. 300). In actuality, the temptation to consider Cornford's views a godsend remains strong among theorists of comedy. Consider, for example, Wylie Sypher's remarkable essay "The Meanings of Comedy," one of the four parts of which deals with comedy's ritual origins. In this section Sypher accepts Cornford's stress on sacrifice and feast (in the sacrifice the representatives of death are subjected to a purifying destruction; in the feast the community rejoices in rebirth) as the solution to the contradictions by which the comic temper is possessed. "Behind my whole discussion of [the fertility] rite," Sypher declares, "and my whole account of the inconsistent theories necessary to explain comedy is Francis M. Cornford: *The Origin of Attic Comedy*, 1914. Cornford's interpretation seems to me to offer our only means of understanding the incompatibles in comedy without laying ourselves open to a charge of willful illogicality."[28]

As a result of his adoption of Cornford's findings, Sypher's conspectus of the comic terrain is far more illuminating than that of theorists trammeled by single vision.[29] We can easily observe an improvement over Langer and Campbell, for instance. In "The Comic Rhythm," Langer offers us a comic hero whose egoistic, organic verve logically compels him, more often than

[28] "The Meanings of Comedy," in *Comedy*, ed. Sypher, pp. 256–257, n. 8.

[29] Most monistic studies of comedy are slanted toward satire or humor. For example, Bernard N. Schilling's *The Comic Spirit: Boccaccio to Thomas Mann* (Detroit: Wayne State University Press, 1965) could easily be retitled "The Spirit of Humor," inasmuch as Schilling stresses the "kindly smile" (p. 13) and the "humanism, discernment, and tolerance" (p. 14) of the comic spirit. The latter are also identified as the basic elements of the reconciliatory "comedy of sympathy" (p. 16).

not, to engage in guerrilla tactics at the expense of society. On the other hand, in "Tragedy and Comedy," Campbell delineates a cosmic-comic hero who is ultimately enlarged by selfless dedication to mankind. Sypher's receptivity to comic incompatibles permits him to embrace both views, along with other apparent irreconcilables. Thus he sees the comic hero as rebel and sage, satyr and scapegoat, buffoon and deliverer, madman and ironist; and he describes comedy itself, quite properly, as radical and conservative, rational and illogical. (Hence he fully rehabilitates the disorder and violence, the saturnalian revels and fantastic foolery, that Meredith's social refinement seeks to erase from literary comedy.) But after a while, unfortunately, the term "comedy" gets buried beneath an avalanche of miscellaneous, conflicting attributes, so that comedy threatens to become all things to all men.

In his remarks on ritual origins, moreover, Sypher scrapes his interest in comedy's complexity down to the familiar monolith unearthed by anthropology. Comedy, he states, following Cornford, "is essentially a Carrying Away of Death, a triumph over mortality by some absurd faith in rebirth, restoration, and salvation."[30] At the same time he retains, in attenuated form, a scale of values that sets "low" comedy against "high." Thus he describes farce as a mechanical type of comedy whose "characters need only be puppets" (p. 209). And as his essay moves to a close he celebrates a humane, kindly-thoughtful social comedy, thereby muffling the Pan element (primitivism, revelry, fantasticality) whose value he had earlier resuscitated in a Cornfordian context.

Cornford himself, one is surprised to realize, in discussing comedy in general resists the implications of his own anthropological discoveries. His evaluation of the nature of comedy might have been made by Meredith himself. "The Sophrosyne of Comedy," he writes, "is the spirit of genial sanity. . . . Its antagonist is pretense, assumption, arrogance, conceit, all the less serious and tragic species of imposture. . . . The duel of

[30] "The Meanings of Comedy," p. 220.

Comedy is everlastingly fought out between them."[31] The irrelevance of anthropological data in this passage could scarcely be more marked. If the chief merit of comedy is its abiding interest in "genial sanity," comedy need never have consorted with the ritual propensities of Attic man in the first place. But this reflection of Cornford's is ironically not the portion of his text that has attained canonization in contemporary comic theory. Students of Cornford persist in gravitating toward the sexual-seasonal compulsions and communal affirmations that are presumably situated at the roots (but not at the heart) of comedy.

Moreover, in their anthropologically based theorizing about comedy as the affirmation of life, the frequency with which comedy, which may indeed have been drama-bound genetically, is discussed as though it were still drama-bound generically is surely astounding. Northrop Frye is an exception—yet even he will not admit to a breaking of the mold as comedy moves from drama to fiction. When Frye claims, in *Anatomy of Criticism*, that fictional comedy is "mainly descended" from dramatic comedy, which, "remarkably tenacious of its structural principles and character types" to this very day, can be gotten at primarily through Greek New Comedy "as transmitted by Plautus and Terence,"[32] he binds many of the new, multiple energies of the comic novel into a throttling fixity of form, purpose, and characterization. To be told, for example, that "in *Huckleberry Finn* the main theme is one of the oldest in comedy, the freeing of a slave" (p. 180)—as though Twain and Plautus were now to be considered firm allies in the history of comedy—is to be offered only a specimen of archetypal homogenization.

When Frye attempts rather more systematically to squeeze a great comic novelist into the narrow world of Latinized New Comedy, as in his essay "Dickens and the Comedy of Humors," the results are still disappointing. Dickens' "humor" characters

---

[31] *The Origin of Attic Comedy*, p. 184.
[32] Northrop Frye, *Anatomy of Criticism: Four Essays* (Princeton: Princeton University Press, 1957), p. 163.

are viewed in this essay as functioning on both sides in a collision (prototypically evinced in New Comedy structure) between an obstructing society and a festively congenial one, the latter representing "the world of an invincible Eros."[33] Sexual magic and magic solidarity (the enlightenment of the comic hero may involve some degree of detachment, however) shine through a glorious world of nonsense and absurd plotting in order to expel a sterile, deathlike power. In an analysis of this sort, Frye returns to Cornford's Aristophanes, not merely to New Comedy. On the other hand, Dickens' humor, which is hardly identical with a display of "humors," gets short shrift in Frye's essay. The point is that New Comedy does not reveal an essentially indulgent, tolerant, democratizing humor; and it is therefore not basically germane to the essence of Dickens' comedy (which, to be sure, can be rather wicked at times), just as it is not germane to the spirit of *Huckleberry Finn*.

Since there is much satire in Dickens, as well as humor (and a great deal of farce), it may be noted here that satire has received its own share of anthropological attention, especially in Robert C. Elliott's *The Power of Satire: Magic, Ritual, Art*, a study which explicitly recurs to the work of Cornford, among others, and which aims to trace manifestations of the magically abusive, death-delivering sting in protosatirical ritual and poetry up to the contemporary period. The last section of Elliott's book attempts to show how satire's "original connection" with magic, ritual, and myth "survives, in underground and distorted ways, in satire written today."[34] Actually his final chapters are devoted only to Wyndham Lewis' theory of satire and Roy Campbell's satiric practice. But if one finally emerges into today's satire only with Lewis and Campbell, the voyage from ritualism to modernism seems hardly worth the effort.

The reason Elliott selects Wyndham Lewis and Roy Camp-

[33] Northrop Frye, "Dickens and the Comedy of Humors," in *Experience in the Novel: Selected Papers from the English Institute*, ed. Roy Harvey Pearce (New York: Columbia University Press, 1968), p. 79.

[34] Robert C. Elliott, *The Power of Satire: Magic, Ritual, Art* (Princeton: Princeton University Press, 1960), p. vii.

bell as sole specimens of contemporary satiric energy is that
they either speculate on, or demonstrate, precisely the kind of
outright fury of derision that harks back to archaic sources of
deadly vituperation. Elliott himself is perfectly aware of the
huge gap between the magic ferocity of the ritual curse and
its distant sublimations in complex satiric art. He fully realizes
that "it would be folly to suggest that satire in Western civilized society has any but the most remote affiliations with its
ritual origins" (p. 282). But if that is so, why does he insist
that it is "crucial" for our "understanding of the image of the
satirist as it develops over the centuries, as it exists in our own
day" (p. 15), to see in him an inheritor of killing laughter, of
verbal assassination? Satire's mortifying mockery—a kind of
death by ridicule—is a powerful phenomenon, but its ancestry
of ritual maleficence, while surely interesting, is hardly crucial
for an understanding of any great modern satirist.

In any case satire, whether blistering or benign, is anger
that has been alchemized into comedy. Much too often, unfortunately, the kind of bile that eats up levity and dissolves
detachment is erroneously equated with satire. (Similarly, the
term "tragical satire," for all its considerable reputation, is a
misnomer.) Thus Thersites, in Shakespeare's *Troilus and
Cressida*, has a marvelously satiric wit, but it is often ruined
by unalloyed rancor, which should be recognized as such. The
danger of lapsing from comedy into undisguised wrath or disgust is of course the savage satirist's constant liability. Such a
lapse is perhaps best exemplified by the animosities of Juvenal,
only a few of whose sixteen "satires" are actually satiric.

I do not intend the preceding remarks to suggest even re-
motely that the ritual or folklore concept of comedy does not
have its value. A reading of C. L. Barber's *Shakespeare's Festive Comedy*, for example, suffices to demonstrate that value.
Barber brilliantly analyzes, not the final "comedies" with their
presumptive mantic glow of definitive revelation, but rather the
products of what he calls the Aristophanic, "Old Comedy cast"
of Shakespeare's work, which "results from his participation in
native Saturnalian traditions of the popular theatre and the

popular holidays."[35] As Barber sees them, these home-bred traditions of carnival liberty (the May games, for instance, or the Lord of Misrule festivities) correspond to the rhythms of the magic invocation to fertility and the magic abuse of barrenness which Cornford signalizes in ancient ritual: "The same double way of achieving release appears in Shakespeare's festive plays" (p. 7). In comedies like *A Midsummer Night's Dream*, *As You Like It*, and *Twelfth Night*—and in characters like Falstaff— "the poetry about the pleasures of nature and the naturalness of pleasure serves to evoke beneficent natural impulses; and much of the wit, mocking the good housewife Fortune from her wheel, acts to free the spirit as does the ritual abuse of hostile spirits" (p. 7). These hostile spirits (unnaturalness, puritanic decorum, frozen energy, kill-joy intrusiveness) destroy growth, love, vitality, warm pleasure, merriment, and gloriously unfettered folly. Festive comedy lays these destroyers low, and restores spontaneity and joy.

But festive comedy, Barber suggests, provides not merely a visceral and psychic deliverance from sterile controls. It also illuminates the mind. That is, Saturnalian release leads to "clarification," a "heightened awareness of the relation between man and 'nature'—the nature celebrated on holiday" (p. 8). Liberated consciousness does not turn anarchic; it does not produce a splintering of the social code. As Barber puts it formulaically, the process of liberation commences with a leap from restraint to release; but it is perfected only by a complementary movement from license to limits. (In essence, this is Freud's view of the uses of tendentious wit.) The complete sequence, from stereotyped normality to uninhibited revelry and then back to refreshed responsibility, is highly parabolic: misrule is futile unless it generates a sane and, ideally, a more wholesome acceptance of rule, of civilized order and grace. Festivity must finally yield to civility. Failure to follow this pattern is variously punished in Shakespeare's festive comedies: Sir Toby Belch,

[35] C. L. Barber, *Shakespeare's Festive Comedy: A Study of Dramatic Form and Its Relation to Social Custom* (Princeton: Princeton University Press), p. 3.

for example, is tellingly rebuked, while Falstaff is simply cast off.

In raising the question of saturnalianism, Barber asserts that Shakespeare is "more Aristophanic than any other great English comic dramatist" (p. 3). This is a defensible position, but only so long as one realizes that recklessness and fantasticality are far more circumscribed by civility in Shakespeare than they are in Aristophanes, and that the reason for this difference is that whimsy, anomaly, and outrage in Shakespearean comedy are generally pressed into the service of a humorous, tolerant vision of life. The Aristophanic vision is dissimilar: it is primarily a composite of farce and satire. Barber himself informs us that Shakespeare's festive comedies express "the experience of moving to humorous understanding through saturnalian release" (p. 4); in so saying he is pointing to humor as an end and saturnalianism as a means. Which signifies that Shakespeare's humor invites, indulges, and gentles the primitive drive toward release. If the vulnerable revelers in *Twelfth Night*, for example, are shepherded back to security and grace, that is because from the perspective of humor their imperfections are forgivable and even lovable. *The Birds*, on the other hand, does not end in restored civility, but rather in a new civilization, one that has repudiated conventional society and the gods to boot. So despite its consummation in harmony, Aristophanes' grotesque iconoclasm in *The Birds* makes saturnalianism much more than a means; it is also an inviolable part of the end.

Actually saturnalianism (the Golden Age refracted into the revelry of abolished restraints) is pre-eminently both the mode and the fulfillment of farce. And just as the anthropological speculations in Cornford's *Origin of Attic Comedy* provide an initial grasp of the subject, so Freud's *Jokes and Their Relation to the Unconscious* offers the psychological theory that best brings it up to date. That is why Barber quotes Freud to help explain the idea of saturnalianism. And that is why Freud is also cited by Erich Segal, whose *Roman Laughter: The Comedy of Plautus* is, admittedly, to some extent inspired by

Shakespeare's Festive Comedy. Segal, who: interprets Plautus' comedy as a festive liberation from an overdeveloped Roman superego,[36] uses Freudianism to underscore comedy's momentary flouting of the rules of society. Plautus' art, he comments, "does not give rise to 'thoughtful laughter,' but Meredith may not be correct in seeing this as the aim of True Comedy. For True Comedy should banish *all* thought—of mortality and morality. It should evoke a laughter which temporarily lifts from us the weight of the world, whether we call it 'das Unbehagen,' loathèd melancholy, or *gravitas*" (p. 14). But it would be more correct to claim that saturnalian farce, not "True Comedy," lightens both the tension of morality and the burden of mortality.

Comedy itself is too diverse to subserve a single, exclusive quality or function; that is why it is neither the advocate of Meredithian mind nor the exponent of Plautine release. "Comedy" has to be recognized as a matrix term that embraces miscellaneous impulses, which can be sensed empirically as effects before they are regarded as intentions. One such impulse—drastic irrationality—will become progressively the center of attention in the chapters that follow.

[36] Erich Segal, *Roman Laughter: The Comedy of Plautus* (Cambridge, Mass.: Harvard University Press, 1968), p. 13.

2

Cynical Wit

Freud does not sum up comedy as a whole and therefore does not define its central concern as the symbolic overthrow of moral restraint or social power. He analyzes, instead, such matters as wit, laughter, "the comic," caricature, humor, and nonsense. According to Freud, it is pre-eminently wit that permits us to relish a curative recantation of civilization. And along with wit, another comic force allows us to gambol on the green fields of lawlessness: nonsense.

A number of psychoanalytical theorists, however, have made rebellious release the key to comedy as a whole. For example, in 1926, Ludwig Jekels wrote an essay, "On the Psychology of Comedy," in which he took the oedipal guilt of the son in tragedy, inverted it, and applied it in comedy to the father, the "disturber of love."[1] Through this displacement of guilt, the father is "degraded into a son" (p. 430). And the result of this debasement is that the need for a tyrannical superego vanishes: "The ego, which has liberated itself from the tyrant, uninhibitedly [vents] its humor, wit, and every sort of comic manifestation in a very ecstasy of freedom"; indeed, "comedy represents an aesthetic correlate of mania" (p. 431).

Two of Jekels' examples of oedipal comedy may briefly clarify his theory. In Molière's *The Miser*, Harpagon desires

[1] Ludwig Jekels, "On the Psychology of Comedy," in *Theories of Comedy*, ed. Lauter, p. 427.

49

his son's chosen bride; but he is foiled. The play therefore illustrates the basic stage of oedipal comedy, which shows the rebel son successfully struggling against the father for the same sexual prize. In Heinrich von Kleist's *The Broken Jug*, oedipal comedy is less literal: Judge Adam, a father figure, is declared guilty, and the young man Ruprecht, a son surrogate, innocent, after an investigation aimed at pinning down responsibility for a nocturnal erotic disturbance which involves the breaking of a jug in the care of the virgin Eve. Ruprecht therefore represents subversive youth, responding to its erotic impulses by waging war against crusty authority.

Jekels' theory, which he states is derived mainly from his analysis of the comedies of Plautus and Terence, has been frequently adopted by critics. Leslie Fiedler, for example, declares that "the New Comedy, being a comic version of the Oedipus conflict, demands that the initial check to love come from parental opposition, preferably the intervention of an unsympathetic father, whom the son can finally defeat in taking possession of the contested girl."[2] Actually parental opposition without sexual claims is the usual New Comedy threat to the fortunes of young lovers. But oedipal symbolism in comic theory scarcely needs erotic rivalry—or even family roots. Jekels himself widens the oedipal issue to such an extent that sexual competition between youth and age is by no means necessary. That is, so long as the major forces in comedy stem from some kind of "filial" resistance and some sort of "paternal" prohibition, oedipal comedy will have a sufficiency of raw materials. Once oedipal comedy is lifted out of a purely familial or quasi-familial milieu, it can of course include all the funny complications that ensue upon youthful revolt against social tyranny.

Nor is that all. The chain of guilt-laden authority in oedipal comedy can stretch all the way from such conventional symbolic extensions of paternity as police supervision, juridical censure, political fiat, and religious taboos to cosmic predestination itself. In sum, oedipal comedy has become associated with any quest

[2] Leslie Fiedler, *Love and Death in the American Novel* (New York: Criterion, 1960), p. 75.

for liberation—which is why its utility has become rather dubious. For that matter, Jekels' own thinking on the subject is not very helpful. Thus in the latter part of his essay he writes that clarity with respect to the proper attribution of guilt (whether to son or father) may be long delayed in the development of a given play. This means that one may not know for a considerable length of time (perhaps not until the very end of the play) whether one is viewing a comedy or a tragedy.[3] But if that is so, what happens in the meantime to the presumably cumulative "ecstasy of freedom" that is necessary in any "aesthetic correlate of mania"?

In the early part of his essay Jekels makes the even more astonishing claim that if a father figure in a particular work can be shown to be weighed down by guilt, then that work is a comedy. Thus *The Merchant of Venice* is a comedy because Antonio, a father figure, is heavily indebted; his money debt is a "mere substitute for moral guilt" (p. 426). Even more questionable than this juggling with comedy and guilt is Jekels' analysis of *Tartuffe:* "If one regards the hypocrite as a mere derivative of the father Orgon [the latter] becomes the son's rival for the mother's affections" (p. 428). Actually, though, according to Jekels' own oedipal theory, Tartuffe might better be seen as a derivative of the son, slyly attempting to deny Orgon both his wife and his house.

Jekels may be critically clumsy; but it is entirely comprehensible that a simplificative theory of comedy should emerge from the psychoanalytical stress on our painful, obsessive regard for authority and restraint. The arts, Freud himself tells us in *Civilization and Its Discontents*, are among the "palliative remedies"[4] we utilize to cope with excessive disillusion and suffering. And since the "substitute gratifications" (p. 15) supplied by the arts allow us, to some extent, to escape from the oppressions of reality, the reader of Freud may easily conclude that the art of comedy must be especially capable, by virtue of

[3] Jekels, "On the Psychology of Comedy," p. 430.
[4] Sigmund Freud, *Civilization and Its Discontents*, trans. Joan Riviere (Garden City, N.Y.: Doubleday, Anchor, 1958), p. 14.

its frequent levity and irreverence, of temporarily nullifying the authority of the superego, which, as Freud indicates, exhausts us with feelings of guilt (p. 81). For this reason it becomes almost irresistible to derive the satisfactions of comedy from the discontents of civilization, especially those discontents produced by legality and morality. Still, Freud nowhere suggests that "comedy" is an entity marked by a joyous insurrection against authority or that it is, in essence, a gay dechristianization designed to recharge our enfeebled nature and purge us of guilt. Only wit and nonsense are the comic powers that grant us a therapeutic reprieve from our bondage to civilization's rules and scruples.

2

Freud's *Der Witz und seine Beziehung zum Unbewussten* was published in 1905 and translated by A. A. Brill in 1916 as *Wit and Its Relation to the Unconscious.* The English title proved troublesome, for Freud had included under the rubric of *Witz* not only witticisms and puns, but a congeries of jokes, largely Jewish (which often have witty punch lines). That is why Eric Bentley, for one, in his essay "The Psychology of Farce" (1958) flatly rejected Brill's use of "wit" and substituted the translation "jokes."[5] In 1960, James Strachey's new translation of Freud's book made this term official: the title became *Jokes and Their Relation to the Unconscious.* Terminological faultfinding in reverse had been foreseen by Strachey, who admits that his consistent use of the word "joke" for *Witz* wrongs certain of Freud's contexts; but he also maintains that such linguistic difficulties are only superficial.[6] They are liable to be more than superficial, however, if one is convinced that witticisms and jokes ought not to be lumped together indiscriminately.

Strachey does not help matters much when he suggests that

[5] Eric Bentley, "The Psychology of Farce," in *"Let's Get a Divorce!" and Other Plays* (New York: Hill and Wang, 1958), p. xiv, n. 4.

[6] Sigmund Freud, *Jokes and Their Relation to the Unconscious,* trans. James Strachey (New York: Norton, 1960), Editor's Preface, pp. 7–8.

the central distinction between wit and jokes is that the former is "applied only to the most refined and intellectual kind of jokes" (p. 7). For what is at issue here is Freud's concept of wit's relation to the unconscious, which, in spite of his own mixed bag of *Witz* specimens, is alien to the contrived nature of most joke productions. Decades ago Constance Rourke pointed out, in *American Humor*, that the solvent of humor had "often become a jaded formula, the comic rebound automatic."[7] This somewhat elegiac appraisal of the ordinary American's proneness to sure-fire comic rejoinders is foreign to the spirit of works like Stewart Harral's *When It's Laughter You're After*. For this book, like its multitudinous peers, specializes precisely in the prefabrication of the comic rebound automatic. Harral offers tips on ways of compiling and hoarding material for laughter so that jokeless pariahs may rise to the eminence of ready jesters. In fact, he offers fourteen redundant and somewhat sickening recommendations for the systematic accumulation and utilization of successful gags whose "mission of mirth" will help us "replace fear with faith."[8] Jokes are so often consciously manufactured or mechanically applied as the small change of popular dialogue that they can hardly be mentioned in the same breath with the mysteries of the unconscious.

One of the paramount ideas in Freud's analysis of wit (tendentious, instinctually propelled wit) is that its unpremeditated genesis is in the wellsprings of the unconscious. This is not to say that, even if they originate in unpredictable levies on the unconscious, witticisms cannot be widely circulated or thoroughly rehearsed. Both jokes and witticisms, which often depend on comparable verbal techniques and similar psychological impulses, can be committed to memory; but this does not mean that their origins are identical. The immediate relevance of this distinction to the discussion of wit that follows is that I avail myself of a semantic compromise. I refer pri-

[7] Constance Rourke, *American Humor* (Garden City, N.Y.: Doubleday, Anchor, 1953), p. 232.
[8] Stewart Harral, *When It's Laughter You're After* (Norman: Oklahoma University Press, 1962), p. xi.

marily to wit, though I also use the term "jokes" whenever it seems apropos. Actually, there are difficulties in Freud's text that no compromise translation can remove. To put it bluntly, Freud's celebrated study of wit is ungainly. It conveys a sense of laboratory strain, and it often presents sequences of thought that seem to be forged from moment to moment. There are times, moreover, when Freud, cogitating in a wash of backward and forward movements, simply fails to be lucid.

The first important point to make is that Freud distinguishes at the outset between verbal wit and conceptual wit. Verbal wit consists of various word or phrase condensations and fusions; the prime interest is in clever sound coincidence or punning. Conceptual wit accentuates ideas and the process of thinking, not fugitive word and sound play. Once we grasp this distinction, we note a second scheme of classification, which divides wit into the innocent (or harmless) kind and the tendentious (or instinctually purposeful) type. The two systems of wit categorization (verbal or conceptual; innocent or tendentious) are independent of each other, but they constantly merge. Thus both innocent wit and tendentious wit can be either verbal or conceptual in their emphases. (Nevertheless, the most innocent kind of wit remains verbal rather than conceptual.)

Innocent conceptual wit may be stimulating and intellectually valuable. But innocent wit of either sort, verbal or conceptual, provides a gratifying realization that one's mind is functioning brightly. Moreover, insofar as innocent wit is a social performance, it provides an exhibitionistic satisfaction—that of bolstering one's vanity and prestige. Still, "the pleasurable effect of innocent jokes is as a rule a moderate one,"[9] Freud points out, and may be registered only in a slight smile. The pleasures accruing from tendentious wit, on the other hand, are intense, for this kind of wit is a verbal harvest of repressed drives. The tendentious wit maker releases inhibitory psychic energy; as a result, his detonations of the unconscious destroy civilized surveillance, if only momentarily. By evacuating the painful ethic

[9] *Jokes and Their Relation to the Unconscious*, p. 96.

of good breeding and correct form, tendentious wit indirectly restores primary joys (those delights that education and virtue oblige us to renounce).

Freud discerns four kinds of tendentious wit: obscene, hostile, cynical, and sceptical. Both hostile wit and cynical wit minister to our thirst for aggression and reprisal; but hostile wit attacks individuals only, while cynical wit assaults institutional values (or persons symbolizing them): moral ideals, social norms, religious dogmas, and so on. (Cynical wit is instinctually grounded in hostility; but there is a significant leap between the instinct of hostility and its metamorphosis into a cynical witticism.) Sceptical wit, which attacks man's presumptuous claims to knowledge and understanding, is barely noticed by Freud, and may be safely subsumed beneath cynical wit. Whether cynical, hostile, or obscene, tendentious wit represents a confluence of burning primitivism (the world of the id, though Freud did not designate it as such in 1905) and cool sophistication (the world of rhetoric).

Though Freud is not sparing in his specimens of hostile or cynical wit, sexual illustrations of the instantaneous conspiracy between the unconscious and the intellect are lacking in his text. But they are not lacking in G. Legman's *Rationale of the Dirty Joke*, which is specifically indebted to Freud's work on wit, as well as to Martha Wolfenstein's *Children's Humor*. In the introduction to his remarkable analytical anthology Legman acknowledges the existence only of hostile wit and obscene wit. Cynical wit he somewhat facilely resolves into a sexual mockery of authority figures.[10] Another questionable procedure is his merger of two distinctly separate Freudian concepts: tendentious wit and anxiety-alleviating humor.[11] Still, Legman does make a sharper, bolder analysis of sexual jokes than Freud.

[10] G. Legman, *Rationale of the Dirty Joke* (New York: Grove, 1968).

[11] This fusion—and confusion—of wit and humor seems inevitable in psychoanalytical discussions of comedy. Thus Martha Wolfenstein puts into "joking" both the repudiation of pain and the gratification of forbidden wishes (*Children's Humor* [Glencoe, Ill.: Free Press, 1954], p. 11). Similarly, Theodore Reik, in *Jewish Wit* (New York: Gamut, 1962), cites many humorous, anxiety-dissolving jokes.

This is especially valuable because there is some inconsistency in Freud's approach to the subject. Freud states that obscene wit serves the purposes of exposure (exhibitionism). But he makes smut, the raw material of obscene wit, synonymous with attempted seduction or sexual aggression—and also with exposure.[12] It is almost as though, in refining the vulgarity of smut, sexual wit were obliged to soften its aims. Cutting through this inconsistency, Legman forthrightly equates sexual jokes with verbal rape or verbal seduction (but sometimes with self-denudation too), depending on the degree of cleverness the jokes display.[13]

Just as sexual wit is an admirable substitute rape or seduction (society—Freud's "third person"—would show disgust at an outright violation of erotic good taste), so hostile wit is a laudable equivalent for direct physical assault (society would be repelled by fisticuffs in the drawing room). Similarly, even while it sternly polices subversive flare-ups in the streets, society hugs to its bosom the maker of cynical witticisms who ruins authority with poise and polish.

But the third species of wit, cynical wit, best retaliates against compulsory virtue and renunciation. (The kind of psychic deliverance which cynical wit provides for the few, Freud observes, is procured for the many by vulgarized epicurean laxity.) Unfortunately, the injustice and emasculation that cynical wit attacks are not ultimately curable. Society is a system of constraints; and Freud is interested, not in differentiating between degrees of constraint in various societies, but rather in underlining the changeless common denominator of all social control: instinctual impoverishment.

Only once in his study of wit does Freud inveigh against a source of social villainy—when he refers to the unfair moral rigors of a Christianized capitalistic society:

The wishes and desires of men have a right to make themselves acceptable alongside of exacting and ruthless morality. And in our

---

[12] *Jokes and Their Relation to the Unconscious*, pp. 97–98.
[13] *Rationale of the Dirty Joke*, pp. 12–13.

days it has been said in forceful and stirring sentences that this morality is only a selfish regulation laid down by the few who are rich and powerful and who can satisfy their wishes at any time without any postponement. So long as the art of healing has not gone further in making our life safe and so long as social arrangements do no more to make it more enjoyable, so long will it be impossible to stifle the voice within us that rebels against the demands of morality.[14]

But though he belabors the ignoble rich in this passage, Freud makes no direct plea for social justice or political reform. He is too conscious of the eternal conflict between society's necessary demands and the individual's equally necessary liberties to commit himself to a radical or utopian stance.[15] That is why cynical witticisms and jokes are indispensable: they defy the forces of reaction and suppression; and they permit the powerless, if only indirectly, to cope with the irrationality and onerousness of authority. To entrust oneself to the shapers and preservers of a "ruthless morality" would be a psychological impossibility without such underground resistance. Somehow, the psyche must gratify its insurrectionary impulses against society.

To a political activist, the elevation of cynical wit and jokes above the direct purgation of social ills—with the result that the hypocrisy of society's "repressive tolerance," to use Marcuse's phrase,[16] is merely confirmed—must appear to be a monstrous surrender to social intimidation. But Freud has in mind the difficulties posed by certain perennial factors in cultural

[14] *Jokes and Their Relation to the Unconscious*, p. 110.

[15] In a much later work, *New Introductory Lectures on Psychoanalysis*, trans. James Strachey (New York: Norton, 1965), Freud maintains that the analyst, for professional and practical reasons, cannot adopt a partisan position against the established social order. More specifically, he declares that psychoanalytical education cannot undertake to "mould its pupils into rebels. It will have played its part if it sends them away as healthy and efficient as possible." But if psychoanalysis does not produce revolutionary children, Freud adds, "it itself contains enough revolutionary factors to ensure that no one educated by it will in later life take the side of reaction and suppression" (p. 151).

[16] For a compact treatment of this kind of hypocrisy, see Herbert Marcuse's essay "Repressive Tolerance," in Robert P. Wolff, Barrington Moore, Jr., and Herbert Marcuse, *A Critique of Pure Tolerance* (Boston: Beacon, 1970), pp. 81–123.

and psychic life. Thus, in *Civilization and Its Discontents*, he deprecates socialism's "idealistic expectations" because they ask too much of human nature. And he accuses the "communistic system" of basing itself on the psychologically "untenable illusion" that the human instinct of aggression can be stamped out by abolishing private property.[17] Similarly, in *New Introductory Lectures on Psychoanalysis*, Freud points out that the role of both the superego (through its retention of traditional ideologies) and the instinctual impulses (through their preservation of aggressiveness and their drive toward pleasure) has been underrated by Marxism and other materialistic theories of history that endorse the primacy of economic motivation. Marxism in Russia, he comments, has become a prohibitory religion with many unprovable illusions; and its attempt to create a new order of society without friction, while in the meantime redistributing outlets for aggressive tendencies, involves a highly improbable transformation of human nature. Even a drastically improved social order will have to "struggle for an incalculable time with the difficulties which the untameable character of human nature presents to every kind of social community."[18]

This brings us back to Freud's observation that cynical wit remains an essential mode of therapy in an epoch not yet equipped to treat all the sores created by the pathology of the social structure. One might expect that the malfeasances of the classes that wield social power would be the major targets of cynical wit. But the fact is that marriage, not political injustice or capitalistic fraud, is the chief institutional victim of cynical wit. For it is in marriage that society's regulations pinch most agonizingly: "There is no more personal claim than that for sexual freedom," Freud remarks, "and at no point has civilization tried to exercise severer suppression than in the sphere of sexuality."[19] This is especially painful because "mar-

[17] *Civilization and Its Discontents*, pp. 103, 63. Freud states that the fight against economic inequality deserves one's good will; but he also avers that human inequalities are ineradicable (p. 63).
[18] *New Introductory Lectures*, pp. 67, 178, 180, 181.
[19] *Jokes and Their Relation to the Unconscious*, p. 110.

riage is not an arrangement calculated to satisfy a man's sexuality" (p. 111).

Freud's examination of marriage in *Jokes and Their Relation to the Unconscious* is followed by brief excursions into two other constrictive areas of civilization that have been traditionally subjected to cynical digs. The first is national or racial character and circumstance (under the heading of racial phenomena, Freud investigates self-critical Jewish joke lore); the second is religious belief. If, then, we add national, racial, and religious vexations to iniquitous morality, social tyranny, and marital claustrophobia, we can see that cynical wit has values enough to rebel against.

As it happens, most of the cynical witticisms and jokes Freud deploys (a number of them are borrowed from predecessors who wrote on the theory of laughter) are extraliterary—not the least important reason being that newspaper selections, personal anecdotes, and social tidbits offer particularly graphic evidences of the energy of wit. It is true that he recurs frequently to Lichtenberg and Heine; but Lichtenberg, the Enlightenment satirist, is generally cited for innocent witticisms, and even Heine is quoted as often for his harmless word play as for his cynical demolitions. Other literary wit makers rarely appear in Freud's pages. Voltaire, for example, is represented but once, and then only on a topical matter; he is quoted as having remarked about Jean Baptiste Rousseau's "Ode to Posterity," "This poem will not reach its destination" (p. 68). For equally good examples of the literature of wit, we shall have to search outside Freud's text.

3

To begin with, we had best not muffle the distinction between witticisms and aphorisms, a distinction which is often hard to establish but which must be made in order to give cynical wit its psychological due. Cynical witticisms are comic utterances that derive their power from sly disruptions of psychic censorship and of verbal expectations. On the other hand, aphorisms are noncomic: their tone can be solemn, exalted, bitter, rhapsodical, poignant, apocalyptic, and so on. Nor do they ordinarily strive for structural cleverness. Instead of offering psychic relief, the sobriety of aphorisms may very well reinforce the disciplinary superego by accentuating moral and social lapses (although this effect is somewhat counterbalanced by the intellectual pleasure of a well-wrought revelation). Witticisms, on the other hand, give easement to the id. Delight of this sort is abundantly available, for example, in *The Devil's Dictionary*, that cynic's wordbook in which Ambrose Bierce plays the role of a superior, wickedly smiling diabolist who extorts from us a wry smile of disenchantment at the collapse of the ideal or the fatality of folly. Moreover, since irony, along with sulphur and brimstone, is among the chief natural resources of hell, it is not surprising that Bierce's demonic dictionary is a breviary of ironic attitudes—attitudes which are meant, like all Mephistophelean mockery, to put mankind in its absurd, damned place.[20]

When Bierce informs us that a Christian is "one who follows the teachings of Christ in so far as they are not inconsistent with a life of sin," his cynically witty view of the human tendency to hold on to moral weaknesses at any cost delightfully disburdens the id of its repressed nihilism; but it also communicates a measure of truth. These two aspects of cynical wit (tenable truth and psychic release) are not equally important. Actually, cynical wit is likely to be more valuable as a destroyer of psychic repression than as a vehicle of veracity. That is because the truths of cynical wit are the instinctually rooted, dangerous half- or quarter-truths which society officially suppresses. Certainly Bierce's wit supplies more psychic alleviation

[20] Ambrose Bierce, *The Devil's Dictionary* (New York: Sagamore, 1957). In his introduction, Carey McWilliams declares that the *Dictionary* contains "the best of Bierce's satire" (p. vii) and that Bierce himself is "the greatest American satirist in the classic tradition" (p. x). McWilliams also states that Bierce is not a cynic but is instead a severe moralist (p. xi). Yet the satanism of the *Dictionary*, nourished by defunctive idealism and expressed as trenchant cynicism, casts a pervasively ironic, absurdist look at the perennially benighted tendencies of human nature.

than trustworthy truth when he defines a beggar as "one who has relied on the assistance of his friends," or logic as "the art of thinking and reasoning in strict accordance with the limitations and incapacities of the human misunderstanding," or opportunity as "a favorable occasion for grasping a disappointment." Obviously these cynical epigrams do not play fair. But fairness is not the point. The epigrams strike home because their partial but powerful truths allow us to throw off our forced respect for received ideas.

Advocates of the aphorism not only scant the epigram's power to gratify repressed subversiveness but minimize its intellectual impact. For example, Louis Kronenberger, in his introduction to La Rochefoucauld's *Maxims*, sees the aphorism, at its best, as a distillation of wisdom or a diamond of compressed insight. The epigram, on the contrary, is incapable of being both profound and pithy. "An aphorism," he writes, "must seem not just shrewd but pointed, not just true but trenchant. . . . At the same time, the true aphorist must be serious—his gift for polish must adorn something more than clever epigrams or flashy paradoxes; indeed he must be not only serious but honestly investigative."[21] Now an epigram may not be "serious" in the conventional sense, and may not be shaped by a sage. But its lightness is often conveyed by an investigative honesty of its own; and its partial truths may be stunning eye openers. Epigrams may be flimsy, just as aphorisms may be flat. Many epigrams, however, have an amusing, clever gloss that has by no means been purchased at the expense of probing intellection. Kronenberger himself speaks of Wilde's gift (also Emerson's and Johnson's) of the "pregnant or witty saying" (p. 14). (I assume the "or" establishes synonymity, not antonymity.) And what is an epigram but wit that is turned out with particular finesse and finality?

In the foreword to *The Viking Book of Aphorisms*, Kronenberger and Auden declare that "aphorisms are essentially an aristocratic genre of writing," but only in the sense that "im-

[21] *The Maxims of La Rochefoucauld*, trans. and intro. Louis Kronenberger (New York: Modern Library, 1959), p. 21.

62   *Comedy*

plicit in the [aphorist's] assertion is a conviction that he is wiser or more intelligent than his readers. For this reason the aphorist who adopts a folksy style with 'democratic' diction and grammar is a cowardly and insufferable hypocrite."[22] The two anthologists distinguish aphorisms not only from folksy wisdom but from limited epigrams. They argue that "an epigram need only be true of a single case . . . or effective only in a particular polemical context" (p. v), whereas an aphorism conveys universal or, at least, general truth. But this comment translates only into the fact that tendentious epigrams may be individually hostile or sexual. Tendentious cynical epigrams, on the other hand, are quite skillful at disseminating general truths, even if these are fractional—as what social and moral truths are not? In any case, *The Viking Book of Aphorisms* harbors more than a few epigrams. Auden and Kronenberger suggest that aphorisms "need not make the reader laugh," but their final hope is that they have incorporated in their selections some of the less frequently exported aspects of "our technological culture . . . such as humor" (p. vi). But if Auden and Kronenberger mix aphorisms and "humor," they are bound to come up with witticisms. For example, under the anthological rubric "Religion and God," Kierkegaard's aphorism, "Prayer does not change God, but it changes him who prays," follows Sydney Smith's witticism, "There is not the least use preaching to anyone unless you chance to catch them ill" (p. 87). Similarly, Simone Weil's aphorism, "God gives himself to men as powerful or perfect—it is for them to choose," is preceded by the epigram of the Polish wit Stanislaw Lec, "The finger of God never leaves identical fingerprints" (p. 86).

Lec's *Unkempt Thoughts* is the subject of an essay by Clifton Fadiman titled "Lec and the Art of the Aphorist,"[23] in which Fadiman more or less equates aphorisms with witticisms. An aphorism, he remarks, "sells the part for the whole. Its plausibility derives from its concision, which stuns, and its wit,

[22] *The Viking Book of Aphorisms: A Personal Selection*, ed. W. H. Auden and Louis Kronenberger (New York: Viking, 1962), pp. v–vi.
[23] Stanislaw J. Lec, *Unkempt Thoughts*, trans. Jacek Galazka, intro. Clifton Fadiman (New York: St. Martin's, 1962).

which dazzles. Hence our pleasure in it depends upon the partial arrest of our reasoning faculty." He goes on to say that this is true also of the aphorism's "flashy younger brothers, the epigram and the paradox" (p. 5). Whether our reasoning faculty is actually arrested (even if only partially) by aphorisms is highly debatable. Much less debatable is Fadiman's unsatisfactory merger of aphorisms and witty utterances. At one point, it is true, he declares that the classical literary aphorism "may or may not be witty" (p. 16). But one of his several definitions of the aphorism unambiguously makes it out to be "a perfectly phrased general comment, salted with true wit, on human life" (p. 15). And his notes on Lec's anticlassical, chillingly unkempt thoughts highlight the Polish writer's "piercing epigrams, some of them just lightly flecked with blood" (p. 20). The truth, of course, is that Lec produces aphorisms that may—but often do not—tend toward the amusing (for example, "In some lands exile is the greatest punishment; in others the greatest humanitarians should fight for it") (p. 59) and witticisms that are unmistakably comic (for example, "On the neck of a giraffe a flea begins to believe in immortality") (p. 28). His aphorisms (which, like all good specimens of the genre, proffer relief from triteness) often overhaul our superegos by substituting new moral freight for old, or by identifying the old more sharply; his epigrams, on the contrary, gratify the id by desanctifying traditional values.

In the final analysis, the detection of aphoristic "seriousness" or epigrammatic "comedy" may very well hinge on individual assays: one man's aphorism may be another man's epigram. But in general the question of tone ought not to be overly problematic. Thus if we pick up Blake's counterbiblical "Proverbs of Hell," we shall very probably fall under the spell of a number of remarkable aphorisms, clearly recognizable as such because of their burningly sober transvaluations of morality, which attack debased ruling ideas and glorify what should supplant them: the wonder and defiance of human creativeness. When Blake writes, for example, that "the road of excess leads to the palace of wisdom," he is taking a stand against a cultural surfeit of prudence and moderation; his message is that it is more fruitful to live by the gospel of romantic expressiveness than by the laws of contractive rationality. To see how this aphorism differs from a tendentious witticism, we have only to glance at Bierce's definition of "twice": "Once too often." Bierce's epigram instantly appeals to our cynical intelligence, that fact-finding agency which is so often a more reliable guide to human experience than a Blakean heart. Many epigrams do as much: they cut into the blubber of romantic enthusiasm, or clear the air of varieties of humbug. They often do so, moreover, with ravishing insolence.

When Aristotle observed that wit is "educated insolence,"[24] he was defining hostile rather than cynical wit. Imaginative malice attaches to all tendentious wit, but it is true that epigrammatic assassination has always been the preserve of lords and ladies of aggressive wit. Lady Sneerwell's aphorism in *The School for Scandal*, "Pshaw! there's no possibility of being witty without a little ill-nature" (I.i) would therefore seem to understate the case. Yet Sir Peter Teazle's distinctly post-Restoration rejoinder one act later, "Ah, madam, true wit is more nearly allied to good nature than your ladyship is aware of" (II.ii), cannot be dismissed out of hand.

In the land of Eldorado in Voltaire's *Candide*, wit actually sparkles—at least at the royal level, which is the only level we hear about. The king of Eldorado is apparently not only adept at making witty remarks but, to the amazement of Candide, is witty even in translation.[25] Though wit in a perfect world would have to be entirely innocent, problems of wit gestation would exist even in utopia, since innocent wit, according to Freud, betrays elements of exhibitionism and vanity. And if we travel from utopia to heaven, we might justifiably expect a witty angel, by definition, to be damned or at least to be heading straight for Miltonic insurrection. On the other hand, we can imagine hell—not Dante's Inferno, for his punitive mytho-

[24] Quoted in *Unkempt Thoughts*, Introduction, p. 8.
[25] Voltaire, *Candide*, trans. Lowell Bair (New York: Bantam, 1959), p. 70.

logical monsters are mostly mental sluggards—to be over-
charged with wit's venom, especially when the use of other
tortures is temporarily in abeyance. Because the wit of the king
of Eldorado is not actually exemplified by Voltaire, we are
spared the task of judging the quality of His Majesty's benevolent pointedness. Nevertheless, we may agree that there is no
reason why blissful wisdom should not overflow in gracious
wit. After all, the exhilaration of animal spirits—to take a not
unrelated phenomenon—often crackles with playfully ingenious phrases.

There is also, to be sure, a literary tradition of intertwined
love and wit, though that tradition is not entirely edenic. According to its rules, hostile wit, flashing in simulated combat,
is indispensable in establishing romantic affinities and expectations. In *Much Ado about Nothing*, for example, Beatrice and
Benedick disclose a charming compulsion to engage in witty
sexual warfare. They cannot do otherwise, for lovers who exemplify the literary convention of wit combats paradoxically
solidify their courtship by flaunting their reciprocal incompatibility. Beatrice and Benedick are of course not engaged in
comic acerbity anywhere beneath the surface of their speech.
Their attacks seem to draw blood, to be sure. Thus Benedick,
recounting to Don Pedro the manner in which Beatrice (Lady
Disdain, Lady Tongue, harpy) has flung at him one barbed
jest after another, avows that "she speaks poniards, and every
word stabs. If her breath were as terrible as her terminations,
there were no living near her, she would infect to the north
star" (II.i). For all that, the mock assaults of Beatrice and
Benedick are basically amorous invitations tricked out as mirth-
ful, provocative indignities. At first their mutual amorousness
is not conscious; each has to be prompted by a conspiracy of
friends to plunge explicitly into the mood of love. In the end,
love and deprecatory playfulness are still busily entwined:
Benedick tells Beatrice he must love her for pity of her condition, while Beatrice replies that she is yielding to him to save
his life.

Wit, then, need not always be a species of civil savagery.

Yet this does not mean that wit suggests primarily happy, warm-hearted, harmonious perceptiveness. Marie C. Swabey, in *Comic Laughter*, more or less makes such an affirmation, claiming that wit is generated by a spirit of integrative joy, and adding that its supreme attributes are rational cogency and logical truth. But what Swabey prizes is, as it happens, fully accredited by Freud: she is actually talking about innocent conceptual wit, which Freud points out is not only pleasurable but (potentially, at any rate) intellectually valuable. Unfortunately, Swabey does not acknowledge a distinction between innocent wit and tendentious wit. She simply rejects the Freudian intimation that wit of any sort can be anchored in a shadowy, alogical (and for her, mythical) entity called the unconscious. Her way of explaining the intellectual aptness of wit (this aptness is all she recognizes; she considers sexual, hostile, and cynical witticisms to be more or less bizarre irrelevancies) is to appeal to the resources of the lightning-swift "intuitive reason," from whose matrix, she is convinced, wit springs full-blown. To her mind the role of wit, moreover, is the key to the function of comedy, which she identifies as the improvement of consciousness and the discernment of value, harmony, and (ultimately) cosmic beneficence.[26]

Because Swabey believes that wit is the foe of illogic, that it is indeed a pathfinder for reason, she attacks Freud's theory of wit as "essentially a weapon against logic" (p. 71). But she misrepresents Freud. For though it is true that logic in tendentious wit is usually the tool of instinct, logic is also perfectly at home (and untouched by motivated malignity) in innocent conceptual wit. If Freud does not elaborate on the wit maker's capacity for heightened lucidity and logical congruence, that is because his major interest is in tendentious wit; and tendentious wit, which is far more potent than innocent wit, is above all a psychological, not a logical, phenomenon.

[26] Marie C. Swabey, *Comic Laughter: A Philosophical Essay* (New Haven: Yale University Press, 1961), p. v.

4

In any event, Freud's opinion of the wit maker's intellectual powers is no mystery. He simply takes it for granted that a maker of witticisms is by definition clever and mentally stimulating, and that wit is bestowed on a small, select group of people.[27] He does, it is true, suggest that the creator of tendentious wit is a "disunited personality disposed to neurotic disorders" (p. 142). Thus Freud links Lichtenberg's wit to his hypochondria, while he locates the source of Heine's wit in the poet's early experience of suffering and rejection. But Freud adds that "the insufficiency of documentary evidence . . . will certainly prevent our setting up a hypothesis that a psychoneurotic constitution of this kind is a habitual or necessary subjective condition for the construction of jokes" (p. 142). It is safe to say no more than that the most favorable condition for the creation of tendentious wit is "the presence of numerous inhibited instincts, whose suppression has retained a certain degree of instability" (p. 143). On the other hand (and Freud also takes this for granted), tendentious wit can hardly be engendered unless the mind's crafty rhetoric merges instantaneously with the id's restive appetite. If Freud does not state axiomatically that one must be bright as well as balked in order to produce tendentious wit, that is because he knows, as everyone else does, that repressed dolts are seldom witty.

A number of literary wit makers, to be sure, plant authorial epigrams in the mouths of characters whose subjective determinants have been inadequately or even carelessly charted for the amount of wit they generate. Consider Mark Twain's *Pudd'nhead Wilson*. How is one to identify the true owner of the fretful unconscious that foments the chapter epigraphs in this novel? Actually these epigraphs are studded with both witticisms and aphorisms, at times mild, at times savage. If we eliminate the harmless witticisms and the innocuous aphorisms,

---

[27] *Jokes and Their Relation to the Unconscious*, p. 140.

there remain a score or so of brief assertions that soberly or comically establish disgust as the chief fact of life. Twain presents these epigraphs as Pudd'nhead Wilson's personal thoughts, though they are curiously sundered from the latter's tranquil, conscious (though not unsly) preoccupations.

But Wilson's unconscious has to be profoundly aggrieved, for a gratuitous sick joke he has perpetrated about a dog, a joke smacking of the casual cruelty of American frontier drollery, has branded Wilson a fool, a "pudd'nhead," in the eyes of the townspeople of Dawson's Landing almost immediately upon his arrival there. One might think that this public reaction of scorn would suggest to a sensible outsider like Wilson the probability that he has landed in an asinine community.[28] Common sense does not prevail, however. Wilson decides to live down his unlucky joke by residing among the very provincials who have relegated him to the status of a nitwit nonentity. Furthermore, he manifests no bewilderment or indignation in enduring his overwhelming setback; nor does he harbor any plan of reprisal. As the years go by, he accepts with preternatural calm the fact of being persistently bypassed on the road to local distinction. But though Wilson lives his decorously quiescent life in virtual isolation, he does gradually prove his worth to a very small number of acquaintances and one good friend. And at long last, without ever betraying a glimmer of hostility toward the society that has ruined his ambitions, he succeeds in capturing the good opinion of the citizens through his clever handling of a sensational murder case. He even garners the glory of a folk hero.

In this extremely protracted experience of social redemption, Wilson's ego, to all outward appearances, has never had to engage in any kind of moral struggle over the reality of his degraded condition. He has cultivated, instead, an uncomplicated and uncomplaining patience and humility. This self-

[28] F. R. Leavis, however, is convinced that Dawson's Landing, while provincially suspicious of originality of mind, "represents a society that has kept its full heritage of civilization" (Mark Twain, *Pudd'nhead Wilson* [New York: Grove, 1955], Introduction, p. 17).

effacement (it is not wholly candid) is all but unbelievable. To be sure, Twain's novel of slavery, miscegenation, confused identities, and loathsome betrayal abounds in fractures of credibility. But that a sudden, apparently irremediable disgrace caused by the unregenerate joke of a moment can persuade a promisingly unsaintly young man to nourish through the years a psychology of (apparently) blameless good will is among the least digestible premises of *Pudd'nhead Wilson*. That is why we cannot help paying special attention to a countervailing element in Wilson's behavior. This is his habit of studying improper mankind in silence and then pinpointing his conclusions in a calendar of frequently bitter aphorisms and epigrams. Now if this calendar—or rather, the noninnocent portion of it—is a faithful index of Wilson's repressed feelings, it becomes clear that while his ego has for decades maintained a pleasant, uninjured front, his id has been boiling all along in unadjusted fury. From the psychic recesses of his damaged but intelligent personality a culturally acceptable mode of retaliation and relief has emerged to settle society's hash—though Wilson prefers not to publicize his calendrical vindictiveness.

But Twain never clarifies the inverse relationship between Wilson's forbearing, conscientious, astute public personality and his subterranean nausea and ferocity. In fact Twain introduces the calendar without the slightest reference to Wilson's years of unmerited scorn and obscurity. The tone of the introduction, furthermore, is marked by a levity which trivializes Wilson's intellectual efforts (though these, in turn, are used by Twain to make fun of the uncomprehending village mind). We may infer that this mocking disclaimer of profundity (and pain) is designed to soften the effect of the calendar's frequent epigrammatic nihilism and aphoristic gloom:[29]

---

[29] Leslie Fiedler, notes that "it is, perhaps, only a final twist of Twain's irony to pretend to dismiss such bitterness as trifling, but it is a protective irony, too, a defense of himself as well as Pudd'nhead" (*Love and Death in the American Novel*, p. 440). In effect, the vindictive aspects of the calendar wind up as a flimsy disguise for Twain's moments of misanthropy.

For some years Wilson had been privately at work on a whimsical almanac, for his amusement—a calendar, with a little dab of ostensible philosophy, usually in ironic form, appended to each date; and the Judge [Wilson's only friend] thought that these quips and fancies of Wilson's were neatly turned and cute; so he carried a handful of them around one day, and read them to some of the chief citizens. But irony was not for these people; their mental vision was not focused for it. They read those playful trifles in the solidest earnest, and decided without hesitation that if there had ever been any doubt that Dave Wilson was a pudd'nhead—which there hadn't —this revelation removed that doubt for good and all.[30]

The satire on the opaque citizens is warranted, and clear enough. But Twain's suggestion that Wilson is only a doodler of whimsical, playful trifles (in spite of the fact that their theme is often man's moral perversion) does a disservice to Wilson's disjunctive personality and therefore to the subjective determinants of Wilson's wit.

It is true that the benign notations on the calendar make Wilson out to be reasonable, avuncular, and even at times kittenish. But the following five epigraphs demonstrate the darker and more pungent aspect of the calendar (I cite both grave aphorisms, which set us pensively on edge, and light epigrams, which take our psyches off the rack): "The Holy passion of Friendship is of so sweet and steady and loyal and enduring a nature that it will last through a whole lifetime, if not asked to lend money" (p. 39). "April 1. This is the day upon which we are reminded of what we are on the other three hundred and sixty-four" (p. 131). "October 12, the Discovery. It was wonderful to find America, but it would have been more wonderful to miss it" (p. 142). "All say, 'How hard it is that we have to die'—a strange complaint from the mouths of people who have had to live" (p. 53). "If you pick up a starving dog and make him prosperous, he will not bite you. This is the principal difference between a dog and a man" (p. 99). The last utterance reveals more persuasively than most of Wilson's epigrams the source of cynical wit in a nimble but bruised spirit.

[30] *Pudd'nhead Wilson*, p. 68.

Had Wilson been presented as a calamity-stricken Dostoev-skian character, the genesis of his tendentious wit would have been instantly transparent. We are not, for example, perplexed about wit motives in Dostoevsky's *Notes from Underground*. In this work the protagonist hungers for nihilistic wit with good reason. He is abnormally cognizant of the world's revilement; hence he is maniacally intent on the malicious thrills of retortion—though he is generally obliged to gnash his teeth over his failure to produce corrosive wit at the right moments. Actually, the underground man can do little with the suspected mockery or verified contempt of others except to allow such abuses to fester within him. But whenever his maimed psyche actually succeeds in elevating spite to the order of annihilating wit, he becomes fatuously and deliriously proud. By the same token, whenever his attempts at wit fail egregiously, revealing themselves to be merely despicable efforts to show off, this tormented clown proceeds to lacerate his pride inordinately (but with much morbid pleasure).

Actually the underground man cannot be successful in his pursuit of retaliatory witticisms because he is usually too wrought up to be able to frigidify his feelings. A complementary factor further inhibits his wit: his sick soul thirsts for humiliation (the exact counterpart of his spite); and though he can at times convince himself that to feel humiliation to the point of ecstasy is the crown of human sensibility, he regularly subsides into an awareness that he is wallowing in spiritual depravity. This kind of handicap can hardly engender wit. Still, in the first part of *Notes from Underground*, Dostoevsky's protagonist does, from time to time, crystallize malice into a first-rate cynical witticism or aphorism worthy of a Bierce or a Wilde. For example: "One may say anything about the history of the world—anything that might enter the most disordered imagination. The only thing one cannot say is that it is rational."[31]

[31] Fyodor Dostoevsky, *Notes from Underground*, in *Three Short Novels of Dostoevsky*, ed. Avrahm Yarmolinsky (Garden City, N.Y.: Doubleday, Anchor, 1960), pp. 204–205.

5

The underground man's sardonic disrespect for civilization has strong affinities with Oscar Wilde's cynical wit, which at its best discloses a destructive impatience with official verities that have gone stale or turned trumpery. Wilde's wit is delivered in so nonchalant and patrician a manner that it does not seem designed to slay restraint. Thus Lord Henry Wotton's epigrams in *The Picture of Dorian Gray* are disseminated in a tone of dandiacal aloofness that seems almost to make wit's crafty mollification of forbidden impulse quite irrelevant.

The reason Lord Henry's wit overturns the entire cart of social pieties while seldom offering impressions of spillage is that he is much too amused by his ironic vision of life as a condemned playground to allow his sense of satire to be dominant. If he appears to estrange himself from his peers in the ruling class by virtue of his witty impertinences (only the dullards are offended by him; the others adore his unorthodoxy), he is nevertheless fully aware that his delightful demoralizations owe much of their success to his unmistakable association with society's vested interests. Thus he will satirically impugn his own social class for doling out bread and circuses to the downtrodden poor. But he himself will take no step toward the eradication of beggary and injustice, mainly because one of the absurd facts of life Lord Henry particularly enjoys is his own privileged position (besides, he sympathizes with beauty, not suffering). To be sure, the satiric scandal of his wit (which gratifies our need for rebellion) is more immediately striking than his ironic complaisance (which satisfies our taste for quiescence); but the latter is finally his more impressive, and certainly more enduring, comic quality.

As it happens, the Swiftian sin of wit (the hazard of blame which the perceptive critic incurs in penetrating the respectable arrangements of church and society) is transformed, in the mind of Lord Henry Wotton, and far more in his influence on Dorian Gray, into the wit of sin—that is, the sin of intellectual concupiscence and infidelity. It is true that Lord Henry's aesthetic, ironic dandyism perfectly immobilizes his insurrectionary energies. Nevertheless, his wit is a true instrument of immoralist curiosity and boldness; indeed, Lord Henry is virtually an epigrammatic antichrist. We never actually see this lord of wit as an immoralist in action. But why should we? He himself is fond of pointing out, for one thing, that society values manners far more than morals;[32] and his manners are impeccable. Besides, he seems, however implausibly, to have experienced everything worth experiencing by his mid-twenties —so his wit is to be viewed less as a surrogate for desired sin than as a verbal recapturing of achieved sin. Not crime, moreover, but sin. Lord Henry would never be guilty of an infraction of legality, for such a violation of dandiacal aloofness would be unforgivably vulgar. One must never do anything, he reminds Dorian, that cannot be talked about after dinner. Unfortunately, Dorian Gray weds wit to actual lawlessness, with the result that he becomes a prey to ultimate damnation. In fact Dorian Gray (Prince Charming) slides all the way from the cult of beauty to the passion of murder, while Lord Henry (Prince Paradox) continues to rule over his amusingly defective social domain with an indefatigably witty gentility. Lord Henry's gay survival is the reward of wit untainted by the superfluity of action.

It is Dorian Gray who gives Lord Henry the accolade of Prince Paradox, and indeed paradox is the core of his wit. A cynical paradox flaunts an iconoclastic countertruth whose hackneyed antithesis (received truth) serves only as a foil. Take, for example, the trite idealistic "truth" that romantic passion is vowed for eternity. Wilde superimposes on this cliché a more revelatory, though officially frowned on, countertruth: the cynical insight that romantic passion is often a fleeting delusion born of sexual desire, ignorance, and literary yearning. The result: "The only difference between a caprice and a life-long passion is that the caprice lasts a little longer" (p. 166).

[32] Oscar Wilde, *The Picture of Dorian Gray*, in *The Portable Wilde*, ed. Richard Aldington (New York: Viking, 1955), p. 300.

As one might expect, the most seductive paradoxes Lord Henry utters—for example, "The only way to get rid of a temptation is to yield to it" (p. 159)—are a form of topsy-turvydom applied to the principle of moral restraint. More specifically, his most successful paradoxes (these are generally condensed into inversions which dispense with the coexistence of truth and countertruth in the same syntactical frame) especially lay waste the institution of marriage and the cult of romantic love, as when he remarks, "The worst of having a romance of any kind is that it leaves one so unromantic" (p. 153), or "The one charm of marriage is that it makes a life of deception absolutely necessary" (p. 143), or "Faithfulness is to the emotional life what consistency is to the life of the intellect—simply a confession of failure" (p. 194).

Most of Lord Henry's paradoxes, by implication, berate unimaginativeness or mental stupor. His contempt for arrested development, moreover, bears directly upon his tutorship of Dorian Gray. To this beautiful young man he preaches a peculiar brand of neo-Hellenism, a style of life which, meant only for rare individuals capable of "insincerity" (that is, sinuous, developmental inconsistency—an idea Gide was to enshrine), pits hedonistic sensationalism against the "maladies of medievalism." The latter, Lord Henry believes, are rooted in the "self-mutilation of the savage," and linger in the puritan self-denials of the dull, morbid, utilitarian nineteenth century. This hedonistic Hellenism is nevertheless antithetical to Lord Henry's own temper. His heart is no longer available for emotional transactions, nor are his senses accessible to extraordinary pleasures.

Lord Henry's heart has in truth been metamorphosed into pure brain. His major interest now is a subtle preoccupation with beautiful surfaces and fascinating individuals. (He likes persons better than principles, he remarks, and persons without principles best of all.) He has derived a cardinal value (and an immunity to suffering) from impassive spectatorship; and from the Tennysonian sin of aestheticism he has plucked non-Christian godlike attributes that make ridiculous the need for ethical valuation: "I never approve, or disapprove, of anything now," he comments. "It is an absurd attitude to take towards life. We are not sent into the world to air our moral prejudices. I never take any notice of what common people say, and I never interfere with what charming people do" (p. 222). For Lord Henry, common people and ordinary feelings are little more than avoidable bacterial infections. If we adopt Baudelaire's definition of the dandy in "The Painter of Modern Life,"[33] Lord Henry might even be seen as the last aristocrat in an increasingly bourgeois world.)

Though youth, charm, beauty, and grace (egoistic grace is infinitely preferable to dowdy humaneness) are among the reigning gods in Lord Henry's pantheon, cynical wit is clearly the chief daimon by which he lives. With his wit he kills off "the world's original sin,"[34] creeping common sense (allied to appallingly earnest goodness); and with it he disinfects society (his small circle of society, at any rate) of ill-smelling religion, callous philanthropy, political bungling, and all the other fiascos and frauds nonwitty flesh is heir to. It is clear that the exploitative vulgarity of commercial and political corruption, among other gross social phenomena, is a very important external determinant of Lord Henry's wit. The subjective determinants of his wit are less easy to arrive at. Nothing in Lord Henry's private circumstances—no conjectural or actual inner frustration (the annoyance of his ludicrous, slightly irksome marriage, for example)—seems as powerful a force in the production of his epigrams as the disgusting nineteenth century.

If Lord Henry's wit has become a second skin, part of the credit for that accomplishment must go to his intellectual and

[33] See "The Dandy," section ix of Charles Baudelaire, "The Painter of Modern Life," in *"The Essence of Laughter" and Other Essays, Journals, and Letters*, ed. Peter Quennell (New York: Meridian, 1956), pp. 46–50.
[34] *The Picture of Dorian Gray*, p. 185.

social distinction (although Wilde fully reveals that witless fatheads are endemic to the aristocracy). Certainly Lord Henry lives in an ambience of wit expectation. And if he should happen to encounter a kindred spirit, like the pretty Duchess of Monmouth, insipid dialogue becomes unthinkable. There is a certain amount of school-for-scandal death-dealing in such meetings; but hostile wit (although he proffers a few excellent specimens) is not Lord Henry's forte. He is too little a gossip to spend much of his time epigrammatically raking up the irritating or ridiculous trivia of mere personalities. He would doubtless not bother, for example, to perform anything comparable to Georges Feydeau's witty aggression recorded in the following anecdote: "There was an actress, popular in revues at that time, pretty, talented but incredibly sloppy about her person. As a matter of truth, she was just plain dirty and was said to take a bath only twice a month. Meeting Feydeau on the Boulevard one afternoon, she announced coyly that the next day was her birthday and the farce writer, with a courtly bow, promised to send her a present. What he sent her was a box containing three tiny cakes of soap and his card on which was written 'For Life!' "[35] Nor would Lord Henry, inasmuch as he is no longer impelled by erotic appetite, figure as an ideal member of the society of "elegant wits and grand horizontals" assembled across the Channel. One cannot, for example, imagine him taking the place of that witty womanizer Aurélien Scholl, about whom the following incident has been related: "When one little married woman, wanting to give way yet struggling with her conscience, pleaded piteously, 'Let me be for a time, my friend! Let me retire into myself,' Scholl replied with gallant ardor: 'Allow me, madame, to accompany you' " (p. 101).

The scrappy zest of a Whistler is even further from Lord Henry's style. Wilde himself was bested by Whistler in their public exchanges over the authenticity of Wilde's propagation

[35] Cornelia Otis Skinner, *Elegant Wits and Grand Horizontals* (Boston: Houghton Mifflin, 1962), pp. 107–108.

of ideas about the new art.[36] But Whistler was a superbly witty destroyer of anyone who impinged on the world of art without sufficient knowledge. Even Ruskin, in the role of Slade Professor of Art at Oxford, was wittily trounced for being pontifical: "A life passed among pictures," wrote Whistler, "makes not a painter—else the policeman in the National Gallery might assert himself. As well allege that he who lives in a library must needs die a poet" (pp. 26–27). Lesser lights were more thoroughly extinguished. Consider the case of P. G. Hamerton, who in the *Saturday Review* criticized Whistler's third "Symphony in White" for being imprecisely white, since the painter had depicted one lady with a yellowish dress and one girl with reddish hair, and had also given them flesh-colored complexions. Rejoined Whistler: "Bon Dieu! did this wise person expect white hair and chalked faces? And does he then, in his astounding consequence, believe that a symphony in F contains no other note, but shall be a continued repetition of F, F, F? . . . Fool!" (p. 45). This type of sparkling belligerence requires more polemical commitment than Lord Henry is willing to muster. He prefers, instead, cynical generalizations virtually devoid of personal animus, as when he says of women that they "represent the triumph of matter over mind, just as men represent the triumph of mind over morals."[37]

6

Lord Henry's nonchalance is played out in the midst of a century which he describes as sick with Christian hypocrisy and bankrupt with philistinism. And since many of Lord Henry's cynical epigrams combat the puritan hangover from the "maladies of medievalism" (p. 159), as well as the middle-

---

[36] See James McNeill Whistler, *The Gentle Art of Making Enemies* (London: William Heinemann, 1953), pp. 164–165, 237–238. Whistler did not, of course, consistently score off his opponents. Thus Swinburne's critique (in the *Fortnightly Review*, June 1888) of Whistler's flippancy in the latter's "Ten O'Clock" lecture was only weakly rebutted (pp. 250–261).

[37] *The Picture of Dorian Gray*, p. 192.

class accommodation to the golden calf, one might conceive the existence of a strong kinship between Lord Henry and a number of cynical wits, also antipuritan and antiphilistine, in Restoration comedy. But Restoration wits like Dorimant, Horner, and Mirabell are activists as well as wits. Moreover, their wit is not only brilliantly cynical; it is also keenly aggressive and, not infrequently, sexually barbed. Nor do they preach a neo-Hellenic reinvigoration of sensation while paradoxically locking defiance in a deep freeze.

On the other hand, it may be claimed that no single Restoration comedy quite matches Lord Henry's infernal wit virtuosity. Lord Henry's wit shines with a unique cynical radiance in the mentally and morally sluggish Victorian world of Wilde's novel (morally sluggish, that is, until Dorian Gray's Greek godhood fastens itself to a program of decadent Faustianism). Such wit isolation is not characteristic of the true Restoration wit maker, who is more abundantly supplied with gifted peers than Lord Henry, and for whom the social compulsion to create wit is as natural as a breath of (perfumed) air. In Restoration comedy, wit is a normative, not an exceptional, phenomenon, though for the silly or vulgar practitioner of false wit, true wit is an unachievable prize, a distinction which provides, among other things, entrée into social cliques and select beds. (However, as Restoration comedy develops from Wycherley and Etherege to Congreve and Farquhar, tendentious wit yields more and more to innocent wit, just as biting satire yields more and more to indulgent humor.)

Also separating Lord Henry's wit from Restoration wit is a crucial difference of form. Though brilliant and bold, the thrust of Restoration tendentious wit is not contained in radical paradox or stunning inversion. Thus Wycherley's *The Country Wife* is dependent for its wit structure on the seventeenth-century rhetorical techniques of similitude and (less important) antithesis.[38] Whatever the moral outrage perpetrated by

---

[38] For a discussion of similitudes in Restoration comedy, see Thomas Fujimura, *The Restoration Comedy of Wit* (Princeton: Princeton University Press, 1952), pp. 29–33.

Wycherley's wit, his use of similitude and antithesis implies a certain reliance on order and balance. Wilde's paradoxes, on the other hand, compound their immoralism by means of their startling construction, which implies a certain taste for disarrangement and disintegration.

Of course, one can always argue that nothing is more unsettling than heresy or scandal transmitted in orderly fashion. And Wycherley's wit, especially as it is delivered by Horner, his protagonist in *The Country Wife*, certainly conveys subversiveness. Horner, who wishes the fraudulent report of his impotence to be universally broadcast so that he may approach the ladies and cozen their husbands with impunity, congratulates himself, at the very outset of the play, on the false medical news a doctor acquaintance has consented to spread throughout the town. "A quack," Horner reflects, "is as fit for a pimp as a midwife for a bawd; they are still but in their way both helpers of nature."[39] The structure of this witticism is symmetrical, its thinking logical (in its own way), and its impact incisive; yet for all its sense of order, it caters abundantly to the unruliness of instinct ("nature"). Horner, the hunter of women, invokes "nature" partly because he is rationalizing an itchy cosmopolitan satyriasis and partly because he has a real regard for the value of naturalness. He is rarely in better form than when he attacks violators of nature and spontaneity, especially the high-toned sluttish hypocrites who disclaim a mercenary interest in the amorous intrigues they seek. Such a disclaimer on the part of Lady Fidget elicits this charmingly deadly similitude from Horner: "I beg your pardon, madam, I must confess I have heard that great ladies, like great merchants, set but the higher prices upon what they have, because they are not in necessity of taking the first offer" (V.iv).

Though Horner, driven by a prodigal but coolly controlled and wittily engineered sexuality, is a great schemer, as Lord Henry (whom in any case one cannot imagine lecherously

[39] William Wycherley, *The Country Wife* (I.i), in *Six Restoration Plays*, ed. John Harold Wilson (Boston: Houghton Mifflin, 1959).

ensconced between adulterous sheets) is not, in deceiving husbands who are boors and exploiting wives who advertise that
they are fair game, Horner is deceitful in order to be genuine,
that is, as genuine as a frank animal and epicurean dandy
can be. Horner knows that ruse is necessary in a world where
instinct cannot be authenticated without the help of artificiality.
It is true that Horner, whose naturalism is not distorted by
sermonizing sophistries (a false medical report, for example,
is not an odious moralistic refrain), pays no particular attention
to the eye of heaven. But by the same token there is no hint of
diabolism in him. Lord Henry's wit depletes moral principles
from a broadly cultural quasi-satanic standpoint. Horner, on
the other hand, belongs to the devil's party only in a limited
sense. Thus he does not, like Lord Henry, seek to identify
Christianity with spiritual emasculation or psychic cowardice.
Horner's gay, inventive testicularity rules out any traditional
allegiance to Christianity. But his carnality and his wit do not
so much dissolve the core of morality as remove its thick rind
of fakery. Though his own morality is clearly pagan and as a
result his intrigues are not elevating, the scandal of his illicit
fun (which is based on a more or less courageous acceptance of
the world's ridicule) is perhaps the most palatable phenomenon
in Wycherley's play.

Horner is a trickster, not a hypocrite. Rose Zimbardo maintains, in *Wycherley's Drama*, that "Wycherley used a satiric
spokesman who, though he draws our attention to the vice
and hypocrisy before us, yet illustrates it in his own nature as
well. Horner . . . himself is the most outrageous example of
vice masquerading as innocence that the play affords."[40] But
Horner is not vice masquerading as innocence. He is conniving
and deceiving; yet for all that, he is not morally double-faced:
he pretends to a biological deficiency, not to virtue. More pre-

[40] Rose Zimbardo, *Wycherley's Drama* (New Haven: Yale University Press, 1965), p. 16. Zimbardo's inflexibility on this point is related to her rigid segregation of satire from comedy. She declares that
The Country Wife, like Wycherley's *The Plain Dealer*, is not a comedy
at all, but rather "a new English conception of formal satire" (p. 3).

cisely, he does not claim to be innocent, but impotent. In any case, he is sportive, not canting.

Virginia Ogden Birdsall, in *Wild Civility: The English Comic Spirit on the Restoration Stage*, is surely right when she describes Horner as a comic hero who is "on the side of instincts and of freedom, life, and health."[41] Moreover, Horner is never a despoiler of chastity or a wrecker of honorable households. He puts horns on husbands who deserve them, and makes love to women who find either fulfillment (like Margery Pinchwife, the country wife) or profit (like Lady Fidget) in the act of adultery. The fact that Horner's love-making is marked by the tactics of a courtier-satyr is simply a matter of style: the courtier arranges assignations by means of Machiavellian opportunism, while the passionate (but ever witty) satyr falls to with gusto. Besides, Horner's virtually instant libertinism is certainly preferable to Pinchwife's ludicrous school-for-wives credo (which involves molding a gracious, innocent chick into a slavishly loving hen), or Sir Jasper Fidget's eunuch-as-pet theory (which involves providing for one's wife's pleasure while one goes about one's own dishonest business).

In any event, Horner has an especially sharp eye for the signs of corruption which the marital condition precipitates. This may be seen in the manner in which he greets Pinchwife: "Well, Jack, by thy long absence from the town, the grumness of thy countenance, and the slovenliness of thy habit, I should give thee joy, should I not, of marriage?" (I.i). Marriage in *The Country Wife* is often slighted, badgered, and damned for being unnatural, ugly, and debasing. Nor is Horner alone in flinging sharp witticisms at marital love and honor. One of the best epigrams in the play, "Marrying to increase love is like gaming to become rich; alas! you only lose what little stock you had before" (IV.i), is not uttered by a major character but by Alithea's servant, Lucy, who has presumably been bribed by Harcourt—by his merit as well as by his money—to dissuade

---

[41] Virginia Ogden Birdsall, *Wild Civility: The English Comic Spirit on the Restoration Stage* (Bloomington: Indiana University Press, 1970), p. 147.

Alithea from marrying Sparkish, the play's fatuous false wit. But Sparkish himself utters a number of telling remarks on the staleness of wedlock. Consider, for example, his self-gratulatory comment, "Gad, I'm witty . . . considering I was married today" (IV.iii). All in all, Wycherley's play, like a good many other Restoration comedies, is an excellent illustration of Freud's views on the antimatrimonial bias of cynical wit.

3

Truth, Humor, and Nonsense

Is every comedy fundamentally a comedy of errors in which understanding vanquishes misconception? Several decades ago Scott Buchanan made precisely this claim; in fact, he defined the basic drive of both comedy and tragedy as the pursuit of truth. In *Poetry and Mathematics*, he argues that just as science banishes ignorance by developing more and more inclusive spheres of truth, so literature dissolves inadequate convictions through its continuing discovery of illuminating assumptions and relationships. In his last chapter, "Tragedy and Comedy," Buchanan compactly restates his thesis that literary intention is comparable to scientific and mathematical investigation. And he affirms that a rational substructure (a process of mental enlightenment) underlies the moral problems of tragedy and comedy.

Buchanan's discussion of tragedy, which is more comprehensive than his remarks on comedy, may be briefly reviewed. In Greek tragedy (*Oedipus Rex*, incidentally, is the only literary work Buchanan refers to) the protagonist's hybris (insolence or arrogance) is the product of misjudgment; hence his tragic disaster is the result of misinterpretation. Catastrophe is inflicted by Nemesis acting as "the vengeance that the ignored factor in a situation takes on man and his virtues."[1] Ultimately,

[1] Scott Buchanan, *Poetry and Mathematics* (1929; rpt. Philadelphia and New York: Lippincott, 1962), p. 147.

benightedness yields to comprehension; and the protagonist's liberation from ignorance becomes his purgation. The dynamism of tragedy, in Buchanan's view, is thus a complex act of clarification. The protagonist initially possesses a false idea of possibility and destiny; and for this he suffers. But his shattering experience radically alters his ideas; and he is left with a catharsis that is equivalent to the elimination of a false hypothesis.[2]

The search for truth is also, according to Buchanan, the ruling impulse in comedy. And it is possible to infer from Buchanan's remarks that comedy is even more suited than tragedy to the "clarification and definition of the properties of . . . ideas"; for comedy offers numerous, heterogeneous occasions for corrective strategies. In a comedy, "every turn in the action marks an inconsistency discovered, a plan gone wrong, a platitude rendered paradoxical, a principle disproved, a fact caught in duplicity. . . . In a good comedy every idea must be deflated and purged by the ordeal of laughter."[3]

It is surely noble to argue that comedy is a mode of combating the tendency of the human mind to harbor faulty knowledge. Nevertheless, the comedy of truth is not all the truth about comedy. Undeniably, the ends of comedy are often served by a quest for clarification and wisdom; and this quest may reasonably be considered the analogue of a series of laboratory experiments. But a razor-edged awareness of the illogical stresses and strains in human thought and conduct is not the whole preoccupation of comic energy. Whereas satiric comedy (Buchanan's real subject) delights in the laughing murder of untenable ideas, ironic comedy treats ideas only as colorful or

[2] Buchanan binds the drama of antiquity to the modern laboratory by claiming that the late-medieval era and the Renaissance converted the Greek humanistic criticism of life into a scientific investigation of reality (p. 149). Northrop Frye, in his *Anatomy of Criticism*, improves on this idea. Frye suggests that the "two great developments of tragic drama, in fifth-century Athens and in seventeenth-century Europe," actually parallel the rise of Ionian and Renaissance science; his point is that both tragedy and science are committed to "an epiphany of law" (p. 208).

[3] *Poetry and Mathematics*, p. 149.

intriguing toys. Farcical comedy is more devastating: it promotes a subversion of mind itself by seeking out the powerful pleasures of irrationality. And humorous comedy not only tolerates man's proneness to make mistakes, but even cherishes his fallible biases and pieties.

The fact is that attitudes toward truth are more important in comedy than truth itself. Literature as a whole, it must be granted, does in some sense endeavor to purge consciousness of its inferior insights. Edmund Wilson once affirmed that the writer, like the scientist or the mathematician, is bent on discovering true relations in the confusing and cluttered human environment. A writer, Wilson declares, "who is to be anything more than an echo of his predecessors must always find expression for something that has never yet been expressed, must master a new set of phenomena." Each literary or scientific victory of the human intellect, moreover, provides us with a deep satisfaction, for "we have been cured of some ache of disorder, relieved of some oppressive burden of uncomprehended events."[4] One may nevertheless point out that the victory of the human intellect is not always curative. Why else would humor strive to lighten the burden of historical events and psychological phenomena that are, alas, all too well comprehended? And why else would farce encourage, rather than cleanse, man's irrational propensities?

Consider the relationship of farce to the comedy of errors. What follies of mental darkness—what erroneous assumptions and deficient perspectives—are laughingly castigated in Plautus' *Amphitryon*, for instance? Whatever the number of errors and illogicalities one may find in *Amphitryon*, their rectification is virtually the last thing Plautus is interested in. In this comedy modifiable ideas are associated mostly with mistaken identities. Alcmena, who has been impregnated both by her husband, General Amphitryon, and by that philandering Olympian mimic, Jove, gives birth to twins; each infant is the

[4] Quoted in Frank Kermode, *Puzzles and Epiphanies* (New York: Chilmark, 1962), p. 57.

progeny of a different father. Shooting off some thunder and a few flashes of lightning, Jove clears Alcmena of all blame, and with divine deviousness legitimizes his erotic fancy by proclaiming that the child (Hercules) sprung from his seed will make Amphitryon's name forever great.

Amphitryon himself returns from war duty just in time to be flabbergasted by his wife's peculiar insistence that they have just spent the night together (a supernaturally protracted night, at that). Not only is he flummoxed by his perfectly innocent wife; he is also knocked out by Jove's thunder and lightning. After he has regained consciousness, Amphitryon indicates that he is not one to quarrel with divine appetite, or with the involuntary adultery his wife has been subjected to. "Well," he philosophizes, "I certainly have no cause for complaint when I'm given the chance to share my goods with Jove."[5] Since, moreover, celestial aid in the form of family benefits and wide repute will be coming his way, how could he dream of being a fool and challenging the ethics of the almighty Olympian?

To the extent that we laugh at Amphitryon (and his slave, Sosia) for being hoodwinked and rendered witless by an Olympian "miracle" (of which we are more critical than he), we are doubtless enjoying an intellectual triumph in the Buchananesque sense. That is, Plautus' comedy has disclosed to us the misconceptions of two men bedeviled by an "ignored factor." But ignored factors that cannot be approached by human beings are scarcely ideal material for the purification of consciousness. The comic keynote in *Amphitryon* is not the clarification of truth at all (unless the "truth" is that fantasticality betrays the imprint of the gods), but rather the exhilarating defeat of reason in an absurd world.

That nonsense, or farcical irrationality, is thoroughly capable of deflecting a Buchananesque bent toward the mind's

[5] Plautus, *Amphitryon* (Act V), in *Six Plays of Plautus*, ed. and trans. Lionel Casson (Garden City, N.Y.: Doubleday, Anchor, 1963), p. 64.

solution of life's befuddlements may be illustrated in another
of Plautus' plays, *The Menaechmus Twins*. The situation here
is that Menaechmus of Syracuse has been seeking his fraternal
double for six years. Though evidence starts accumulating pell-
mell in the city of Epidamnus, his latest stop, that he is being
mistaken for someone else, he is blinded to the twinship he has
finally stumbled onto, not only by a perdurable dramatic convention which requires that sensible inferences be suspended in
favor of pleasurably giddy elaborations of error, but also, more
specifically, by Epidamnus' notorious way of scalping foolish
foreigners. This local skill is expatiated on by Messenio,
Menaechmus' slave: "The hardest drinkers and worst rakes are
right here in Epidamnus. Besides, the town's full of crooks and
swindlers. And they say the prostitutes here have a smoother
line of talk than anywhere else in the world. That's why this
place is called Epidamnus: nobody stays here without a
damned lot of damage."[6] When, therefore, Menaechmus of
Syracuse is rather familiarly approached, owing to a natural
error, by the whore Lovey (who is being cheerfully kept by her
next-door neighbor, Menaechmus of Epidamnus, a somewhat
loosely married man), we understand that he will be on his
guard: Messenio has convinced him how clever and well rehearsed the sharpsters in Epidamnus are. But Menaechmus of
Syracuse begins enjoying so many favors in Lovey's house
that his good fortune, which satisfies a strong predisposition to
opportunism, helps chase suspicion away.

The extramarital hanky-panky whose benefits Menaechmus
of Syracuse thus inherits suggests that if there is any satiric
clarification to be found in *The Menaechmus Twins*, it revolves
around the fortunes of marriage. In *Amphitryon* marriage, at
least before the contretemps created by that lecherous prankster, Jove, has apparently been an unoppressive relationship. In
The Menaechmus Twins, on the other hand, a more character-

istically Plautine marital derangement prevails.[7] That marriage is a hornet's nest, at least in the opinion of Menaechmus of Epidamnus, is indeed among the first attitudes expressed in the comedy. Nor is good-time Menaechmus particularly gallant toward his wife: "If you weren't so stupid and sour, / Such a mean-tempered bitch, such a shrew," he tells her, they might get along. But her excessive supervision galls him: "Every time that I want to go out," he squawks, "I get called, I get grabbed, I get grilled. . . . Why, the way I declare every act of my life, / It's a customs official I wed, not a wife" (Act I, p. 184). That is why he spends so much of his time seeking his pleasure with Lovey.

The Menaechmus Twins is thus a comedy of release both from the bondage of matrimony and the tyranny of rationality. Insofar as it has a satiric component, the comedy serves Buchanan's theory rather better than *Amphitryon* does. In *The Menaechmus Twins* one can actually demonstrate that a set of ideas, as distinguished from a series of nonsense imbroglios, has been put through an ordeal of laughter. But the single beneficiary (within the play) of this comic "experiment" in truth-finding must be Menaechmus' wife; for the unideal truth that overturns (if it does) her erroneous notions about wedlock is that marriage is liable to be a morbid miscalculation if it is acted out in accordance with strict standards. There is no corresponding discovery of a false hypothesis by her husband; as far as Menaechmus of Epidamnus is concerned, the only ideas which have been tested, evaluated, and condemned in the crucible of comedy relate to the inappropriate purloining of his wife's wardrobe and jewelry. But that is not a very meaningful eluci-

---

[7] Erich Segal points out that "as a general rule, Plautine characters prefer love without marriage, 'komos' without 'gamos.' For Plautus the words of Shakespeare's Don Armado, 'the catastrophe is a nuptial,' represent not merely a pun but a philosophy" (*Roman Laughter*, p. 165). This is a useful reminder, for New Comedy (which in its Roman derivation is, after all, Plautine as well as Terentian, although Terence is closer in spirit to Menander) is often referred to as the matrix from which the theme of boy-meets-girl-and-marries-same (rapturously) is conveyed to European drama and fiction.

dation of the shadowy places of the human mind. Plautus' comedy, in short, has little to do with the correction of ideas, but it has much to do with a strategy of farcical errors designed to retard as long as possible the very process of clarification.

In *The Nature of Roman Comedy*, George Duckworth informs us that the one feature which the comedies of Plautus and Terence have in common is "mental error, or misapprehension,"[8] and that this condition is divisible into three categories: "innocent mistakes," "guileful deception," and a blend of the two. But Duckworth does not point to a Roman comic goal that is related to Buchanan's theory of the elucidation of ideas. Nor, for that matter, does he stress an opposing concept: the liberation of impulse from sense (and authority). He simply transfers the importance of Aristotelian anagnorisis (discovery) from Greek tragedy to Roman comedy, and points out that the transition from ignorance to recognition often coincides, as in tragedy, with peripeteia (reversal of fortune) —except that reversals in comedy are rarely catastrophic (p. 140). Into this theoretical void, Buchanan's intellectualism may legitimately enter. But so can Freud's stress on irrationalism—for example, via Erich Segal's *Roman Laughter*, which argues for festive release as Plautus' great theme.

Certainly Shakespeare, in his *Comedy of Errors*, does not forsake the privileges of nonsense bequeathed to him by Plautus. As is well known, the chaos resulting from mistaken identities in Shakespeare's comedy is richer than in Plautus, for we have not only identical Antipholi from Ephesus and Syracuse but also identical Dromios. Moreover, Shakespeare's special twist in his complication of character and circumstance—the idealizing passion of Antipholus of Syracuse for Luciana (the sister of Adriana, who is the wife of Antipholus of Ephesus)—introduces a natural ally of nonsense: romantic unreason. The two irrationalities (lunatic misidentification and romantic passion) harmonize in *The Comedy of Errors* largely because disparate aggressors against reason tend to become partners willy-nilly,

---

[8] George Duckworth, *The Nature of Roman Comedy* (Princeton: Princeton University Press, 1952), p. 140.

one incredibility helping to beget another. (To be sure, Shakespeare also permits nonsense to buttress realism: the conjugal exasperation already prevailing between Antipholus of Ephesus and Adriana is only reinforced by confusions of identity.)

The magic of love which instantly attracts Antipholus of Syracuse to Luciana, and which is enhanced by the bewildering novelties floating about in the atmosphere of Ephesus, is not consistently radiant. When the famous magic arts of Ephesus begin to reveal what seems to Antipholus their darker side, his acceptance of the unusual comes to a stop. He gets ready to quit both the cheating town and his beguiling love—but to no avail, for he becomes ensnarled in perplexities and even accusations (presumably hatched as the duperies of a town practicing the "liberties of sin") that rob him of his freedom. And in truth the later acts of *The Comedy of Errors* breed nonsensical situations that have a much greater impact on the flesh and bones of Antipholus of Syracuse (not to mention those of his brother) than on his heart.

The extraordinary family reunion that takes place in the last act, when father, mother, twin sons, and twin servants are all recovered, is a soothing fantasticality but also a weak one (getting rid of the elations of incoherence at the end of a comedy of errors is always a letdown); and it hardly alters one's realization that the nonsense in Shakespeare's play is immune to Buchanan's scientific concept of comedy, though, as in *The Menaechmus Twins*, there is a certain amount of clarifying mockery applied to the marriage question.

Harry Levin compares *The Menaechmus Twins* with *The Comedy of Errors* in an interesting essay, "Two Comedies of Errors," and generalizes as follows: "Comedy may be described as an exercise in understanding. . . . It is a planned confusion, created in order to be clarified: a series of misunderstandings brought about, under the guise of chance or contrivance, by the playwright himself."[9] Levin's commentary seems for a moment to suggest, in Buchananesque fashion, that

[9] Harry Levin, "Two Comedies of Errors," in *Refractions: Essays in Comparative Literature* (New York: Oxford University Press, 1966), p. 128.

comedy travels an intellectual road from obscurity to light, from knots to solutions, from false relations to true. But Levin, who believes that Shakespeare's title is generic and that it "sorts with any comedy or revel" (p. 134), is not arguing that the comedy of errors is symbiotically related to the comedy of ideas. Inasmuch as Levin focuses on revel, the kind of comedy he evokes signifies an indulgence in, rather than an instructive erasure of, farcical misunderstandings. Yet comedy-revel suggests other elements too—especially a radical irresponsibility and unorthodoxy—that are not characteristic of *The Comedy of Errors*.

Actually, a comedy of misapprehensions may sort only in part with revel, because nonsense (or illogic), however madcap, is only one facet of comic saturnalianism. That contingency, and therefore irrationality, is king in *The Menaechmus Twins* and *The Comedy of Errors* is indicated in Levin's apt metaphor: "We are at the roulette table, not the chessboard, here. There is no plotting or counterplotting in a Machiavellian sense" (p. 136). But Levin is tempted to transform the whirligig of chance into more drastic and more modern comic mischief; and in his analysis of *The Comedy of Errors* he finally embraces both the metaphysics (not just the presence) of contingency and the madness of farce. Paying homage to Shakespeare's daring in presenting the absurdity of two sets of twins, Levin suggests that there is really nothing astounding here: "Absurdity is man's lot as the Existentialists have redefined it, and what should a farce be if not wholly absurd?" (p. 137).

But, in the first place, it is irony that plays comically with the absurd, not existentialism (which only incidentally, as in Sartre's *Nausea*, extracts comedy from the everlasting grotesque). And, in the second place, a "wholly absurd" farce would contain impieties and outrages that are nonexistent in *The Comedy of Errors*. Shakespeare's farce is a delightfully tricky dislocation of logic and sense, but in other respects it is a small solvent for psychic repression. Levin's metaphor of the roulette table suggests well enough that the nonsense in Shakespeare's comedy has its boundaries: it leaps about within a patterned chanciness and a comparatively polite ambience. It is no step toward nihilism and no summons to festive riot. Thus *The Comedy of Errors* does not exemplify Levin's assertion that the "carnival spirit" is "the first condition of comedy," comedy itself being "a release from the rules, a dispensation from the routine duties of existence" (p. 138). Nonsense in Shakespeare's comedy is a dispensation from the pressure of reason, and also an emancipation of sorts from an inevitable psychic undertow of anxiety. But it is not gloriously irreverent. *The Comedy of Errors* may break the rules of reliable inference, but it does not open the floodgates of carnival.

Nor do its quirky contingencies, which are no more than skin-deep rufflings of reality, have much to do with the intellectual or moral experimentation that Buchanan postulates for a comedy of errors. It is therefore misleading for Levin to conclude his essay with the following translation from Etienne Souriau's *Les 200,000 situations dramatiques:* "A comedy of errors—or ignorance—is inherent in the condition of men, who are perpetually groping through moral shadows and playing a game of blind man's buff with their souls" (p. 150). In Shakespeare's play there are no moral shadows (unless one chooses to make something of Antipholus of Ephesus' marital problems, including his acquaintanceship with a courtesan), and there is no soul blindness (unless one chooses ungallantly to focus on Antipholus of Syracuse's infatuation with Luciana). In Shakespeare's comedy of ignorance, error arises chiefly from optical illusion, not from ethical delusion.

2

Souriau's observation may not fit *The Comedy of Errors;* but it clearly accords with Buchanan's way of thinking. And it can easily bring to mind a large number of comedies in which moral and mental shadows are in fact dissolved while truth is amusingly groped for and found. For example, the silly idea of affected language and factitious manners is hilariously exposed in Molière's *Precious Damsels*, though the play shows that too ready a reliance on "naturalness" may also be a mistake, as Gorgibus, father of Magdelon and uncle of Cathos—the two girls who have been applying cosmetics to their vocabulary and their feelings—funnily demonstrates. On the other hand, satiric anatomies may be notoriously one-sided, as in the case of the academy of Lagado, in *Gulliver's Travels*, where hundreds of projectors form a battalion of lunatics mired in impractical research. In detailing the academy's grotesqueries, moreover, Swift appeals at least as much to the id as to the intellect.

The same farcical piling-up of grotesque "evidence" characterizes the satire in Voltaire's *Candide*. If we invoke Buchanan's theory, we may assume that Voltaire has been able to shatter the idea of optimism because he has tested it—and found it ludicrously wanting—in numerous situations that are vaguely parallel to a series of experiments in the discrimination of truth from error. But the "experiments" in catastrophe Voltaire furnishes are hardly fair probes into the mentality of rebounding hope in a world peculiarly susceptible to bad news. Furthermore, just as it is the lunacy of farce that brings off the triumph of Swift's slam at the academy, so it is the buffoonery of events and appetites that makes Voltaire's comedy successful.

The farce in *Candide* works mainly by means of a huge, illogical accumulation and acceleration of disasters which are attended by a comic devastation of moral and religious taboos. The story of the old woman who, acting on behalf of Cunégonde, succors Candide after he has been flogged at the auto-da-fé is a representative cameo of the story's frightful, zany occurrences. As a youngster, this daughter of a pope and a princess is devirginized by a black pirate captain and almost slaughtered in the hideous factional wars in Morocco, wars in which "no one ever missed the five daily prayers prescribed by Mohammed."[10] She is resurrected from a mass of bleeding corpses with the help of a eunuch (one of thousands of Catholic *castrati* coerced into a consecration to music), who, wriggling against her still voluptuous body, laments more than once the loss of his testicles, and who later, feigning saintly solicitude, sells her into slavery. The ultimate result of this transaction is a religiously superintended cuisine (in the midst of siege and famine) in which she loses one of her buttocks to the

[10] *Candide*, p. 44.

cooking pot (she refers to her incomplete backside with almost Wagnerian insistence). So while the reader's intellect is being strongly positioned against optimism by nasty evidences of human barbarity, his id is enjoying a farcical spectacle of virtually incessant eroticism, scatology, aggression, and lunacy.

Buchanan's theory obviously requires subtler comedies of ideas that provide a noticeable give and take—Shaw's, for example. Yet Shaw's expulsion of error (the morally humdrum or the intellectually shoddy), not the secure discovery of truth, is his chief glory. In *Major Barbara*, for instance, Undershaft's recommendation that worn-out moralities, religions, and political systems be scrapped with as little hesitation as obsolete machinery[11] is breath-taking. But how experimentally irreverent has Undershaft's own life been? Like his predecessors, this "mystical" munitions maker seems to have translated the illegitimacy of the bastard into the daring of ethically unprecedented principles. He has boldly declared that killing "is the final test of conviction, the only lever strong enough to overturn a social system." In fact, as a young man faced by the horror of poverty, Undershaft had vowed that not reason or morals or the destruction of other lives would stop him from becoming a "full-fed free man" (Act III, p. 143). For all that, Shaw did not allow him, while he was on his way to freedom and greatness, to murder one or two obstructive individuals; nor did the history of his morals become the scandal of the century.

As for the utopian city Undershaft has built for his workers, his daughter Barbara is convinced that its citizens, with their filled bellies, sanitary plumbing, and smug temperaments, are (without realizing it) waiting for someone who will announce thrilling new truths about how they may save their souls. Barbara's religious experiment among the well-fed may of course fail; she may discover that physical comfort and economic ease militate against the soul's redemption as decisively as indigence and suffering. Nevertheless, in discarding the collapsed experiment of winning souls through the bribe of bread and in undertaking a more promising experiment in salvation among the

[11] George Bernard Shaw, *Major Barbara* (Baltimore: Penguin, 1965), Act III, p. 140.

economically contented, Barbara does achieve a Buchananesque illumination of ideas.

Cusins' experimentalism, which involves deeper responsibilities than Barbara's, will provide material for a more heterogeneous essay in clarification. Basically, he is being challenged by Undershaft to effect one great change: to make war on war (this has never been Undershaft's obligation, but the unashamed armorer is not averse to being a harbinger of more humane things to come). He is thus being invited to become what the world has always needed: a philosopher-king (in this instance a professor of Greek who is also a maker of gunpowder). The paradox he must build his wisdom and power on is the realization that "the way of life lies through the factory of death" (Act III, p. 152), that power for good can be exercised only through possession of the means of destruction. Though it is arguable that the use of power may corrupt Cusins' Dionysian energy and cripple his compassion, it is obvious that in his case Shaw's experimentation with ideas is authentically Buchananesque. Shaw has clearly engaged Cusins in an ideal war for the beneficent transformation of reality. Major Barbara's voyage from error to enlightenment is perhaps more convincing than Cusins' because it follows a more striking pattern of crisis, ordeal, and rebirth. But Cusins is more impressive as a verifying agent, as a keen (and partly Undershaftian) mind that has seen through the impotence of mere humanism and now ventures into a practical union of power and grace for the sake of long abused mankind. Buchanan is therefore vindicated—with one enormous qualification: Shaw himself has pointed out that social and moral ideas lose their relevance in varying degrees; they may therefore also lose their bloom of truth in the literary works in which they are embodied.[12]

Would the ideas in a highly intelligent futuristic comedy be

[12] Cf. Eric Bentley's comment: "If, as Shaw holds, ideas are a most important part of a work of art, and if, as he also holds, ideas go out of date, it follows that even the best works of art go out of date in some important respects and that the generally held view that great works are in all respects eternal is not shared by Shaw" (*The Playwright as Thinker* [Boston: Meridian, 1957], p. 114).

less likely, then, to fade away? Consider *Brave New World*, a work in which Huxley apparently seeks, in the life of society over half a thousand years from today, a clarification of ideas relating to stability and individualism. Huxley clearly experiments with values by compelling contrary sets of postulates to clash. In his third chapter, for example, today's problems of love, marriage, and the family are presented as the cultural obscenities of the "brave new world." But because the chapter is contrapuntal in its technique, tomorrow's reversals of today's ethics, psychology, and legality are exhibited with their own freakish inadequacies. Huxley's ironic plague on both houses of culture can be sensed especially in his treatment of sex. It may be a tossup whether sex saturation in A.F. (After Ford) 632 is funnier than prolonged chastity in A.D. 1932; but Huxley's juxtaposition of these equally undesirable antithetical mores helps to make the civilization of the future as absurd as that of the present.

Huxley has cast three major characters (Bernard Marx, Helmholtz Watson, and John the Savage) into experimental situations that bear directly on the novel's comic counterpoint of indictments. The experimental premise behind Bernard's role is that an accidental enhancement of self-consciousness will produce a misfit whose alien vision will expose the insanity of a robotistic utopia. But Bernard is no hero; his gutlessness is in fact an embarrassment to Helmholtz Watson, who also disdains herd psychology. A lecturer at the College of Emotional Engineering (Department of Writing), Helmholtz has become more and more dissatisfied with the aesthetic juvenility he is professionally occupied with. But the catalytic agent that finally makes him break away from the "brave new world" is the lost art of emotional intensity and lyrical imagination to which John the Savage introduces him in the salvaged works of William Shakespeare. The latter's verbal magic and heightened feeling make it clear to Helmholtz once and for all that the flaccid phrases and silly rhymes he employs as a propagandist for the masses must go, along with the higher authority that sanctions them. Yet Helmholtz cannot swallow Shakespeare whole. He realizes that a neo-Shakespearean linguistic effort can be provoked only by mad, violent, excruciating situations. But in listening to *Romeo and Juliet*, he reacts to the emotional crises of the young lovers—crises based on a desperate, archaic craving for exclusivity in love—with guffaws of disbelief. Other obsolete matters, such as Juliet's smutty reference to her sweet mother, or the failure to dispose of Tybalt's uncremated corpse wasting its phosphorus on a dim monument, also precipitate his laughter.

Huxley is obviously using Shakespeare as an index of his ambivalence toward the old and the new civilizations. This is especially evident in his characterization of John the Savage, that complete (though not completely enlightened) Shakespeare worshiper. Shakespearean magic has exalted John the Savage with the discovery of wonder and love and time and death and God; but it has also magnified his bent toward perverse irrationality. Shakespearean love, for example, has given him visions of perfection—and also a disproportionate sense of betrayal and horror. Inspired by the image of Juliet's "pure and vestal modesty," he can feel only shame at his desire for the deliciously pneumatic Lenina Crowne. But Lenina Crowne is not Juliet Capulet. Unzipping her pink zippicamiknicks with rakish rapidity, she offers John her naked embraces, together with a poetical effusion that unfortunately falls short of Shakespeare's genius:

> Hug me till you drug me, honey;
> Kiss me till I'm in a coma:
> Hug me, honey, snuggly bunny;
> Love's as good as soma.[13]

The shocked young man cannot endure the melting of honor into lust; he furiously repels the impudent strumpet, after which, in full Shakespearean fever, he torments himself with Lear's maddening lines about the fiend's bequest of sulphurous stench beneath the girdle (IV.vi.129–131).

[13] Aldous Huxley, *Brave New World* (New York: Bantam, 1958), p. 112.

Clearly there is a burlesque imbalance on both sides in this erotic situation; but this imbalance also characterizes Huxley's larger portrait of two mutually repellent cultures. In the sixteenth and seventeenth chapters of *Brave New World*, this double lopsidedness is presented soberly. Mustapha Mond claims that it is better to have an unpicturesque civilization permanently cleansed of poverty, old age, anxiety, and war than an exciting civilization in which passion is often catastrophic and in which nobility and heroism are no more than symptoms of political inefficiency. John the Savage takes the opposing view: he anathematizes a "brave new world" immersed in comforts, artifices, surrogates, and sterilities. Needless to say, neither Mond nor John unambiguously wins in this contrapuntal intellectual struggle.

Does this mean that Huxley's comedy of ideas has been played out genuinely in the service of Buchananesque truth? Only superficially—for the principal truth Huxley himself derived from the writing of *Brave New World* (or so he said in his 1946 preface) was the ineluctability of social insanity, whether in the form of a queer primitivism (which may be enlarged to include the pathology of the Fordian-Freudian age) or of an abnormal utopia (p. vii). But this kind of truth scarcely corresponds to Buchanan's belief that comedy possesses an inherently melioristic proneness to eradicate error. Actually, Huxley's is an ironic truth, relished by an "amused, Pyrrhonic aesthete" (p. viii)—an ironic truth which signifies an absurd equivalence between two invalid systems of ideas. In 1946, Huxley posited another possible truth: a religious final end. But in 1932, his ironic indeterminism made a mockery of the progressive principle of verification which Buchanan posits at the core of tragedy and comedy.

3

The ironist destroys the Buchananesque formula for comedy by playing the game of ideas in such a way as not to permit an intrusive, impertinent "discovery" of a dominant truth; but the humorist destroys the formula even more effectively. The major concern of humor, Freud observes, both in his early work on wit and in his late essay on humor, is the repudiation of suffering (and not, therefore, the clarification of truth). Moreover, Freud upholds humor's metamorphosis of pain into pleasure as the noblest of man's defensive processes. He considers humor to be superior to wit, for example, because while the latter is invaluable as a force for the recoupment of instinct and the cancellation of guilt, it is also vindictive. Humor, on the other hand, is a liberation from the wounds of life, not a release for lawless desires; and it does not outjest agony at the expense of others. That is why humor's ability to transmute misfortune into gaiety (the Figaro factor) makes it incomparable among the uses of adversity. And that is why humor, it must be added, is at times overpraised. Thus Freud insists that "the triumph of narcissism, the ego's victorious assertion of its own invulnerability" in humor is evidence of a capacity for rebellion.[14] The truth of the matter is probably less heroic. Still, it is not difficult to accept Freud's verdict that the ego's refusal to suffer has a dignity of its own. Humor embraces the pleasure principle, to be sure; but Freud points out that it does not shirk the claims of mental sanity; its procedure is neither narcotizing nor neurotic.

What apparently takes place in our psyches when humor is operative is a relenting of the superego's rigorous attitude toward the ego. Acting as a kindly parent, for once, rather than as a demanding one, the superego helps the ego to survive its troubles by reducing them to the proportions of a child's disturbances. The meaning of this momentarily benevolent guardianship, Freud suggests, can be boiled down to the following reassurance: "Look here! This is all that this seemingly dangerous world amounts to. Child's play—the very thing to jest about!" (p. 268). Whether we are being humorous about ourselves (one of the great psychical achievements of humor, in Freud's opinion, is the healing resourcefulness it affords us in our stricken solitude), or whether we are observing a humor-

---

[14] Sigmund Freud, "Humor," in *Character and Culture*, ed. Philip Rieff (New York: Collier, 1963), p. 265.

ous treatment of other people, humor makes life and calamity, if not quite compatible, at least reconcilable. "Gallows humor," which carries out this function in the teeth of death, represents a special grandeur of spirit for Freud; but it is well to add that stereotyped gallows humor may flaunt only a calloused sensitivity. Genuine "sick humor" is a pathological variety of gallows humor: it does not so much exorcise dread and the fear of death as pander to a dehumanizing appetite for the macabre.

Other kinds of "humor" are likely to be merely generic synonyms for "comedy." Thus the essays in *Veins of Humor* betray the familiar baffling variety of impulses "humor" seems to include. The essay by Robert Alter on Jewish humor is actually untypical of the book's contents, though it is a natural extension of Freud's own essay on humor. Alter points out that Jewish humor deflates the awesomeness of suffering: it not only shrinks inevitable pain to the dimensions of "a world of homey practical realities" but conceives of it as "incongruous with dignity"; the result is that an "aura of ridicule" succeeds in relieving sad hearts and overburdened shoulders.[15] Matthew Winston's essay " 'Humour noir' and Black Humor," on the other hand, is symptomatic of humor's notorious promiscuity. After tracing the genesis of the phrase "black humor" to André Breton's *Anthologie de l'humour noir*, Winston divides the darker "black humor" of the last two decades (which has specialized in the blending of frightfulness and farce) into "absurd black humor" (where the accent is on the "humor," as in the "theatre of the absurd") and "grotesque black humor" (where the emphasis is on the "blackness," as in—surprisingly— *Lolita*).[16]

[15] Robert Alter, "Jewish Humor and the Domestication of Myth," in *Veins of Humor*, ed. Harry Levin (Cambridge, Mass.: Harvard University Press, 1972), pp. 256–257.

[16] Matthew Winston, " 'Humour noir' and Black Humor," in *Veins of Humor*, p. 277. André Breton's *Anthologie de l'humour noir* (Paris: Editions du Sagittaire, 1940) contains a galaxy of rather disparate "comic" writers. Baudelaire, Kafka, and Gide, for example, rub shoulders with Lewis Carroll, O. Henry, and Synge. Still, one can detect among Breton's selections the power of extreme, absurd, bizarre comedy. Swift is the great initiator of ferocious and funereal jokes (p. 15);

The kind of humor Freud has in mind may be described as disaster-humor, so that it may be distinguished from two other traditional kinds of humor in literature: the whimsical-humor of tender hearts and eccentric minds, and the sanguine-humor of devotees of cakes and ale. Whimsical-humor is a fusion of oddity and kindness that begins its democratic career essentially in the eighteenth century.[17] Its typical protagonists, such as Sterne's Uncle Toby, Jean Paul Richter's Maria Wutz, and Dickens' Pickwick, are, on the whole, relatively immune to reality, suffering, and maturity. Indeed Uncle Toby, Maria Wutz, and Pickwick are lovable, ingenuous, infantile, and sexless. Their minds are delicious lunacies, having been pleasurably and permanently warped by whimsical ruling passions; but their hearts are extraordinarily charitable.

Sanguine-humor characters are rather different. Most famously represented by the Wife of Bath and Falstaff, such char-

---

Sade practices sinister mystification (p. 28); Lichtenberg has a gift for philosophical absurdity (p. 35); De Quincey knows how to mingle levity with grief (p. 41); Villiers de L'Isle-Adam is proficient in lugubrious comedy (p. 87); and so on. Christian Dietrich Grabbe's *Jest, Satire, Irony, and Deeper Significance* (1827), incidentally, is hailed by Breton as an unsurpassed work of buffoonery (p. 48). Yet Grabbe (who influenced Jarry) does not wed nausea with blitheness, agony with clowning—though he himself believed his comedy was rooted in despair. His farce belongs, if anywhere, to the commedia dell'arte tradition. But though Grabbe is no farceur of the vomitous void, there is an obvious mingling of dread and crazy drollery in much contemporary black humor. See, for example, "Sick Jew Black Humor," in Albert Goldman's *Freakshow* (New York: Atheneum, 1971), Part II. The link between Freudian disaster-humor and black humor (Breton himself relies on Freud's analysis of humor) may be noted in Goldman's analysis of Bruce Jay Friedman's *Stern* (1962). This novel, he remarks, "is pure black humor which, if presented seriously, would be an unbearable nightmare; instead it is all played on a note of absurdity and intense hilarity, the fears made funny and thus tolerable" (p. 182). For a more comprehensive study of black humor, see Max Schulz, *Black Humor Fiction of the Sixties* (Athens: Ohio University Press, 1973). And for a first-rate essay on "sick humor," see Kenneth Alsop, "Those American Sickniks," *Twentieth Century*, 170 (July 1961), 97–106.

[17] Stuart M. Tave, in *The Amiable Humorist* (Chicago: University of Chicago Press, 1960), has admirably traced the change from the seventeenth-century aristocratic tradition of wit and raillery to the democratic emphasis on humor in the eighteenth century.

acters are zestfully self-confident. Like whimsical-humor characters, they are comparatively impervious to pain; but unlike
whimsical-humor characters, they are not marked by infantile-
angelic eccentricities; nor are they detached from the experience
of maturity. They generally enjoy, for example, a healthy sexuality; and they have an exhilarating sense of humor. Often
they are like untrammeled, toughly innocent children for whom
life is lightheartedness and an invitation to perpetual carnival.
Their "innocent," lovable imperfections, together with their
temper of affirmation, link them not only to whimsical-humor
characters but to disaster-humor characters as well.

The note of affirmation in disaster-humor is relatively subdued, however, and is generally authorial. The substance of
disaster-humor always involves some kind of devictimization.
Thus if we are shown a pitiful protagonist—a little man, an
underdog, a misfit—disaster-humor will rehabilitate him (at
least in our eyes) and leave him (or us) with some intimation
of happiness, reconciliation, or feasible survival. This rehabili-
tation is possible because the protagonist, whatever the way in
which he has become a cipher or a creature of misfortune (like
Akaky Akakyevich in Gogol's "The Overcoat," or Olenka in
Chekhov's "The Darling"), has a good heart that counterbal-
ances his physical, mental, or social inadequacies. Among these
inadequacies, the characters' lack of a sense of humor is often
conspicuous—though some disaster-humor characters, like
Sholom Aleichem's Tevye and H. G. Wells's Mr. Polly, are familiar with laughing chagrin. Disaster-humor, in short, is an
index of thoroughly humane vision. It invites us to regard the
ordinary, the lowly, or the stricken with amused but compassionate and affectionate attention; and it suggests that human
dignity can be vindicated at even the lowest levels of society.
(But disaster-humor can be mixed with satire. Thus, in "The
Overcoat," Gogol's charity and pathos are queered by amused
contempt, though there is enough humorous indulgence in
Gogol's tale to evoke from his protagonist's weaknesses a
pledge of our affection as well as a stimulus to our scorn.)

Disaster-humor's principal beneficiaries are the world's op-

pressed groups, such as the ignorant and impoverished southern Italian peasants who make up much of the population of
Ignazio Silone's *Bread and Wine* (1934). Though the peasants can occasionally exercise a crude but foxy sense of humor
for survival purposes, most of them, owing to their endless capacity for suffering and "their almost geological resignation,"[18]
face every calamity, whether it be a natural disaster or a change
in the government (the latest such mutation is fascism), like
stubborn beasts of burden, knowing nothing of the powerful
solace of humor. For these (at least by way of the reader's involvement) Silone's comedy constitutes a redemptive force. Humor, it is true, does not dominate Silone's main theme, which is
the indispensable merger of political revolt and religious brotherhood; but disaster humor does flow through the novel's major
articulations of human misery.

Pietro Spina, Silone's protagonist, secretly returns from exile
to the soil of Italy in order to rouse the downtrodden peasants
from their ignorance and lethargy. One sympathizes with
Spina, but one soon notes that his vision of life is less comprehensive than Silone's. It is quite clear that Silone is more pa-
tient than Spina, more indulgent, more cognizant of barriers to
progress. While he supports his protagonist's revolutionary
ardor, he also pokes fun at Spina's misunderstandings of the
peasant mind and at his misconstructions of presumptive opportunities for revolt. Certain ironies in the novel are in fact shared
only by Silone and the reader, who cannot help smiling at
Spina's bafflement when he discovers, time and again, that his
covert attempts at revolutionary proselytizing among the peasants are futile.

Spina persists in his pedagogy. At one point he believes
he has hit upon an excellent, if oblique, way of teaching the
lesson of political revolt. A group of card players at the inn are
debating whether they dare depose the king of diamonds,
whose card is too worn out not to be easily recognizable, and
substitute for it the three of spades. Some are worried by this

[18] Ignazio Silone, *Bread and Wine*, trans. Gwenda David and Eric
Mosbacher (New York: New American Library, 1960), p. 172.

reckless change of authority. But Spina points out that the value of the king was given to him only by the printer, and that the players are therefore free to do what they want with this card. In an attempt to rub in the lesson, he goes on to say that a big country in the East formerly had a king, but one day millions of peasants stopped obeying him, so he lost all his power. This hint of revolution seems to bear fruit: the king of diamonds is disenthroned by the players. But Spina's symbolism is laughably wasted: though the peasants discuss the dethronement for days, it has no political carry-over whatever. For the peasants, cards are cards; but real kings and dictators are destiny.

When Spina goes to Rome, hoping to find members of resistance groups among the workers in order to build a revolutionary bridge between the city and the country, he encounters two extraordinary nonconformists. One is his former socialist friend Uliva, who is now bitterly convinced that every revolution starts with an ideal of liberation but ends only with a new kind of repression. The other nonconformist also signalizes the uselessness of revolution, but this time in a comic vein. He is "Fleet-footed" Achilles Scarpa, who comes to the rescue of unescorted women tourists (preferably Nordic types, or at least women from countries with a favorable currency) when they are assaulted by the "Monster Outside the Gates." The "Monster" is an old man named Mannaggia Lamorra, whom Achilles has hired to be defeated in combat (the old man confesses to Spina that at times the foreign ladies he pretends to attack yield to him at once; as a consequence he has been compelled by the furious Achilles to look as dirty and repugnant as possible). The young ladies whose honor has been saved show their gratitude to Signor Achilles (who naturally loses his wallet in the fray—but only when he has run out of money) not only with currency and food but with uninhibited, earthquake lovemaking.

This is the only kind of commotion Scarpa is interested in; but though international in scope, it is perversely nonpolitical. Which does not prevent this reprobate from convincing himself, not only that he is genuinely rescuing ladies in distress while risking his own life, but that he is actually achieving glory in doing so. His unauthentic risks, spurious glory, and sybaritic rewards are too funny to condemn, however. And it is a measure of Silone's fair-minded and humorously balanced view that he makes Achilles Scarpa one of the memorable characters in *Bread and Wine*. As idler, opportunist, parasite, and confidence trickster, Achilles is a farcical symbol of the sleazy struggle for survival in the Italian lower depths. But his romantic autosuggestion and his cunningly preposterous ideas make him the kind of sympathetic fool and fraud that humor dotes on. The portrait of Scarpa is one of Silone's salutary reminders (it is hardly his first) that the attempt to stoke up revolutionary thinking, let alone altruistic fervor, among the Italian people must be qualified by a recognition of profound aversions (historically understandable and often amusingly forgivable) to fraternal self-sacrifice.

At key moments later in the novel, when the crisis of national ignominy becomes most acute, Silone continues to temper Spina's heroic aspirations with a humorous authorial acceptance of human weakness. Thus Spina's revulsion from the madness and degradation of the government's calculated war with Abyssinia is exhibited in the midst of a flock of comic absurdities. These include the confessions of the young cowherd on whose politically awakened assistance Spina has been counting in this emergency. The cowherd reveals that he is being driven mad by an overamorous but very religious baroness who sins throughout Europe and then records her weekly totals on postcards which she sends to him. Just to keep in touch with her (they have been friends since childhood), the cowherd has undertaken to do penance for the baroness' sins: he licks as many crosses on the ground as correspond to the baroness' illicit acts of love-making. The poor cowherd is himself never sexually rewarded, and he is all too conscious of what he is missing now that the baroness has returned to Italy with an ancient but tireless lover. In fact the cowherd cannot think of anything else, just as Spina can think of nothing but the horror of the war that has just started. In arranging this counterpoint of intensities, Silone reveals his amused tolerance of hindrances to urgent idealism—a tolerance that refreshingly moderates, without invalidating, his hero's purposes.

Silone, one can only assume, ultimately found this kind of humor suspect. Two decades after its original publication, he revised, and spoiled, his novel. He suggested in 1962 that his intention in reworking *Bread and Wine* was to tone down elements of "exaggeration, sarcasm and melodrama," as well as excessive topicality—elements produced by an untranquil and novelistically unprofitable state of mind.[19] But another explanation is more probable, especially since the elements of the original novel which Silone claims he wished to purge are more fictive than fictional. The key to the revision, it would seem, lies mainly in the shrinking of Silone's sense of humor. Although he has preserved a sizable number of comic incidents and details, Silone has eliminated the juiciest and most imaginative— for example, the conflict between Achilles Scarpa and the "Monster Outside the Gates," and the history of the baroness' flagrant sins and the cowherd's penitential licking of crosses. Other comic features in the original novel, moreover, have been altered in the direction of desirable normality or realizable progress.

It is likely, in other words, that Silone believed the drastic elements of his humor might suggest a betrayal of revolutionary integrity, a capitulation to the political and moral sluggishness of mankind.[20] One must admit that humor may at times

[19] Ignazio Silone, "A Note on the Revision of *Bread and Wine*," in *Bread and Wine*, trans. Harvey Fergusson (rev. ed.; New York: New American Library, 1963), pp. vi–vii. In the afterword to this edition, Marc Slonim accepts Silone's rationalization of his revision and suggests that the greatness of the novel is unimpaired. But it would be closer to the truth to say that Silone has turned his fictional masterpiece into a second-rate novel.

[20] It is worth noting, in this connection, that Van Wyck Brooks once argued, in *The Ordeal of Mark Twain* (New York: Meridian, 1955), that Twain's courageous, regenerative satire yielded, "on pain of social extinction" (p. 208), to the accommodations of humor, which, among other things, allowed the American business man to maintain his "psy-

signify a spineless acceptance of the status quo, a cowardly adjustment to ignoble realities. But the kind of humor that suggests a camouflaged surrender to evil and oppression, or a willingness to accept the hardships of existence because disasters are forever to be swallowed and never regurgitated, is hardly the humor Freud lauds or that Silone once utilized. Silone's disaster-humor in the original version of his novel is never less than an act of affirmation and courage. There is nothing in it that smacks of aborted idealism or a masochistic preservation of injustice and pain.

Disaster-humor is not only an honorable antidote to suffering; it is by definition an irrational, wryly reverent yea-saying to life. (What does it matter if its convictions are logically indefensible?) As such, its great value lies in its transformation of weakness into strength, indignity into hope. Moreover, when disaster-humor is compounded with sanguine-humor, it can actually convert misery into creative joy. In Joyce Cary's *The Horse's Mouth*, for example, the laughter of disaster-humor (tolerant, woe-dissolving, buoyantly forgiving) is omnipresent, for it is needed to alleviate the sorrowful facts, gruesome images, and desperate experiences that mark the protagonist's world. The life of Gulley Jimson, Cary's unsuperannuatable artist, is not unlike the history of Ikey's junk shop, which constantly changes hands because the owners keep getting hit by catastrophe and grotesquely die, often voluntarily. Unlike the various Ikeys, however,—and even though he is, or looks, down and out most of the time—Gulley is undefeatable. His anarchic antics, like his disaster-humor (which is never in danger of becoming an art of accommodation), prevent life from tumbling down on him. But his art is his most successful form of resistance to life's mishaps. His painting, after an intricate evolution, has become haunted by an epic thirst and a Blakean feeling for

chic equilibrium" (p. 211) but spoiled the artist in Twain himself by robbing him of the energy of indignation (p. 219). Somewhat similarly, in *The Quintessence of Ibsenism* (New York: Hill and Wang, n.d.), Shaw pitted the critical drive of Ibsen against the jolly assimilation of folly and failure in the early Dickens (pp. 161–169).

generation and regeneration (which does not prevent him from regularly burlesquing the Blake he reveres). Art can nevermore be tidy or timid for Gulley; like all real art, it must be waspish and subversive; it must sting the Establishment and undermine propriety, that "old fly button."[21]

For Gulley himself, madness, art, and gaiety are meat and drink. The playfulness of this sanguine, indestructible scarecrow, stuffed with genius and devilry, is at large as walls and as small as words. But there is one character in *The Horse's Mouth* who excels even Gulley in reckless verve. This is the sculptor Abel, whose aesthetic inhumanity is a fiendish parody of Gulley's own consecration to art, just as his zaniness is a fantastic extension of Gulley's own outrageous oddities. Gulley may plunge into nonsensical or lawless capers; but Abel's aberrations are often strictly mad. For example, he is constantly committing suicide; just before expiring, however, he is always struck by an aesthetic sensation that calls him back to life. Twice he tired to drown himself, his wife Lollie informs Gulley, but the first time "the chap who fished him out had no lobes to his ears, and gave him an idea for an abstract bit of stuff he was doing, an urn or something; and the second time he put all his hammers in his pocket and jumped off Waterloo Bridge, but as soon as he hit the water, he got such a strong feeling of the horizontal that he shouted for the police" (p. 215).

This kind of life-and-death clowning belongs to the world of farcical irrationality. It is a world which Gulley himself often inhabits and which is peculiarly sanctified by the horse's mouth itself—that is, by divine revelation, which encourages the fructifying force of unreason and nonsense. Humor, to be sure, is alive with fecund or protective unreason. But farcical nonsense goes even further: it glorifies irrationality.

4

Nonsense saps the prestige of the comedy of truth far more effectively than humor does—that is, if we accept the Freudian

[21] Joyce Cary, *The Horse's Mouth* (New York: Harper, 1959), p. 118.

interpretation of nonsense, which emphasizes the delights of obstructed or annihilated rationalism. Insofar as Freud's analysis of nonsense is associated with wit techniques and wit motives, it is bedeviled by a certain lack of clarity and a certain confusion of priorities. But in the fourth chapter of Freud's *Jokes and Their Relation to the Unconscious* ("The Mechanism of Pleasure and the Psychogenesis of Jokes"), there is a brief, autonomous, perfectly lucid section on nonsense which notably defends comic irrationality. Here Freud gives human nature's intermittent rejection of sense (that stuffy and severe symbol of civilization) a thoroughgoing psychological validation.

Freud sees little cultural support (clearly, things have changed since 1905) for the proliferation of nonsense, which he believes "is concealed in serious life to a vanishing point"[22] because it is too often thought to signify intellectual imbecility. This is a pity, he comments, for nonsense is enjoyable and useful: it allows us to "withdraw from the pressure of critical reason" which a prolonged education in careful thinking has imposed on us. In other words, nonsense permits us to escape from the percipience associated with maturity, which naggingly requires us to distinguish truth from falsehood. Because logic and a sense of reality make the inability to differentiate between fact and fiction a cause of shame and pain, our "rebellion against the compulsion of logic and reality is deep-going and long-lasting" (p. 126). That is why nonsense is so attractive: it laughs jubilantly at what is forbidden both by reason and the responsibilities of adulthood.

Nonsense is not the only restorative of the joys of infantile freedom. Actually the most efficient, Freud observes, is alcohol: "A change in mood is the most precious thing that alcohol achieves for mankind" (p. 127). Such changes in mood can dissolve ethical restraints; but Freud's emphasis is elsewhere. He underlines only the dethronement of intellect—for example by the deliberately nonsensical desecration in the *Kneipzeitung*, or "tavern newspaper," which lampoons the discoveries (and hence the added burden of knowledge) announced at scientific

[22] *Jokes and Their Relation to the Unconscious*, p. 125.

congresses (p. 127). In this instance, a bit of saturnalian merriment satisfies the indestructible need to get rid of chafing rationality. But however it is fermented, nonsense gratifyingly restores the liberty, wonder, and giddy euphoria which the demands of rational development have quashed.

In Freud's compact exposition, it is noteworthy that nonsense is quite separable from wit: while tendentious wit satisfies repressed impulses of sexuality, aggression, and cynicism, nonsense gratifies the urge to liberate the mind from significance. But elsewhere in Freud's text, wit and nonsense are considerably intertwined. The connection exists from the moment Freud recognizes nonsense as one of several techniques of wit. It continues as Freud, exploring the purposes of wit, sees nonsense and its ally, wordplay, take on a more generalized role—especially in innocent wit. Freud states at one point (p. 94) that innocent wit is bound to permit a purer investigation than tendentious wit into the nature of wit itself, because it is uncluttered by the purposes of sexuality, aggression, and cynicism. And as Freud endeavors to get at the earliest roots of wit in his fourth chapter, nonsense and wordplay, even in relation to instinctual gratification, finally assume a primordial function: "The psychogenesis of jokes has taught us," Freud declares, "that the pleasure in a joke is derived from play with words or from the liberation of nonsense, and that the meaning of a joke is merely intended to protect that pleasure from being done away with by criticism" (p. 131).

Nevertheless, the powerful drives of tendentious wit, which surge up from the unconscious, provide satisfactions so much more intense than those of innocent wit that they hardly fit the generalization quoted above. For a while, in fact, Freud has a certain amount of difficulty in making the earliest roots of wit (nonsense and wordplay) compatible with its deepest penetrations (sex, aggression, cynicism). The continuing sovereignty of the infantile mind is somehow made accountable for both types of phenomena. But in the long run, Freud does move away from the suggestion that sexual, hostile, and cynical witticisms carry meanings that serve merely to protect the pleasure

of illogic from rational repudiation. As he ultimately and persuasively puts it, the enticing form of wit (nonsense or wordplay) operates in its tendentious stage by the "principle of forepleasure" (p. 137); it serves to release the much greater
pleasure derived from repressed impulses of sex, hostility, and
cynicism. Nonsense is thus a trigger, not the bang itself.

The application of the sexual role of forepleasure to the functioning of tendentious wit might therefore appear to settle, once
and for all, the question whether nonsense or instinctual release
has priority. Just as an orgasm is not inherently a prelude to a
kiss, so sexual, hostile, or cynical witticisms are not basically
prologues to nonsense.[23] Cynical wit, for example, does not discredit social forms and moral values primarily for the sake of
recovering the joys of childhood irrationality.

Yet the question of priorities has not been settled, after all.
In a long and obscure footnote on nonsense jokes appended to
the concluding paragraph of the fourth chapter (the very paragraph in which nonsense or wordplay is made only a bribe or
an incitement that leads to the profounder gratifications of tendentious wit), Freud writes that "the pleasure in jokes exhibits
a core of original pleasure in play and a casing of pleasure in
lifting inhibitions."[24] But how can the forepleasure be the core?
And how can the climactic pleasure be the casing? Freud's new
metaphor does not stay buried in a footnote, moreover. He re-
peats it in his seventh and final chapter, "Jokes and the Species
of the Comic": wit, he says, contains a "core of verbal pleasure
and pleasure from nonsense, and a casing of pleasure in the lifting of inhibitions or in the relief of psychical expenditure" (p.
185). The metaphor is reinforced by a number of scattered
summarizing statements to the effect that the original intention
of wit is to recapture the delights of nonsense and wordplay.

[23] Freud applies the sexual forepleasure principle not only to tendentious wit but to literature as a whole (and rather more weakly) in his
essay "The Relation of the Poet to Day-Dreaming," in which he claims
that form, or the aesthetic element in literature, acts as a forepleasure
which releases the deeper pleasure stemming from the writer's disguised fantasies (*Character and Culture*, p. 43).
[24] *Jokes and Their Relation to the Unconscious*, p. 138.

This iteration virtually cancels, except for a single late reference which is perfunctory and fugitive (p. 221), the sexual analogy of nonsense and wordplay to forepleasure. What we are left with is a confusing homage to—of all things—the genetic fallacy. But in the matter of nonsense and tendentious wit, "original" and "earliest" are simply not synonymous with "deepest" and "most gratifying." In order, therefore, to get a clear view of Freud's attitude toward nonsense in the life of culture, it is necessary to return to the independent section on nonsense in the fourth chapter, where we learn that reason and reality need periodically to be shoved aside or dismantled.

There is another view of nonsense to contend with first. Elizabeth Sewell, in her thoroughly non-Freudian study *The Field of Nonsense*, affirms that Nonsense (which she capitalizes) is "a carefully limited world, controlled and directed by reason."[25] That is, logic and system are the lords of Nonsense, not its victims. Sewellian Nonsense is rather rarefied, however; only Lewis Carroll and Edward Lear dwell within its confines. These two masters of Nonsense, Sewell explains, play a mental game, a purificatory intellectual exercise, with one basic tool: serially related items—discrete units that can be numbered but that cannot be glued together by causal connections or psychological associations or poetically imaginative equivalences.

Disunity and incompatibility are obviously not the usual instruments of the mind, for ordinary mental activity betrays an incorrigible thirst for relation and unification. That is why these are the prime bogeys of Nonsense. More specifically, Nonsense, in Sewell's scheme, is the enemy of (1) feeling, which works by integration; (2) poetry, which capitalizes on the metaphoric imagination; (3) dream, which amalgamates shadowy, disrelated images and events (the dream form of the *Alice* books is exonerated, since it is a device of isolation from reality, not a sign of disorder); (4) beauty, which invites attachment; (5) love, which is "supremely unitive" (p. 153) and

[25] Elizabeth Sewell, *The Field of Nonsense* (London: Chatto and Windus, 1952), p. 5.

is powered by feeling, poetry, and even madness; and (6) satire, which invites entrapment by conventional social standards and contamination by reality.

Nonsense exposes erroneous fantasies or strategies of unification by clarifying the real disconnections between things. Consider the riddle which the Mad Hatter proposes to Alice: Why is a raven like a writing desk? The point of the riddle, says Sewell, is precisely that it has no solution; no fusion of the two mutually alien halves of the riddle is conceivable. If we have actually been teased or alarmed, like Alice, into searching for an underlying congruence between ravens and writing desks, we receive a salutary and pleasurable rebuke (from ourselves) upon further reflection; and we learn better to respect the law, not of synthesis, but of succession—that is, of serial numbering: one and one and one, instead of "one big One" (p. 51).

Sewell takes pains to segregate Nonsense even from satirizable real life, which she insists would be a grossly imperfect model for Nonsense precisely because of its irrational tendency to embrace trumped-up coherences. But surely she is exaggerating the chastity of Nonsense here. It is doubtful whether the reader of the *Alice* books apprehends the leakages of reality and satire into Nonsense as violations of a special Nonsense decorum, and equally doubtful whether he enjoys primarily the logic of a Nonsense universe which is, in Sewell's words, "the sum of its parts and nothing more" (p. 98). That the dissociative game of logic is a vital part of Carroll's nonsense can be granted without hesitation. The *Alice* books do curtail, with inexorable whimsy, budding sequences of conversation and discovery, and they do thrust upon us delightfully disconcerting incongruities in the realm of objects and ideas. But the intellectual pleasure derived from playing a game of capricious logic (however "pure" it may be in game terms) cannot be isolated from the psychological satisfaction resulting from the derailing of normality. Excessively purified logic, in short, easily takes on the look of antic irrationality.

The coexistence of rarefied logic and burlesque irrationality in *Alice's Adventures in Wonderland* not uncommonly takes the form of a lunatic premise, a mad conclusion, and a bit of quiet, superb logic sandwiched between them. The most significant thing about such disjointed triptychs is Carroll's relaxed refusal to penetrate the absurdities he perpetrates, especially when the sense of initial and terminal insanity swallows up the power of intervening logic. Consider the tale told by the customarily dozing and ineffectual Dormouse in "A Mad Tea-Party." His story about three little girls (Elsie, Lacie, and Tillie) who live at the bottom of a well is inevitably interrupted by Alice, who attempts to explore this fantasticality with her usual mixture of curiosity and good manners:

> "What did they live on?" said Alice, who always took a great interest in questions of eating and drinking.
> "They lived on treacle," said the Dormouse, after thinking a minute or two.
> "They couldn't have done that, you know," Alice gently remarked. "They'd have been ill."
> "So they were," said the Dormouse; "*very* ill."
> . . . "But why did they live at the bottom of a well?"
> "Take some more tea," the March Hare said to Alice, very earnestly.[26]

Note the pattern of this dialogue, which is more or less repeated in Alice's other interrogations in "A Mad Tea-Party": an absurd commencement (human habitation in a well) is followed by a plausible unfolding of logic (gobs of treacle will inevitably make little girls sick), which in turn yields to a final irrationality (why would desperately ill little girls incessantly ingest treacle at the bottom of a well?) that cannot possibly be plumbed. The March Hare suspends this major absurdity in the void by shifting to lower-key, extraneous illogic: Alice is invited to take more tea, though she has not yet had any.

The treacle-well story contains further zany details; for example, the three girls draw all kinds of things beginning with an M. When Alice asks, "Why with an M?" the March Hare easily ripostes with a ludicrous counterquery: "Why not?" (p.

[26] Lewis Carroll, *"Alice's Adventures in Wonderland" and "Through the Looking-Glass"* (New York: New American Library, 1960), p. 71.

73). This rejoinder, which silences Alice, seems to be less an exemplification of the mind's organized sportiveness than a specimen of logic giving up the ghost. Still, the intermittent death of mentality in *Alice's Adventures* is too delightful to be cause for alarm. Illogic, like violence and grotesquerie, has from the opening pages of the book been cozily domesticated by an authorial voice that casually and confidently and whimsically melts the fantastic into the familiar, and the marvelous into the matter-of-fact.[27] If, then, we ask which is dominant in *Alice's Adventures*, the strange Sewellian game of logic or the Freudian disruption of sense, the answer will be that though absurd unreason (the Freudian element) has its say, the voice of a playful but self-controlled mind testing its own resilience (the Sewellian element) is the more powerful.

Yet Carroll (who was variously appreciated by the French surrealists) is cited in Martin Esslin's *Theatre of the Absurd* as a forerunner of contemporary absurdists. In a number of dramatizations of *Alice in Wonderland*, Esslin asserts, one "will find a venerable example of the traditional Theatre of the Absurd, wholly delightful and not in the least obscure."[28] But the absence of obscurity is a minor point. What separates Carroll from other, more immediate predecessors of the "theatre of the absurd," such as the dadaists, is the relatively innocuous use he makes of his nonsense. Whereas nonsense in Carroll is

---

[27] Recent criticism has inevitably tended toward the perception of fearful absurdist elements in the *Alice* books. Martin Gardner, in *The Annotated Alice* (New York: Potter, 1960), suggests that the deepest significance of these two books is their "vision of the monstrous mindlessness of the cosmos" (p. 15). Donald Rackin basically expands this questionable assessment in "Alice's Journey to the End of the Night," in which he claims that *Alice's Adventures* "embodies a comic horrorvision of the chaotic land beneath the man-made groundwork of Western thought and convention" (*PMLA*, 81 [October 1966], 313). Sewell is an excellent corrective for such forays into metaphysical nightmare and world anarchy.

[28] Martin Esslin, *The Theatre of the Absurd* (rev. ed.; Garden City, N.Y.: Doubleday, Anchor, 1969), pp. 281–282. Esslin treats Sewell's book rather oddly, as though it supported the idea that Carroll's nonsense signifies a "mystical yearning for unity with the universe" (p. 298).

often a restorative gift of childhood wonder, nonsense in dadaism is a species of exuberant infantile nihilism. Carroll's levities
are unjarring to social equilibrium and philosophic certitudes.
Dadaism, quite to the contrary, is a funnily shocking destructiveness prompted by contempt for society and system.

Carroll's "innocent" kind of nonsense and dadaism's nihilistic
type are indeed utterly separated by the latter's mad murder of
inherited culture—or, rather, by its recognition of cultural
death, for the dadaists' outrageous negations signified that
"civilization was already in a state of total disintegration and
decay."[29] One may of course confuse individual verbal fragments of dadaist nonsense with Carroll's or with Lear's at his
looniest or, better, if only because of her chronological closeness
to dadaism, with Gertrude Stein's. Take, for example, a scrap
of dialogue in Tristan Tzara's *The First Celestial Adventure of
Mr. Antipyrine:* "This bird has come white and feverish as /
from which regiment comes the clock?"[30] This piece of gibberish is obviously meant to be an unilluminating dislocation of
language. So is the whole of Tzara's *Symphonic Vaseline,*
which Esslin describes as "a cacophony of inarticulate
sounds."[31]

The lines about the bird in *Mr. Antipyrine* resemble many
of Gertrude Stein's perplexing fragments in *Tender Buttons:
Objects, Food, Rooms*—for example, "A Box. Out of kindness
comes redness and out of rudeness comes rapid same question,
out of an eye comes research, out of selection comes painful
cattle."[32] But, as Edmund Wilson observes, Gertrude Stein's
verbal grotesqueries were presumably intended to be prose analogues of Cubist still lifes "composed of unidentifiable fragments."[33] They were, therefore, however nonsensical they ap-

---

[29] Georges Lemaitre, *From Cubism to Surrealism in French Literature* (Cambridge, Mass.: Harvard University Press, 1945), p. 169.
[30] Quoted in *The Theatre of the Absurd,* p. 319.
[31] *The Theatre of the Absurd,* p. 320.
[32] Gertrude Stein, *Tender Buttons: Objects, Food, Rooms* (New York:
Claire Marie, 1914), p. 11.
[33] Edmund Wilson, *Axel's Castle* (New York: Scribner's, 1931), p.
242.

peared (they are certainly deleriously nonsensical in effect) meant to be experiments in novel, creative associations, not pointless dissociations in the somewhat later dadaist fashion.

Dadaism's penchant for the sort of deranged phrasing that signifies a buffoonish repudiation of civilization does not, in any event, hold up well aesthetically. There is no dadaist desecration that has the continuing appeal of the sustained nonsense in *The Importance of Being Earnest*, for example. Though it exists within a coherent framework, Wilde's illogic is nevertheless outrageous enough to qualify as a centerpiece in any Freudian elucidation of the psychic enfranchisement effected by nonsense. Eric Bentley would not agree: he maintains in *The Playwright as Thinker* that the satiric impact of *The Importance* (or, rather, the near-satiric impact, for Bentley seems to think that satire must be bitter) is central to the comedy: "Wilde is as much of a moralist as Bernard Shaw but . . . instead of presenting the problems of modern society directly, he flits around them, teasing them, declining to grapple with them. . . . Wildean 'comment' is a pseudo-irresponsible jabbing at all the great problems."[34] Bentley claims that Wilde, in *The Importance*, is in fact a rebel availing himself of a bohemian, insouciant mask.

On the other hand, Louis Kronenberger's analysis of Wilde's comedy, in *The Thread of Laughter*—an analysis which seems to have been designed as a nullification of Bentley's argument—concludes that Wilde's satire is so detached from reality that it is virtually without leverage: "Here nothing can seem bogus," he asserts, "because nothing pretends-to-be-real." He adds, "There is a complete sense of the joke for the joke's sake," since the piece is marked by "a scrupulous avoidance of meaning"[35] and is played out in a uniquely absurd world. While this opinion seems more persuasive than Bentley's, Wilde's comedy is not actually nonsense-in-unreality; it has not eliminated all familiar social and psychological patterns in order to feature a

[34] *The Playwright as Thinker*, p. 144.
[35] Louis Kronenberger, *The Thread of Laughter* (New York: Knopf, 1952), p. 222.

group of dotty Carrollian duchesses and Learian Yongy-Bonghy-Bos.

Having made this reservation, let us scrutinize three techniques that Wilde uses to neutralize his satire with farcical nonsense so that our mental delight in detecting idiocy is subordinated to the joys of unreason. The first of these methods—and the best known—is the preposterous inversion of received ideas. The second, the ludicrous nonsequitur (which is as likely to be built on ridiculous premises as to collapse into silly conclusions), is the technique that provides the principal nonsense savor of the comedy—in the form of crackpot opinions, zany observations, lunatic repartees, foolishly fey quips, and mad bons mots. Wilde's third method, the crazy juxtaposition of incongruous contexts, might be classified as an especially daffy species of nonsequitur. But in a nonsequitur, what stands out, strictly speaking, is a wacky progression from one point to another. In an absurd juxtaposition, emphasis is not on a jolting advance from a possibly sound premise to an obviously cracked deduction, but on a collision of two weirdly incompatible worlds.

Nonsensical inversions in *The Importance* become especially memorable when they are uttered by Lady Bracknell, who is capable of revealing a sense of values which is at times positively demented. For example, after she has exhausted all major documentable topics during her detailed interview with Jack (who is suing for the hand of her daughter Gwendolyn), she makes ready to descend to trivialities: "Now to minor matters. Are your parents living?" She even suggests, in the same fantastic interview, that God is an urbanite, rather than the author of rural innocence: "You have a town house, I hope? A girl with a simple, unspoiled nature, like Gwendolyn, could hardly be expected to reside in the country."[36]

Though many of the comedy's nonsensical inversions of hackneyed attitudes release us from the tyranny of triteness, the fact that they adhere to a fairly mechanical formula pre-

[36] Oscar Wilde, *The Importance of Being Earnest* (Act I), in *The Portable Wilde*, p. 449.

vents them from achieving the piquancy of Wilde's second nonsense technique, the use of crazy nonsequiturs. At times the
success of the nonsequitur method turns on something as transparent as vagrant wordplay. But Wilde's more complex specimens are generally the result of oddities of opinion or emotion
that are marvelously infatuated with illogic. Thus Algernon's
"death" (in his fictive role as Jack's wicked brother) inspires
several moral and meteorological masterpieces of unreason in
the earnest mouths of Miss Prism and Canon Chasuble:

Chasuble.   Your brother Ernest dead?
Jack.   Quite dead.
Miss Prism.   What a lesson for him! I trust he will profit by it.
. . . . .
Chasuble.   Was the cause of death mentioned?
Jack.   A severe chill, it seems.
Miss Prism.   As a man sows, so shall he reap.
Chasuble. (*Raising his hand.*)   Charity, dear Miss Prism, charity.
None of us are perfect. I myself am peculiarly susceptible to
draughts. Will the interment take place here?
Jack.   No. He seemed to have expressed a desire to be buried in
Paris.
Chasuble.   In Paris! (*Shakes his head.*) I fear that hardly points
to any very serious state of mind at the last.   [Act II, pp. 465–
466]

Miss Prism is particularly deranged here since she hopes that
cadavers may learn to reform; moreover, she identifies hostile
weather patterns as the product of one's moral pollution. But
Dr. Chasuble's nonsense is not far behind: he synonymizes
moral imperfection with sneezes and colds, and he pronounces
Parisian cemeteries to be hotbeds of frivolous decadence.

Most of Wilde's examples of the third nonsense technique,
absurd juxtaposition, mangle mature judgment as obtrusively
as do his nonsequiturs, of which, to be sure, they may be seen
as variations. The difference between them is that the nutty nonsequitur bankrupts logic by burlesquing its patterns, whereas
absurd juxtaposition registers pure infantile irrationality—especially when fixed or uncontrollable facts (physiological data,
above all) are improbably subjugated by the human will. In-

evitably, the fatuously imperious Lady Bracknell makes of will power a monumental force capable of reducing all obstacles to rubble. When Jack confesses to her in his interview that he was found as a baby in a leather handbag in the cloakroom at Victoria Station, both Lady Bracknell's blue-bloodedness and her faith in firmness of will are outraged by this insurrectionary impropriety: "Mr. Worthing, I confess I feel somewhat bewildered by what you have just told me. To be born, or at any rate, bred in a handbag . . . seems to me to display a contempt for the ordinary decencies of family life that remind one of the worst excesses of the French Revolution. And I presume you know what that unfortunate movement led to?" (Act I, pp. 450–451). Acting on her extraordinary insight into the rise of bloody dissonance, Lady Bracknell decides to abort the makings of an English revolution by dismissing Jack's pretensions to her daughter's hand. But Jack soon turns out to be Algernon's older brother—that is, Lady Bracknell's other nephew—and his name is importantly discovered to be, in truth, Ernest. These findings pleasantly cap Wilde's farcical toying with the civilized imperative that man is to be defined by his cultivation of the faculty of reason.

However delightful and psychically emancipatory Wilde's nonsense is, it has become somewhat old-fashioned by now. Even Freud, in the 1912 edition of his study of wit, added three footnotes which illuminate several post-Wildean aspects of literary nonsense. That is, the footnotes contain illustrations of spoofery which are more extravagant than any discussed in 1905. (But Freud does not declare that they strike him less as a wholesome vacation from logic than as a potentially unworthy subversion of mind.) In the first footnote Freud cites a nonsensical joke reported in Von Falke's *Memoirs* (1897; p. 271): "Is this the place where the Duke of Wellington spoke those words?"—"Yes, it is the place; but he never spoke the words."[37] The nonsense here is based on two disjunct, irremediably contradictory items whose merger ruins the reasoning process.

[37] Quoted in *Jokes and Their Relation to the Unconscious*, p. 61, n. 1.

The second footnote deals with what Freud calls "idiocy masquerading as a joke." Here is an illustration he cites: "A man at the dinner table who was being handed fish slipped his two hands twice in the mayonnaise and then ran them through his hair. When his neighbor looked at him in astonishment, he seemed to notice his mistake and apologized: 'I'm so sorry. I thought it was spinach' " (pp. 138–139). The third footnote concerns *Scherzfragen*, or "facetious questions," which often use the technique of displacement. For example: "What is a cannibal who has eaten his father and his mother?"—"An orphan." —"And if he has eaten all his other relations as well?"—"The sole heir."—"And where will such a monster of that kind find sympathy?"—"In the dictionary under 'S' " (p. 153). This series of "facetious questions" sets up a maddening discordance between a teasingly "rational" query and an outlandish rejoinder (which possesses a queer pseudo logic of its own).

The interest of Freud's three footnotes is that they present anarchic nonsense material whose senselessness has remained thoroughly modern. "Facetious questions," "idiocy masquerading as a joke," and other, allied kinds of irrationalities figure importantly in contemporary mad comedy. They are certainly prominent in Heller's *Catch-22*, which is a cornucopia of nonsense tactics. Consider, for example, the technique of the sudden mental blank and ricochet, in which a preposterous ignorance or total black-out of the mind is precisely duplicated by someone who should know better (much better) but inexplicably does not. An illustration: Doc Daneeka tells Yossarian about a husband and his still virginal wife who wore a "medal of Saint Anthony hanging down inside the most beautiful bosom I never saw."[38] Doc Daneeka made a joke in their presence about Saint Anthony's temptation. The husband knew nothing about the saint, so he asked his wife, "Who's Saint Anthony?" His startled wife threw the question back at him: "Saint Anthony? . . . Who's Saint Anthony?" The husband might better have asked about the Greek goddess of love, for

[38] Joseph Heller, *Catch-22* (New York: Dell, 1962), p. 42.

Doc Daneeka subsequently discovered that the husband, for all his boasting about his virility in bed, had never learned the facts about sexual intercourse. With both the husband and wife looking on, Doc Daneeka helpfully demonstrated the proper mode of love-making by using rubber models of the reproductive organs of both sexes—rubber models which were usually "locked up in separate cabinets to avoid a scandal" (p. 42). A few days later the husband returned, called Doc a wise guy, and punched him in the nose. Doc Daneeka confesses to Yossarian he still can't figure out why. "Maybe it had something to do with Saint Anthony?" Yossarian brightly asks. "Doc Daneeka looked at Yossarian blankly. 'Saint Anthony?' he asked with astonishment, 'Who's Saint Anthony?' " (p. 43). This is not a deliberate put-on (which would in any case make for a cheap laugh); Doc Daneeka's sudden ignorance is thoroughly illogical, true, but it is also absolutely genuine. In *Catch-22* remembrance of things past may madly, unaccountably dissolve from one moment to the next.

Contagious lunacy is in fact Heller's most reliable comic stratagem. Another nonsense method, the vertiginous nonsequitur, illustrates this contagion especially well. Take the episode (which aptly conjoins logical laxity and sexual looseness) in which Yossarian is erotically avenging himself on Mrs. Scheisskopf. The latter's husband, Lieutenant Scheisskopf (Shithead), lives only for parades, and is therefore one of the horrendous monomaniacs in the novel. The best thing about Lieutenant Scheisskopf "was his wife and the best thing about his wife was a girl friend named Dori Duz who did whenever she could" (p. 71). Yet she generally wouldn't for Yossarian, who nevertheless "loved Dori Duz so much that he couldn't help flinging himself down passionately on top of Lieutenant Scheisskopf's wife every week . . . to revenge himself upon Lieutenant Scheisskopf for the way Lieutenant Scheisskopf was revenging himself upon Clevinger" (p. 72)—a friend of Yossarian's who gets in the way of military balderdash. Lieutenant Scheisskopf's wife, moreover, was "revenging herself upon Lieutenant Scheisskopf for some unforgettable crime of his she couldn't recall" (p. 72). This merry-go-round of sex and revenge is virtually unbenumbed by logic. The initial nonsequitur in this scene is somewhat qualified by later information that Yossarian is in love, not only with Dori Duz, but also with Mrs. Scheisskopf. On the other hand, that bit of news is not an authentic escape from illogic, inasmuch as Yossarian, besides being rather frequently an infant, an anarchist, and a lunatic, is also a libertine in love with all women, whether they are like the fat, instantly accessible maid in the lime-colored panties or like General Dreedle's cherry-nippled nurse.

In any case, Heller's protagonist is so often subject to instant irrationality and insanity that it is difficult, and often impossible, to distinguish between his burlesque jokes and his demented goofiness. When Yossarian accuses everybody around him (specifically, those who are either pushing or accepting the war effort) of being crazy, he is in a sense right. But when he further claims that he alone is endeavoring to maintain a decent perspective on things, he is truly potty. If we compare his use of mockery, either as a protective device or as damning criticism, with his gratuitous indulgence in lunatic nihilism, we can only conclude that a love of, or an obsession with, hilarious insanity easily triumphs over defensive or remedial aims. Yossarian's madness is not so much a Hamlet-like putting-on of an antic disposition[39] as it is the very emblem of Heller's uninhibited farce.

Yossarian can, to be sure, express with first-rate lucidity his bitter disillusionment. His condemnation of God, for example, is acidly sober. In Yossarian's opinion, he faces two major en-

---

[39] J. P. Stern, comparing Jaroslav Hasek's *The Good Soldier Schweik* with *Catch-22* (and tilting Heller toward Hasek in the process), underscores this kind of survivalism: "Given that war, as a self-contained pursuit, is an unnatural and irrational activity, it follows that the two heroes, Schweik and Yossarian, being bent on self-protection and survival, must adopt a conduct that has, in that context, the appearance of being irrational or, as Mr. Heller puts it, 'crazy.' . . . [Yossarian's] 'crazy' character is informed by an exquisite balance between sentient openness and protective integrity" ("War and the Comic Muse: *The Good Soldier Schweik* and *Catch-22*," *Comparative Literature*, 20 [Summer 1968], 211, 213).

emies in the war: the top American brass and God. But the latter is first in the field of fiendishness. During a serious discussion with Mrs. Scheisskopf in a hotel bedroom, Yossarian denies that God, that "colossal, immortal blunderer" equipped with a "warped, evil, scatological mind," knows what mercy and love mean—whereupon the atheistic Mrs. Scheisskopf begins screaming and beating him. Yossarian, surprised, asks why an atheist should be so upset. Mrs. Scheisskopf sobbingly acknowledges that she does not believe in God. "But the God I don't believe in," she adds, "is a good God, a just God, a merciful God. He's not the mean and stupid God you make Him out to be."[40] Mrs. Scheisskopf's flagrant self-contradiction (outrageous contradiction is one of the important nonsense techniques in the novel) fittingly reintroduces quirky illogic at the end of Yossarian's clear-headed indictment. For in *Catch*-22 mad farce is more pronounced than critical satire.

The rolling-snowball nonsense technique reinforces this point rather well. Consider Chief White Halfoat's life story, which reveals that the members of his family were haunted by the curse of ceaseless serendipity. To be precise, they were reluctant human divining rods who invariably pitched their tents on petroleum deposits. As a consequence they were forced to move on when oil wells began sprouting up around them. "Soon every oil company in the world," Chief White Halfoat tells Yossarian and Doc Daneeka, "had technicians chasing us around" (p. 44). Crews and equipment promptly joined the technicians. And then came the beginning of the end:

They began to follow us around from in front. They would try to guess where we were going to stop next and would begin drilling before we even got there, so we couldn't even stop. As soon as we'd begin to unroll our blankets, they would kick us off. They had confidence in us. They wouldn't even wait to strike oil before they kicked us off. We were so tired we almost didn't care the day our time ran out. One morning we found ourselves completely surrounded by oilmen waiting for us to come their way so they could kick us off. [p. 45]

[40] *Catch*-22, p. 185.

Luckily the war broke out and plucked Chief White Halfoat out of this infernal circle.

The satiric theme of the white man's sordid exploitation of the Indian—or, in larger perspective, capitalism's monstrous rapacity—is sounded quite obviously here; but it is only of secondary importance in this tall tale. Of primary importance is exploitation's mad momentum, its inconceivably fabulous acceleration—in a word, its embodiment of fantastic farce. One can see the same rolling-snowball technique in the dizzy career of Milo Minderbinder. Milo begins by being whimsically drafted for mess-officer duties. But as a result of true greed, demented ambition, and cannibalistic brainwork, Milo's powers stunningly proliferate; ultimately he succeeds in staking out most of the planet (a good deal of which worships him as a god) for profit. Again, mad nonsense reduces the mockery of capitalism's titanic theology to a secondary position.

Another nonsense technique, the use of shock antithesis to a big build-up, is related to the rolling-snowball method, with the important difference that what has been enormously piling up is suddenly and explosively deflated. Take, for example, the Glorious Loyalty Oath Crusade, sparked by that resentful nitwit, Captain Black (chief intelligence officer). His insane doctrine of "Continual Reaffirmation" (p. 117) has such a rabbity growth that enlisted men and officers spend most of the day signing loyalty oaths, that is, until the moment when the revered and majestic Major——de Coverley, a Jehovah surrogate, returns from Rome, enters the mess hall, and discovers that his way is being blocked by a line of officers waiting to sign loyalty oaths that will permit them to eat. Major —— de Coverley "started forward in a straight line, and the wall of officers before him parted like the Red Sea. Glancing neither left nor right, he strode indomitably up to the steam counter and, in a clear, full-bodied voice that was gruff with age and resonant with ancient eminence and authority, said: 'Gimme eat!' " (p. 120)—rough syllables which shattered the Glorious Loyalty Oath Crusade to bits. Actually there are two shock antitheses here: the lesser converts a quasi deity into an illiterate ("Gimme eat!"); the larger pulverizes a moronic mushrooming of rabid patriotism.

The satire in this last instance is quite plain; but it is devoured, like most of the satire in *Catch-22*, by omnivorous nonsense. The enjoyment of mad absurdity for its own sake, that is to say, becomes more significant than any satiric exposé of military-commercial imbecility. Granted that a Freudian indulgence in the liberties of Hellerian nonsense cannot be unlimited: our critical minds cannot be put wholly off guard by the seductions of unreason. But within our double delight in nonsense, the disruption of sense remains our chief pleasure, while our pride of intellect, our exhilarating mental superiority, takes a subordinate place. Not satire, nor Heller's noncomic moralizing on his theme, nor the prolonged nightmare in Rome, nor the intermittent motif of despair (Snowden's "message" that man is only garbage when his spirit is gone), nor Yossarian's occasionally frightened, sober, intelligent, profound assessments of nearly universal pathology are powerful enough to displace the pre-eminence of farcical lunacy in *Catch 22*.

4

The Imagination of Farce

The connection between Freud and farce is crucial: no other theorist's ideas are more important for the validation of saturnalian comedy. Yet Freud, for all his painstaking analysis of the shattering of inhibitions by means of tendentious wit (and nonsense), does not accentuate the more powerful annihilation of taboos achievable by farce (which has become far more vital in the literature of comedy than it was in his time). No matter; we ourselves can stress the kinship between tendentious wit and farce. Defined somewhat simply, farce is tendentious wit writ large—at least as far as psychological factors are concerned.

In Nietzschean language, farce may be described as our only source of Dionysian comedy—though the early Nietzsche, proclaiming the emancipatory joys of Dionysianism (and the culture-destructive potencies of wit), would not have acknowledged farce as the embodiment of an irredeemable satyr spirit. In *The Birth of Tragedy*, Nietzsche briefly dispatches farce as an impediment to creative vision[1] while strongly suggesting that it belongs among the art forms of decadence. Nietzsche mentions farce in the context of Hellenic decline, which is symbolized for him in Euripides' failure to keep alive the spirit of tragedy. Euripides' drama, Nietzsche contends, was corrupted by the influence of Socrates' optimistic rationality; that is, a

[1] *The Birth of Tragedy*, p. 96.

contamination by the problem-solving intellect sufficed to destroy Greek grandeur, hitherto fertilized by a noble irrationality and a genius for transcendent suffering. Euripidean drama in turn lent its psychological patterns to the erotic trivia of domestic New Comedy, which, when further degraded into mindlessness, ended as farce. Nietzsche implies that farce is to comedy what Euripidean drama is to tragedy: each is a spurious imitation of the real thing; and each represents a wholesale loss of primal ecstasy.

Nietzsche's conviction that farce signifies a low-grade, sham joyousness was hardly a unique animadversion in the later nineteenth century. Strindberg, whose early literary ideas are partly explicable in Nietzschean terms, rejects farce even more pointedly. Announcing in his preface to *Miss Julie* the need in literature for hard, tragic joy, Strindberg condemns his epoch's insistence on easy levity in the theatre. He particularly upbraids those theatrical producers who laxly cater to the vulgar and who therefore keep "demanding farces—as if the joy of life consisted in being ludicrous and in depicting all human beings as if they were suffering from St. Vitus' dance, or idiocy."[2]

To writers like Nietzsche and Strindberg, who were intensely interested in literature's repudiative and transfiguring powers, nineteenth-century farce seemed to be little more than ignoble frivolity or simian nonsense. (On the other hand, Nietzsche thought that Jewish artists like Offenbach and Heine were raising witty buffoonery to new cultural heights.) But Nietzsche's own philosophic wanderer, Zarathustra, suggests, if we may stretch his words, that farce (at its best, to be sure) may promote an exuberant rape of the world's stultified attitudes; he declares that greatness of soul is accompanied by prankishness. "Courage . . . wants to laugh," the prophet affirms. "Not by wrath does one kill but by laughter. Come, let us kill the spirit of gravity."[3] Farce is of course the perfect killer of gravity.

[2] August Strindberg, *Miss Julie*, Preface, in *Seven Plays*, trans. Arvid Paulson, intro. John Gassner (New York: Bantam, 1960), p. 64.
[3] *Thus Spake Zarathustra*, in *The Portable Nietzsche*, pp. 152–153.

It has been maintained that true Dionysian vivacity (as distinguished from the kind of comedy that is generated by anxiety and desperation) is defunct in the modern age. Jacques Barzun asserts that we fail to follow the old Greek saturnalian imperative in our personal lives:

> Unlike the Greeks whom we so admire, with our lips, for their taste and their reason, we make no provision in society for the bacchanalian part of being. We do not know how to laugh or revel. We are serious thinkers or serious alcoholics. Like the late Wolcott Gibbs, we live "with a hard ball of panic in our stomachs." We read Freud's *Civilization and Its Discontents* and approve but do not take heed. The Middle Ages, for all their fits of puritanism and supposed fears of eternal punishment, knew how to wash away panic in laughter and make room in civilization for the dionysiac as well as for its sublimation in work. We . . . can only look for "relaxation."[4]

It is doubtless true that the potential for Dionysian exhilaration has been to some degree sponged out of our lives by neurotic frustrations; but it is hard to imagine that we never engage in the kind of saturnalian revelry that dissolves panic. We are prepared to make our jokes somewhat sick and our "humor" somewhat black; but this does not mean that true bacchanalianism has become a psychological dinosaur.

Moreover, we not only approve of Freud's *Civilization and Its Discontents* but heed its contents so well, together with those of his work on wit, that we find in them clear (if indirect) justification for the propagation of bacchanalian farce. Because Freud, in his little book on the discomforts of culture, speaks of the disinhibitory role of the arts, it would in truth have been appropriate for him to declare that comic art in its most irrational form (farce) is the best single aesthetic counteragent to man's culturally submissive conduct.[5]

In *Civilization and Its Discontents*, which is predicated on the belief that man and society are both inevitable partners and

[4] Jacques Barzun, *The House of Intellect* (New York: Harper, 1959), pp. 254–255.

[5] Yet it would not do to exaggerate, for at one point Freud says that art affects us only as a "mild narcotic" (*Civilization and Its Discontents*, p. 22).

sworn foes, Freud highlights cultural suffering and its alleviation. The arts ease the antisocial hostility in man by indirectly
restoring to him elements of a lost psychic freedom. And among
the arts (here I am extrapolating from Freud's ideas, not summarizing them) farce must be the perfect antagonist of the
cultural superego; for farce is the art that circumvents inhibi-
tion most rebelliously and most irresponsibly. Without such
rebellious irresponsibility, the price of civilization (the for-
feiting of much instinctual pleasure, as Freud says) would be
intolerably high, especially in a Christianized culture where the
obligations of ideal benignity intensify the usual stringencies
of civilization. "The command to love our neighbors as ourselves," Freud writes, "is the strongest defense there is against
human aggressiveness and it is a superlative example of the un-
psychological attitude of the cultural superego."[6] Rather than
follow this unrealistic summons to universal benevolence, we
would do better, Freud suggests, to understand that man's
fundamental wolfishness can be allayed through the use of
substitute gratifications; these will allow him to get rid of some
of the congealed sociality that rankles within him.

In achieving this end, farce is especially helpful. By rejecting
the emasculating forces of propriety and conformity, it purges
the impacted cravings and poisonous resentments that debilitate
the psyche. As the most lawless and lunatic of the arts—it un-
leashes into the drawing rooms of civilization the happy beasts
of sexuality, aggression, scatology, cynicism, nonsense, and
madness—farce, with incomparable outrageousness, helps man
abjure social discipline. In farce there is no sacrifice of impulse
on the altar of virtue. On the contrary, the bones of civilized
decency are disarticulated by an incorrigible outlaw force. That
is why the farceur, that natural enemy of the saint, the sober-
sides, and the good citizen, is the darling of the id and the
thaumaturge of psychological primitivism.

Homage to the spirit of farce is no longer a novelty. Moreover, farce is sometimes celebrated under other names. George

---

[6] *Civilization and Its Discontents*, p. 102.

Orwell, for example, in "The Art of Donald McGill," interprets comic postcards of the McGill type as a delightful break-out from culture's close quarters. Though he does not scare up a whisper of either Freud or the comedy of clownery, his analysis touches the very marrow of farce. Orwell seems to agree that man is a palimpsest (to use one of Freud's favorite metaphors) whose rough instinctual scribblings have been coated with the corrective injunctions of civilization. And in his comments on the McGill postcards, Orwell is just a step away from declaring that it is outrageous comedy that best gets through to man's original animal disgrace and infantile gusto. But Orwell utilizes Cervantes, not Freud, as a source for his theorizing. The McGill postcards, he declares, capitalize on the Sancho Panza view of life, which embraces the rights of the "unofficial self." Sancho is "the voice of the belly"[7] protesting with comic candor against a "world-wide conspiracy" (p. 121) to exalt the values of the soul (the idealizing tendencies of a Don Quixote) and keep instinctual rebellion in check.

Though this Quixote-Panza bifurcation in man is dramatic enough to command attention, Orwell's designations are not wholly satisfactory, largely because Sancho Panza is not a very good example of the uninhibited, debunking antihero who shakes off the demands of social decencies. Very often, in fact, he is the voice of moderation and restraint. Nevertheless, his oversimplified image is sufficiently useful for Orwell's purposes. Sancho is grounded deeply enough in vulgarity and egoistic appetite to be able to stand, more or less, for "the lazy, cowardly, debt-bilking adulterer who is inside all of us, can never be suppressed altogether and needs a hearing occasionally" (pp. 121–122).

McGill's comic postcards, Orwell observes, provide such a hearing. They illustrate jokes, most of which deal with sex and marriage, that center on indiscretions and fantasies which society must discourage in order to ensure its survival. The postcards, in short, are meant to lift the lid off widespread re-

[7] George Orwell, "The Art of Donald McGill," in *A Collection of Essays* (Garden City, N.Y.: Doubleday, Anchor, 1954), p. 120.

pressions (p. 117). They can do so because "whatever is funny," Orwell points out, in a formula that he seems ready to apply to comedy as a whole, "is subversive"; "every joke is ultimately a custard pie. . . . A dirty joke is not, of course, a serious attack upon morality, but it is a sort of mental rebellion, a momentary wish that things were otherwise. . . . Like the music halls [the comic postcards] are a sort of saturnalia, a harmless rebellion against virtue" (pp. 121–122). The Saturnalia (that annual carnival of suspended guilt and inverted social roles) is the perfect Freudian Roman holiday. Freud himself sanctions cynical wit and jokes as the powerless man's pagan means of overthrowing enforced virtue and social inferiority; this idea neatly accords with Orwell's conception of comic energy as the liberation of unfairly suppressed instinct.

McGill's postcards are only thinly saturnalian, however; they by no means apotheosize the spirit of anarchy. Orwell himself admits that the atmosphere of the cards is old-fashioned, and he offers an explanation. The postcards appear to be addressed to the "better off working class and poorer middle class"—a group which, Orwell remarks, is neither adventure-minded nor protractedly youthful in spirit (or at least presumably was not so at the time Orwell's essay was published, in 1941). This is obviously not an ideal audience, then, for farcical nihilism. Moreover, the naughtiness in the postcards presupposes a stable society "in which marriage is indissoluble and family loyalty taken for granted" (p. 117). Thus adultery is eliminated as a motif because it is sensed to be a propensity of those with leisure and money, while homosexuality is excluded because it is apparently a hallmark of the aberrant and the sissified. McGill's obscenities, in sum, are geared to groups ready to enjoy psychic release, but only within the framework of a "fairly strict moral code." That is why the postcards present a "skit on pornography" rather than pornography itself: voluptuous women are given hefty dimensions and Hottentot behinds so as not to appeal too explicitly to secret masculine ideals of lust.

Orwell's position, which derives from the premises of the

postcards, is that saturnalianism has to be defined, not in terms of the immoralism it exhibits, but in light of the massive restrictions against which it detonates. If such restrictions are mildly felt, saturnalianism will be minimal; if they are keenly felt, saturnalianism will be riotous. It is difficult to quarrel with this judgment; but we might add that the releasable saturnalianism in a joke lies chiefly in the id of the beholder or listener. Consider two different interpretations of a familiar marriage joke Orwell cites: "A young bridegroom is shown getting out of bed the morning after his wedding night. 'The first morning in our own little home, darling!' he is saying. 'I'll go and get the milk and paper and bring you a cup of tea.' Inset is a picture of the front doorstep; on it are four newspapers and four bottles of milk." Here is Orwell's comment: "This is obscene, if you like, but it is not immoral. Its implication—and this is just the implication that *Esquire* or *The New Yorker* would avoid at all costs—is that marriage is something profoundly exciting and important, the biggest event in the average being's life" (p. 117). Perhaps. But where Orwell sees a rapt consummation of exciting, important conjugality (so rapt that four nights become as one), a more cynical reader might easily detect a mockery of marriage itself, the point being that marriage is treated in this joke as a cozy legitimization of a tremendously powerful but hitherto suppressed sexual hunger. However pleasant the veneer of tea talk and an enjoyable new home may be, four uninterrupted nights and days of love-making may suggest, not that a venerable institution is being thrillingly worshiped, but rather that the urge to fornicate has finally found all the blessings of a home in which to carry on its immortal business.

It is just this kind of business which is irrelevant to the career of Orwell's hero of the belly, Sancho Panza. Of the belly, yes; but not of the genitals. Sancho returns faithfully to his daughters, his livestock, and his plain-pudding wife whenever chivalrous adventure in the company of Don Quixote collapses. Even more to the point, this wandering squire leaves all love dalliance (it turns out to be imaginary and burlesque) to his master. Surely a successfully (or ruinously) erotic Sancho would more feasibly embody the energies of saturnalian farce. The fact is that Sancho is not naturally irresponsible and anarchic. He is a farmer fascinated by the talk (and occasionally by the actions) of a visionary knight. He is conservative, not unorthodox; peace-loving, not disruptive; paternal toward his donkey, not adulterous toward chambermaids. If we are to think of farcical comedy as a rebellion against the demands of morality and normality, we shall need a stronger representative figure than Sancho—someone capable, among other things, of funnily bashing in the fundaments of marriage.

Antimarital destructiveness is signalized in Eric Bentley's brilliant essay "The Psychology of Farce" as one of the major pleasures of uninhibited comedy. Emphasizing Freud's recognition of the "open secret" that marriage cannot satisfy a man sexually (or a woman, it would have to be added today), Bentley states that bedroom farce, his principal topic, is simply an elaborated cynical joke on marriage. The joke, which acts as a safety valve or "temporary truancy," not only affords release but actually blesses us with a larger quota of matrimonial endurance. (Freud makes the same point about tendentious wit; it increases one's ability to bear social pressure.) In any case, marriage is only a part (an extraordinary part, to be sure) of a larger inhibitory complex: family controls. Since "farces show the disguised fulfillment of repressed wishes," Bentley declares, and since, in addition, "we take the family to be the very center of culture, we should not be surprised that gross wishes are mainly, if not exclusively, desires to damage the family, to desecrate the household gods. . . . Outrage to family piety and propriety is certainly at the heart of farce."[8]

The heart of farce, Bentley might have continued, is capacious enough to include attacks on many irksome cultural extensions of the family. Farce may be seen as a "temporary truancy" from a whole host of proprieties (including academic gentility, vehicular etiquette, and supermarket seemliness) and

[8] "The Psychology of Farce," in *"Let's Get a Divorce!" and Other Plays*, p. x.

an entire army of pieties (for example, sexual virginity, religious awe, and democratic egalitarianism). Farce boldly invites us to smash all decency and discipline, all legitimacy and
logic, all authority and artificiality. Farce is the comedy (at
least potentially) of all the delectable sins and outrages that
the cultural superego plainly denounces.

If this program sounds rather like a mixed bag, we can discriminate among the destructive drives of farce by considering
four character types who variously crystallize the impulse of
farce to permit the impermissible. In his discussion of the immunity to guilt and shame that farce procures for us while
making rubble of our frustrations, Bentley has occasion to cite
a passage from *The Classical Tradition in Poetry* in which
Gilbert Murray states that the central purpose of comedy is to
liberate illicit appetite, a purpose that "must not be spoilt by
any tiresome temperance or prudential considerations of the
morrow." Bentley quite reasonably finds this statement to be an
unwarranted generalization about comedy as a whole. But he is
willing to offer the following selection from Murray's text as a
true guide, if not to comedy, certainly to farce: "The anarchist
and the polygamist, close-prisoned and chained in ordinary life,
enjoy their release in comedy. . . . As for the protagonist,
comedy provides him with an atmosphere in which . . . husbands are recognized as ridiculous and wives as a nuisance,
where Captain Macheath and Don Juan and Célimare find a
world that exactly suits them."[9]

Murray's vital evasionists and rebels—the anarchist and the
polygamist (or, better, the libertine)—are authentic exemplars
of farcical iconoclasm. But we may add another pair of char-

---

[9] Quoted in "The Psychology of Farce," p. xv. It should be added that
Murray's discussion of comedy, like Cornford's, is based on the idea of
the ritual expulsion of evil and the celebration of fertility. See Gilbert
Murray, *The Classical Tradition in Poetry* (New York: Vintage, 1957),
p. 47. In the same paragraph in which Murray discountenances "tiresome temperance" in comedy and approves "a complete surrender to
frolic" (p. 49), he cites Aristotle's stress on "high" characters in tragedy
and "low" characters in comedy. Ridiculous comic characters are thus
wedded by Murray to comedy's exaltation of freedom and fertility.

acters Bentley himself associates with the shenanigans of farce: the unruly child and the lunatic, each buoyant with superb silliness. These four desecrators of "piety and propriety" overlap in the kind of mayhem they perpetrate, to be sure; but each has his specialty. The anarchist obviously obliterates law; the libertine tramples on chastity and conjugality; the unruly child shatters social and household decorum; and the lunatic makes free with chaotic absurdity and madness.

Even this quartet can be improved upon; for the archetypal figure of the clown blends within itself the multiple misrule of farce. I refer to the kind of clown who, far from being the depreciated and ridiculous father figure oedipal theory makes him out to be,[10] is a true nihilistic buffoon, one whose physical antics and psychic frenzy ruin human dignity and unstring the bow of culture. To this kind of buffoon belongs the "demonic verve" of farce, that product of an inner experience which, as Bentley observes, "is so wild and preposterous that it would probably be impossible to exaggerate it."[11] The "real absurdity of life" (p. ix) becomes converted in farce into a "destructive orgy" (p. xiii) whose aggressions demolish society's façade of stability, maturity, and refinement.[12] The iconoclastic clown—a wild fool tempting us to shun the argument of culture and throw in our lot with the joys of chaos—is the very symbol of such gay, gross, instinctual acts of brigandage against the world's custodianship of proper values. He, above all, supplies us with the sensation that we are still marvelously untamed

[10] Martin Grotjahn, *Beyond Laughter* (New York: McGraw Hill, 1957), pp. 92–93. For a more testicular version of the buffoon, see William Willeford, *The Fool and His Sceptre* (Evanston, Ill.: Northwestern University Press, 1969), p. 11.

[11] "The Psychology of Farce," p. xv.

[12] Though his later treatment of farce, in *The Life of the Drama* (New York: Atheneum, 1964), also accentuates the guiltless comic catharsis of the psyche's wild impulses in a traditionally censorious society, Bentley wraps the Freudian justification of farce in a homogenized comic essence which he calls "humor," or the "sense of humor." But Freud's view of humor, as has been noted, has nothing to do with the liberation of reckless wishes. Also, Bentley now disappointingly considers the chief characters in farce to be the knave and the fool. (See pp. 248–250.)

and therefore still capable of uninhibited exuberance in a civilization which would prefer not to acknowledge that to revel is to rebel.

2

Let us concentrate on four special kinds of farce: sexual, psychic, social, and metaphysical. Of these, sexual farce is the most widely recognized. We may recall that Gilbert Murray cites three erotic pathfinders in a wilderness of sexual frustration: Don Juan, Macheath, and Célimare. It should be noted that Murray overestimates the sexual liberation of the last of these three figures. Célimare, whose name provides the title of an erotic farce by Labiche and Delacour, is only at first sight devilishly disrespectable, for in actuality he betrays a solid yen for middle-class stability. Whereas Captain Macheath (in Gay's *The Beggar's Opera*) enjoys ascendancy over a large number of ladies (both distinctly shady and semiproper), and whereas Don Juan scores a thousand and three conquests on the Iberian Peninsula alone, Célimare spends his time grinding out, in strictly consecutive order, two oddly prolonged sexual affairs (at least these are all we hear about). That is because he is essentially a camouflaged bourgeois whose libertine escapades, carried out with the utmost discretion, are clinched in the spirit of domesticity.

Célimare is so steady and reliable in his adulterous loves—so normal and faithful, actually—that he becomes a matchless second husband. Thus when his first mistress, Madame Vernouillet, dies (in consequence of an addiction to mushrooms) after five loyal years of adultery with Célimare, the latter feels himself to be, not an ex-lover, but a widower. The only reason Célimare has chosen to break off his liaison with his most recent mistress, Madame Bocardon, is that he now has an urge to marry an adorable virgin, Emma Colombot. But this apparently drastic step is scarcely an inconsistency in Célimare's conduct. So fixed is the quasi-marital design of his illicit amours that it seems perfectly admissible for him to switch from regularized adultery to marital regularity. The point is that while erotic farce, in theory, thrives on the destruction of marital sanctities, in practice its apparent recklessness may cohabit with a good deal of support for commonplace conduct. *Célimare* is an apt illustration of this kind of compromise: it yields to bourgeois morality in the very act of laughing at middle-class convention; it plays with fire but provides its own fire extinguisher.

The comparative restraint of the Labiche-Delacour comedy is plainly revealed when it is juxtaposed with *Keep an Eye on Amélie*, authored by that prince of erotic farceurs, Georges Feydeau (in a number of whose farces, however, adulterous urges are also ultimately tethered, if not dashed, by bourgeois propriety). *Amélie* offers a richly complicated farcical annihilation of the faiths of the middle class—and also of aristocratic and royal codes. Where *Célimare* is a comedy of mended (and never essentially dangerous) indiscretions, *Keep an Eye on Amélie* is a comedy of droll apostasies never conventionalized by a concealed pull of respectability. In *Célimare* marriage is recognized as every man's destiny (sometimes terrible, sometimes pleasant). In Feydeau's farce, sin is only a bogey of the bourgeoisie, legality is an inherent travesty, and marriage itself is a ghastly error, or at best a hypocritical, last-ditch, purely transitory submission to folly.

Amélie, a blithe coquette who has graduated, from motives of ambition, to the rank of cocotte, is a charming, art-loving alien to virtue. She remembers her lovers not as haunting reminders of waywardness but as playful tidbits from a sweet past. Moreover, Amélie is full of surprises; she is often moved by a harlequinesque appreciation of the fun of fortuitousness. For Amélie and her carefree friends, life is but a game, sex is another, and both are nourished by unfailing youth, charm, braininess, impertinence, irresponsibility, and exorbitant gaiety. Some of Amélie's male friends may belong to the world of business (for example, her present lover, Etienne, is a stockbroker's agent); others are presumably idlers on the periphery of the money-making world. But by their casual immorality they may all be identified as more or less bohemian types. Certainly no moral qualms and no sense of guilt impinge on their way of

life. There are bourgeois intrusions into this hedonic world, but these become only a foil for counterbourgeois antics.

In reality, Feydeau's main farcical interest is not so much the bourgeoisie as the upper and lower classes. These two social groups make a deeper appeal to the heresies of farce than the middle class, since (at least in Feydeau's treatment) they know little or nothing of sobriety and responsibility—especially in the matter of sex. But the representatives of low life are more candid than those of high life: Amélie's band of cocottes and their lovers endorse nonmatrimonial sexuality with cheerful vigor (some of the girls do have their eyes focused on marriage, but they rarely press the point). The representatives of high life, on the other hand, are secretive about sex on the aristocratic level, and predatory on the princely.

Two figures embody the upper-class way of the world in Feydeau's farce. The first is the Countess Irene, who adulterously launches herself into her lover Marcel's bed with all the giddiness of a famished nymphomaniac. The second, much funnier than the preposterously ardent pussycat-snob Irene, and also far more important as a character in the comedy, is the incessantly amorous middle-aged Prince of Palestria, for whom General Koshnadiev, his aide, acts as a peerless pimp. In the Prince's diplomatic-erotic European travels, it is General Koshnadiev who arranges for the satisfaction of his master's imperious sexuality (while getting a ten-percent kickback from the Prince's mistresses). After Koshnadiev informs Amélie that she is the Prince's most recent choice for a command performance in bed, the frustration of this peremptory Slavic sexual monomaniac becomes one of our chief sources of hilarity. Nowhere else in this comedy are authority and dignity so clownishly desecrated.

The Prince, in fact, is a crazy barbarian. His sense of humor is repugnantly antidemocratic, and his bedroom conduct is no better. He brooks no erotic delicacies; he demands instant copulation and proceeds with royal haste to remove his trousers whenever the occasion seems propitious. Amélie accepts the Prince's sexual invitation partly for the luxuries he will furnish (she is not grasping, just provident), and partly because her illicit affair with royalty will, as she herself daffily remarks, provide an unusual tale to regale her grandchildren with. But the Prince and Amélie never get a chance to consummate their project. Not that beds, or even the area under them, are unavailable. The reason for the Prince's defeat derives rather from the fantastic collisions and cross-purposes which run through Feydeau's comedy.

Because the Prince cannot urbanely stifle his sexual appetite (it erupts, in effect, as a powerful burlesque of all the mad lusts of European royalty), whatever vestigial awe we may feel toward exalted personages of his rank (are not princes incarnations of grace and chivalry, as well as veritable ambassadors of God?) is resoundingly punctured. Bumbling royalty is in itself a superb farcical target for psychic release, and never more than when it is exhibited in the full fever of sexual primitivism. Members of the middle class cannot instigate a comparable crashing-out of irreverence, simply because royal sublimity is a much older and much more impressive onus for the average reader's psyche to bear than any bourgeois norms. (It is noteworthy, by the way, that the Prince of Palestria's antics not only permit a gay disintegration of mystery, awe, and ritual; they also invite us to share the pleasures of sexual disinhibition.)

Powerful as the royal farce may be in Feydeau's play, Amélie's own adorable shamelessness provides excellent competition. Amélie is not the eternal feminine. She is something better: she is a beautiful, childlike, witty, fun-loving pagan immoralist. For all that, she becomes the very image of delicacy when placed side by side with the sexual privateers (for example, Henry Miller, Sebastian Dangerfield, and Humbert Humbert) of contemporary farce. How, for example, can one compare her with the autobiographical narrator of Miller's *Tropic of Cancer?* Miller's protagonist belongs to a totally different world: he is an ecstatically restless nihilist who ranges vandalistically over the whole corpus (for him, corpse) of organized culture. By an amazing personal fiat, aimed at releas-

ing him from the doldrums of life so that he may enjoy its suc-
culence, he devotes himself to fecund, formless anarchism; and
in the process he becomes a great life swallower and death
vomiter.

The narrator's fantastic self-metamorphosis suggests far
more than irrepressible antipuritanism; it also involves a readi-
ness to deracinate the whole stale, bloody world—often by
using modes of wild comedy. Miller's spitting and kicking at
phony ideals and rotting shibboleths are so often communi-
cated through monstrously dazzling vulgarity and delirious
zaniness that he must be recognized as one of the great farceurs
of our time. Certainly one gets the impression that there are
oceans of farcically scabrous and scatological upheavals in
Tropic of Cancer. The furious scatological clown in Miller's
persona is inevitably less copious in his contributions to comedy
than his sexual counterpart. Still, scatological outbursts have
always been nonpareil in exploding the system of things, and
Miller is remarkably good at the job. "For a hundred years
or more the world, *our* world," runs Miller's essential gambit,
"has been dying. And not one man, in these last hundred years
or so, has been crazy enough to put a bomb up the asshole of
creation and set it off."[13] But Miller's sexual assaults against
the putrescent world clearly surpass his scatological sorties. In
his characteristic forays into monumental sex, Miller negoti-
ates cuntland (the heartland of the anti-ideal, yet also the seed-
bed of giant energies) and in doing so spills over with the
brazen poetry of some colossal explorer sounding the depths of
a rugged, primeval paradise.

Miller's sexual taboo-smashing can nevertheless be transcendent as well as farcical. He shoots off his crazy orgasms
sometimes in a glory of poetic perceptions, sometimes in a
gaggle of burlesque images, sometimes in an amalgamation of

[13] Henry Miller, *Tropic of Cancer* (New York: Grove, 1961), p. 26.
In *Henry Miller* (New York: Twayne, 1963), Kingsley Widmer rightly
stresses the clown element in Miller. In his last chapter, "The Rebel-
Buffoon," he makes the point that "the rebel-buffoon's one heroism is
his own defiant absurdity" (p. 159).

both. That is, Miller not only rawly reduces psychic repression to zero; he also elevates sexual gyrations into a divine choreography, reminding us that a satyr celebration of life used to be affiliated with divinity. But it would be inaccurate to suggest that reaching heaven is the major motive behind Miller's piledriver eroticism. A good many episodes and characterizations in *Tropic of Cancer* gain merit only because they are hilarious wipe-outs of civilized icons and cultural restraints.

These wipe-outs occur not only when Miller's Dionysian-American bravura is in full play, but also when his cockiness results in fiasco. Moreover, when his manhood suffers derailed erections and failed orgies, Miller's farcical antics become much more pleasingly human than when his virility takes on breezily epic proportions. Thus Miller the daffy hobo hooking impromptu rides in the world's vagina is a delightfully vulnerable sexual clown who is not only the most insatiable of libertines but also the unruliest of children, the wildest of anarchists, and the most intractable of lunatics. As a world misfit, Miller encounters much calamity and sordidness; but more often than not he responds to them like a satyr who has sunlight in his veins and joyous outrage in his genitals.

Karl Shapiro has called Miller "Gandhi with a penis."[14] This is Shapiro's way of indicating the fusion in Miller of spirituality and appetite, of holiness and lust. Yet most of the sexual farce in *Tropic of Cancer* is too wackily promiscuous to be readily sensed as the alloy of soul force. At first, in fact, Miller comes across as a burlesque Priapus, not as a bawdy saint. Or if Miller really is Gandhi with a penis, then the hungry, boisterous, jocularly uncouth penis wags Gandhi far more often than Gandhi wags the penis. Miller the mad prankster and phallic anarchist clearly dominates the poet and mystic that also reside within him.

Sebastian Dangerfield, the intemperate hero of J. P. Donleavy's *The Ginger Man*, also belongs to the tribe of puerile, penile, poetic clowns; and he too has an extraordinary knack

[14] Karl Shapiro, Introduction, *Tropic of Cancer*, p. xiv.

for nihilism. But there is no intermittent itch for cosmic copulation in Dangerfield; he cannot make the grade of transcendental clown because the kind of rumpus he kicks up has no
metaphysical side drift. The Millerian maelstrom can at times
tear asunder the secular self; but Dangerfield's eruptiveness
rarely gets beyond a vertiginous egoism. Moreover, the Miller
persona, overfamiliar with social bondage and universal muck,
never gravitates, like Dangerfield, toward the panacea of an
upper-middle-class income. Miller may be savage, mendacious,
and grotesque; but he does not pump out his shattering energies
in the service of ultimate ease and privilege and conformity.

The America of bogus expectations Miller satirizes and stays
away from in *Tropic of Cancer* is also hilariously ridiculed in
The Ginger Man. The ignoble thing about Dangerfield, however, is that he wittily drools over the cushy American life he
sardonically deprecates. Unfortunately, his plans to indulge his
taste for membership in the capitalistic elite have been temporarily foiled by a rotten marriage and unpicturesque poverty.
And his predicament has hastened the development in him of
certain shady talents and strident tendencies: he has become a
fast-patter charlatan, a boozer, a brawler, a sponger, a wencher,
a petty thief, and a grand vandal. He is also a marvelous (generally retaliatory) prankster, a subtle poet, and an immensely
sad fellow. Because his wife Marion sees him principally as a
disgruntled idler and a nasty vulgarian, aggressive and scatological domestic conflicts are almost a daily dish.

Though Dangerfield's waging of conjugal warfare can be
stunningly forthright, he wins his best battles in his interior
monologues, where he manages to shine forth as a sensitive
ruffian and a soul-searching satyr. But circumstances often have
an absurd rhetoric of their own which no inner opiate (or
irony) can quell. There is the matter, for example, of the
flimsy pipes in Dangerfield's rathole of a rented house:

One morning there was sunshine and I was feeling great. Sitting
in there grunting and groaning, looking over the news, and then
reach up and pull the chain. Downstairs in the kitchen, Marion
screamed.

"I say, Marion, what is it?"

"For God's sake, stop it, stop it, Sebastian, you fool. What have you done?"

Moving with swift irritability down the narrow stairs, stumbling into the kitchen at the bottom. Perhaps things have gotten too much for Marion and she's gone mad.

"You idiot, Sebastian, look at me, look at the baby's things."

Marion trembling in the middle of the kitchen floor covered with strands of wet toilet paper and fecal matter. From a gaping patch in the ceiling poured water, plaster and excrement.

"God's miserable teeth."[15]

Later, after a nasty spat with Marion, Sebastian moves from excremental innocence to scatological turpitude: "In the toilet, Sebastian forced a board up from the floor. He hammered a nail through the lead pipe with the heel of his golfing shoe"; then he left the house, in "bitterness and hazy hatred" (p. 102). His plan of revenge is funnily but viciously infantile. Dangerfield's defections from decency are, in fact, often exorbitantly childish. He is so ill-mannered with Marion's female acquaintances that he is liable to import turd or bordello effusions into the most superficial chatter with them. Since he cannot stop up the toilet pipes of all these unbearable women, he resorts to dislocations of social plumbing. Still, one barely scratches smelly Sebastian's indiscretions by mentioning his horrid social profanities and his rerouting of fecal matter. A more notable rejection of responsibility is his continual adultery. Dangerfield may not be a Millerian phallic titan, but his adventures in carnality constitute the crown of farce in *The Ginger Man*.

In these erotically farcical adventures (there is only one important exception) Sebastian is usually either a helpless, deficient orgiast enmired in adventitious copulations or a brilliantly coy seducer able to avoid any possibility of a disruptive imbroglio. In the first of these two roles, that of the imperfect satyr, Sebastian picks up a stocky girl named Mary at a violently festive, hit-or-miss party. He cultivates her in histrionic,

[15] J. P. Donleavy, *The Ginger Man* (New York: Berkley, 1967), pp. 44–45.

half-nonsensical fits and snatches until he finds himself attacked on a cellar mattress by an increasingly ardent, lubriciously gaga creature who not only swallows his not so phony folderol about running away to England with the thirty pounds she has in the bank but who also presses him to give her a thrillingly novel experience: a complete lay. Dangerfield, who often does his "most penetrating thinking just slopping around with someone else's body" (p. 158), and who is having great mamillary cravings on account of Mary's tremendous breasts, discovers, alas, that he is in a condition of collapsed bacchanalianism.

In his second erotic role, Dangerfield is a foxy tactician rather than a clownish drifter. Consider his subtle approach to Miss Lilly Frost, the gentle, not unattractive spinster to whom he and his wife have sublet several rooms in their third, and this time acceptably middle-class, rented house. Marion herself has just cleared out in a final spasm of disgust at Dangerfield's deceitful pranks, and Dangerfield himself, in order to escape his unpaid former landlord's vigilant snooping, has to dash out of the house with mad furtiveness and get back in the same way. Marion's departure and his own panicky sense of victimization conspire to set up a perfect excuse for erotic solace. Dangerfield therefore goes to work to thaw out Miss Frost. And he is so insinuatingly childlike and helpless as he guilefully nestles closer and closer to Miss Frost on a lonely night that we seem to be watching a heavenly siege, a prelude to the intercourse of angels. Thinned down to his torn, stinking underwear, he waxes beautifully apologetic about the dreadful inconvenience he is causing her by being so melancholy that he is unable to sleep in his own room. Dangerfield first boyishly holds Miss Frost's hand (after proper request), then maturely slinks into her bed (after gracious permission), and finally provides her (after utter consent) with an entirely adult feast of sexual congress. With coition, however, comes guilt: Catholic Miss Frost is much troubled by the idea of mortal sin. Fortunately, after a good deal of spiritual self-questioning (and further sessions in bed with Sebastian), she at last hits upon a solution: anal copulation. "Lilly, why did you want me to do it this way?" "O Mr. Dangerfield, it's so much less of a sin" (p. 227). And fun too, Dangerfield adds.

In the long run, Dangerfield's ironic buffoonery wilts. His flair for outrage lapses into trivial irreverence, then yields to jokeless despair. This ultimate sadness is in reality a culminating point of pain. Dangerfield's clowning has always existed in close concert with suffering; he even avows, for all his mad antics, that misery is his forte (he thereby joins the ranks of literature's anguished comedians). The dark wells of nightmare from which much of Dangerfield's comic lunacy springs also provide him with a doomsday consciousness which, unlike the protagonist of *Tropic of Cancer*, he is incapable of transmuting into cosmic joy. The last, brief chapter of the novel is in fact pregnant with futility and death. As he returns to his empty, parasitical relationship with Mary (now metamorphosed into a brainy beauty), the former God wrecker and fiery clown sinks to the condition of a heart-sick marionette, twitched by prudence, fear, and a sense of the void.

Whereas Dangerfield's comic temper is finally incapacitated, that of Humbert Humbert, in Nabokov's *Lolita*, remains very much alive even in his period of decline (which, after all, includes the time during which he writes his confessions). But Humbert Humbert's affiliations with comedy are more astonishing than Dangerfield's. He is, for example, a romantic ironist: he is moved by exaltation yet at the same time is devoted to absurdity; he ardently believes yet sardonically disbelieves; he dreams yet befouls his dreams in laughter. Humbert the rhapsodist of mystical romantic love is not incompatible with Humbert the parodist of romantic idealism—or with Humbert the sex pervert; for Humbert's romantic intoxication, mocking derogation of the ideal, and abnormal fleshly fever are equally genuine.

The fact that Humbert finds Lolita the nymphet both paradisally captivating and unconsciously demonic suits his dichotomous tendency to idealize and ironize—a tendency which presumably dates from Humbert's comically interrupted ecstasy on a Riviera beach when he and his first love were mere adolescents: "I was on my knees, and on the point of possessing my darling, when two bearded bathers, the old man of the sea and his brother, came out of the sea with exclamations of ribald encouragement."[16] This heritage of rapture and ridiculousness is wickedly intensified after Humbert marries Charlotte Haze in order to avail himself, he hopes, of her daughter. But the palpitations which the image of Lolita evokes in him—it has been a case of romantic re-love at first sight—regularly carom into farce, especially after he is robbed of his nymphet by her mother's decision to send her to a summer camp. Thus one Sunday morning, while Mrs. Humbert is at church, Humbert deceives his wife with—"one of Lolita's anklets" (p. 76). This is erotic farce of an unexampled kind.

Actually, Humbert's masturbatory or semimasturbatory activities blend the incandescence of a visionary with the calibrated delights of an oriental sensualist and the freakish antics of a self-conscious buffoon. But after Lolita has (she thinks) retroactively normalized Humbert's sexless youth by initiating him again into the basic facts of fornication, Humbert's anomalous phallic desires are from time to time fulfilled with amazing ease—as when Lolita the newspaper scanner is phlegmatically ensconced on Humbert's erect penis while picking her nose, lazily following the adventures of comic-strip characters, and girlishly attending to the paraphernalia of photographed local brides.

In any case, Humbert is quite often consciously and cleverly (but also longingly and pathetically) on the lookout for erotic bonuses. He manages to exculpate himself in the reader's eyes by making physical lust more risible than pathological. Consider the initial Humbert-Lolita motel bedroom sequence ("le grand moment"). Not having succeeded in anesthetizing Lolita's nearness, Humbert is compelled to make breathless, microscopically libidinous movements toward her nebulous body:

I had the odious feeling that little Dolores was wide awake and would explode in screams if I touched her with any part of my wretchedness. Please, reader: no matter your exasperation with

[16] Vladimir Nabokov, *Lolita* (New York: Berkley, 1969), p. 15.

the tenderhearted, morbidly sensitive, infinitely circumspect hero of my book, do not skip these essential pages! Imagine me; I shall not exist if you do not imagine me; try to discern the doe in me, trembling in the forest of my own iniquity; let's even smile a little. After all, there is no harm in smiling. For instance (I almost wrote "frinstance"), I had no place to rest my head, and a fit of heartburn (they call those fries "French," grand Dieu!) was added to my discomfort. [p. 119]

Humbert, "burning with desire and dyspepsia" (p. 120), and having to endure the Niagara crashes of the various toilets at the motel while desperately concentrating on keeping Lolita asleep so that his shyly imperious penis may ultimately poke its way to a mere millimeter's distance from a heavenly haunch, is above all a burlesque figure. Besides, this lecherously delicate doe trembling in the forest of his own iniquity, this sensitive flesh scientist, this phallically aroused preserver of virginity, is poised only to be laughably foiled—although later that night Lolita seduces him, thereby consummating the deepest dream of contemporary literature's most complex erotic clown.

A febrile clown, too. Much of the sexual farce in *Lolita* is generated at the point where Humbert's carnal fever—its romantic origins hectically obscured—rages maniacally against prudence and fear, which generally win out. In this coalescence of the comedy of sex and the comedy of guilt, Humbert's imagination is likely to twist things awry. When, for example, Humbert arrives at the Enchanted Hunters Motel for "le grand moment," his greedy but apprehensive sexual excitement projects an aura of swinishness onto ordinary things and commonplace proceedings. Thus the cars parked outside the motel are "like pigs at a trough" (p. 108); and one of the two ridiculous old men who handle the registration looks distinctly porcine. "Would there be a spare cot in 49, Mr. Swine?" this old man is asked. "I think it went to the Swoons," replies Mr. Swine (p. 109). This swine-swoon syndrome is the very index of Humbert's haunted (if still lyrical and redemptively farcical) lust.

Clownish frenzy and terror contort Humbert's recollection of names, especially toward the end of the novel as he prepares to wreak vengeance on Clare Quilty because of the latter's lubricious viciousness toward Lolita. Sick, sleepless, and intent on murder, Humbert plunges into a farcical Gothic melodrama. First he quits Insomnia Lodge, then gains Grimm Road, from which he is able to reach Pavor Manor. Here he seeks out disheveled, drunken, degenerate Quilty, who is shambling about in a purple bathrobe and who only with difficulty gets the message that Humbert, gloating at the entrapment of his subhuman double, is stalking him to the death with his loaded pistol, his metallic pal Chum. After scuffling in a ludicrous, nightmarish ballet of two intellectual buffoons and after rejecting Quilty's attempts to bribe him away from his ghastly intention—"By the way, I do not know if you care for the bizarre, but if you do, I can offer you . . . as house pet, a rather exciting little freak, a young lady with three breasts, one a dandy, this is a rare and delightful marvel of nature" (p. 274)—Humbert fires away. The shots evoke from the wounded Quilty either unpredictable, insanely irrelevant spasms of activity (hysterically vigorous piano-playing, for example) or histrionic rebukes, generally in a British accent. And when the whole affair is over—when loony McFate is slowing Humbert down to a happy disgrace—Nabokov's protagonist dares dreamily to trifle with the law once more, this time by driving on the wrong side of the road. The gesture turns out to be, not simply a pleasant anticlimactic illegality after a history of antic incest and farcical murder, but perhaps the most perfect balm of all—a virtual return to an infantile paradise.

3

Humbert Humbert, romantic ironist and bleeding buffoon, is the victim of a remarkable psychic duality. He may therefore be described as a representative, not only of erotic farce, but also of psychic farce, which prevails when a character's psychological imbalance is the pre-eminent agent of hilarity. Usually the protagonist of psychic farce oscillates unpredictably between reason and irrationality, maturity and infantilism, dignity and dishevelment—often simply by leaping from one emotion to its polar opposite. The essence of psychic farce, in short, is zany mental and emotional instability.

Psychic farce may be illustrated in Chekhov's one-act, one-character play, *The Harmfulness of Tobacco*. The protagonist of this dark little comedy has been forced by his harridan of a wife to give a free lecture to the public. But the lecture he delivers is extraordinarily jumbled; in fact, the protagonist is so ridiculously incompetent as a speaker that he annihilates the whole ritual of lecturing. His ineptness is a boon for farce, inasmuch as lectures, whose formality is propped up by authority and prestige, fairly scream for farcical desanctification. Certainly the chaotic lecture on the subject of tobacco burlesquely ruins any expectation of reason, illumination, or uplift. It furnishes, instead, a relish of emancipation, not only from intellectual inferiority to the gods of the platform, but from the not easily forgotten incubus of academic discipline. When the shabbily dressed, Chaplinesque lecturer observes that a fly in a snuffbox probably dies of a nervous breakdown, we understand that a similar fate may be in store for the lecturer himself (certain of his tics, for example, are obviously indices of repressed psychological earthquakes). But in spite of his boxed-in, insect-like existence, the lecturer has managed to survive the doom of the small. Not without becoming an odd creature, though. "Tobacco, speaking very generally, is a plant," he remarks, with his curiously unscientific predilection for the indefinite. His very next words are peculiarly digressive: "Yes, I know, when lecturing before an audience, I blink a little bit, my right eye blinks. Pay no attention, it's just nervousness. I'm a nervous man, speaking very generally."[17]

---

[17] Anton Chekhov, *The Harmfulness of Tobacco*, in *"The Brute" and Other Farces*, ed. Eric Bentley (New York: Grove, 1958), p. 8. In *The Unknown Chekhov*, trans. Avrahm Yarmolinsky (New York: Noonday, 1958), one may find both the first and the last versions of this play. Yarmolinsky points out that the last version, written sixteen years after the first, is reduced in farcical verve because of its greater stress on "ugly actuality" (p. 18). Chekhov's protagonist, like the comparable figure in his *Swan Song*, belongs to the literary tradition of the crucified clown, whose vulgate embodiment is most notoriously etched in *I*

How could he be otherwise? In his wife's boarding school (it is approximately that), he is forced to undertake all the menial occupations, from the stitching together of exercise books to the extermination of bedbugs. His wife, furthermore, is a stingy shrew who systematically mistreats him—even to the point of starving him. The lecturer does have daughters, but they are no solace to him; in fact, they only laugh at his melancholy fits. Besides, their very birth dates suggest that their father's life is hellish: each of them—he is not quite sure how many he has—was born on the thirteenth. And that is not all. His address is Five Dogs Lane, Number 13. "That's probably the reason I'm a failure," he points out, "living at Number 13. My daughters were all born on the 13th. I think I told you. Our house has 13 windows" (p. 5). This, of course, is the mathematics of madness. But perhaps the lecturer is the victim of a cosmic conspiracy.

Not that he complains about the gods; he confines his animus almost entirely to the formidable tyranny of his wife. And the more he focuses on the tormenting fact that he is her lackey, the more fantastic become his shifts of theme and tone. "I'm always hungry," he laments. "Yesterday, for example, she gave me no dinner at all. 'A dumbbell like you,' she said, 'doesn't deserve a dinner.' However (*looks at his watch*), I see I have strayed a little from the subject of the lecture. . . . To proceed . . . though I know you'd all rather hear a love song . . . (*he breaks into song*). Hear ye the battle cry? / Forward! Be strong!" (p. 5). But this rousing battle chant suddenly gives way to a consideration of business activities as he attempts, without success, to sell the audience prospectuses de-

---

Pagliacci but who is incarnated in many profound interpretations, including several by Baudelaire in *Le Spleen de Paris*. When Heine, that sensitively suffering buffoon-as-writer, describes Laurence Sterne in *The Romantic School*, he is also depicting himself: "Sometimes, when his soul is most deeply agitated with tragic emotion, and he seeks to give utterance to the profound sorrows of his bleeding heart, then, to his own astonishment, the merriest, most mirth-provoking words will flutter from his lips" (*The Prose Writings of Heinrich Heine*, ed. Havelock Ellis [London: Walter Scott, 1887], p. 130).

scribing his wife's school, where he himself teaches all the subjects and also serves as janitor.

His aborted salesmanship now triggers a darker disburdening of woes, expressed in a speech still marked by crazy disconnections. We learn that the lecturer, a self-branded nonentity and suffering fool (who declares he was once young and intelligent, had aspirations, and even attended a university), has compensatory dreams of escape. But so frightening has his trivial existence become that he can no longer envision real freedom. He cannot conceive of liberation in purely human terms, for he hopes only to flee and then "to stop, somewhere far away, in the middle of a field . . . like a tree, a post, a scarecrow, and watch the bright, gentle moon overhead and forget, just forget" (p. 7). (The pathos here derives from his descending series of aims: first he will become a living tree, then a dead piece of wood, and finally a hideous simulacrum of a man.) In the meantime, he occasionally substitutes for his grotesque arcadian dream an inadequate brief revolt. For example, he tears off his threadbare coat, which he first wore at his wedding thirty-three years before, and tramples this hateful symbol of bondage with repeated, antic savagery. But fear of his wife's imminent arrival, as well as a regard for the lateness of the hour, compels him to call a halt to this surrogate assassination. "My time's up," he discloses to his listeners, then incongruously solicits from them their aid in covering up his demented digressions: "If she asks, will you tell her the lecture was . . . will you tell her that her fool of a husband . . . I mean, that I . . . conducted myself with dignity?" (p. 7).

It is precisely a failure of dignity, at once preposterous and poignant, that has characterized his entire absurd "lecture." He has not only publicly abominated his marriage but destroyed the very basis of the lecture system; and he has done this by mingling, in a rage of discontinuity, farcical levity and emotional torture. Chekhov's lecturer is a tragic buffoon, an unwitting clown of agony whose funny futilities symptomatize the aimless, blundering follies of his unlucky and helpless existence. Yet he is not entirely crushed by life, for to some small extent he can shake off the cerements of his anxiety and fear in desultory outbursts of utterly silly (and heart-breaking) confessions and tantrums.

Chekhov's playlet should now enable us to see how psychic farce functions. Whereas the purpose of erotic farce is to subvert the tradition of Christian restraint, the aim of psychic farce is to demolish the repression that is associated with psychological consistency and maturity. Psychic farce, that is to say, explodes conventional stylizations of attitude and emotion; and it blasts the familiar patterns of sanity. Whereas erotic farce is an assault on moral prohibitions, psychic farce is an attack on society's regulative regard for spurious unity and balance of personality. We smile at Chekhov's bamboozled lecturer (we smile right through our compassion) partly because his dizzily changing feelings and opinions betray a shameful failure of self-control. But we also smile because the drastic irrationality and nearly hysterical disequilibrium of the lecturer provide a cathartic occasion for disregarding the suffocating postulate that to be adult human beings, we must show reliably recurrent traits and reject with horror an infantile reversion to seesawing attitudes and an indecorous lapse of discipline. Psychic buffoonery, both in light farces (such as Chekhov's *The Boor* and *The Marriage Proposal*) and in dark, restores to us our pleasure in outrageously contradictory and chameleonic impulses— and, by extension, in whatever is absurdly protean in the larger life of society.

Much of Diderot's *Rameau's Nephew*, for example, assaults both the notion of unity of character and the idea of order in society. This dual assault occurs because the astonishing psychological imbalance of the Nephew is linked to immoralist confessions that disintegrate society's pretentious blandness. Actually, Rameau's nephew has little reason to venerate either psychic or social equilibrium, for basically he considers self-interest to be the only authentic guide to conduct—the kind of self-interest that is ready to play a highly variable game of manners and morals. It is a game in which the Nephew clowns a good deal, often abasing himself, for he belongs to the army of the poor. But Rameau the Nephew (he bears the same name as his uncle, the well-known composer) is a lackey-fool not only by necessity (as Fyodor Karamazov claims he himself was, when as a young man he had to entertain the rich in order to stave off intestinal rumbling); he is also driven to folly by natural inclination—by an imp of comic perversity. Thus solemnity appalls him because of its unnaturalness, which he believes brings on bodily strain and spiritual grouchiness. Similarly, virtue and wisdom are intolerable to Rameau because they are either too cold or too dull. It seems certain that even if it were possible for him to be happy by being respectable, he would prefer the gaiety and freedom disreputability guarantees.

Rameau's Nephew is essentially a dialogue, an interchange of impressions and ideas, between Diderot and Rameau the Nephew. According to Diderot, who presents himself as honorable and moral but also as receptive to risky, even mad notions, Rameau (who permits himself to be uninhibited in Diderot's unforbidding presence) is both psychologically and physically a creature of dualities. Psychologically, he is "a compound of elevation and abjectness, of good sense and lunacy, . . . of decency and depravity."[18] Physically, he alternates between pale, ragged consumptiveness and fat, elegant well-being. But if his flesh is uncertain and his psyche shaky, Rameau is always stimulatingly outrageous. Diderot admits that Rameau's company (once a year, say) is good therapy for the correct, conventional, well-mannered person. Rameau "is like a grain of yeast that ferments and restores to each of us a part of his native individuality" (p. 9). In other words, being with Rameau is like doffing one's social puppetry and returning (not entirely, to be sure, for Rameau often exploits a keen, egoistic opportunism) to the id, with its reanimating cravings, conscienceless demands, and unsettling truths.

All in all, Diderot finds Rameau's frankness as delightful and revelatory as it is dangerous and unworthy. But though at

[18] Denis Diderot, *Rameau's Nephew* (Garden City, N.Y.: Doubleday, Anchor, 1956), p. 8.

times he is troubled by Rameau's delinquencies, Diderot is rarely stuffy about them. Rameau is too exuberantly nonconformist (he cheerfully confesses he is a blackguard) and too unexpectedly zany to elicit starchy disapproval, even if his lifestyle is a scandal. And a scandal it obviously is. Most of the time he is a parasite-clown-swindler who would like nothing better than good food, pretty women, considerable wealth, lordly power, and fine bowels. (Wealth is all-important, for it protects the immorality which is the inevitable idiom of survival and triumph.)

A pauper-clown tends to find his status infuriating; and the suffering buffoon in Rameau has much to exasperate him, especially the revolting conceit and intolerable taste of his patrons. Often he has to suppress his rage (and envy) just to get along. Worse, at times he is liable to forget his role. Recently, he explains to Diderot, he had grown so fatuous and arrogant about his gifts as an irreplaceable comedian—he was sure he was worth a whole lunatic asylum—that he committed an act of unimaginable folly: he used common sense in speaking his mind. His patron for once found him too saucily, too ironically truthful, and as a result threw him out of his house (after all, Rameau's function was to dispel boredom, not to be cuttingly sensible). Naturally, Rameau has vowed to stay away from good sense forevermore. He may badger himself to reach sublime levels of lunacy, but he will henceforth avoid the perils of sound observation.

There is a good deal of cynical truth in what Rameau tells Diderot on the subjects of vanity, power, and buffoonery. And Diderot cannot help recognizing this, although he does not honor Rameau's cult of duplicity. Actually Rameau takes such pride in his chicanery that he wishes to be thought of as belonging to the "great tradition of the master scoundrels" (p. 63). This ambition is not entirely suitable, though; there is so much spontaneous, unpredictable, overwhelming irrationality in Rameau that one wonders how genuine his turpitude can possibly be. One can only find something strangely innocent (and ineffectual) about a character who, like Rameau, can indulge in instant buffoonish histrionics—even to the point of spellbinding himself.

In his essay "The Essence of Laughter," Baudelaire defines droll pantomime as the quintessence of farce; this is a definition which applies especially well to Rameau's gifts, for when Rameau goes into pantomimic action, he drops his affinities with the tradition of the tortured buffoon and becomes a reincarnation of the commedia dell'arte's mad clowns, a veritable Harlequin reborn. His gestural art, which is accompanied by an extraordinary vocal talent, leaps into being with a sudden storm of multitudinous emotions—as though the Nephew's restless spirit of mimicry were intently waiting for an opportunity to crash through the narrow walls of a single personality. For example, as Diderot advises Rameau to go back to his patron's establishment and beg forgiveness, Rameau at once acts out the very scene: he prostrates himself, then sobs a vow to reform himself—only to rise immediately and continue his discussion with Diderot in perfect coolness and sobriety. Later, as he proves to Diderot that his momentarily wooden fingers (which he scolds and punishes) have learned over the years to manipulate keys and strings expertly, he almost dislocates his bones: first he plays an invisible violin, which he stops to tune now and then (with grimaces of dissatisfaction) in the manner of a virtuoso suffering convulsions; then, without pausing, he sits down at a nonexistent piano and ranges swiftly over the keyboard (but he can become annoyed with the invisible piano too, at moments when his fingers begin stumbling and groping in fits of musical illiteracy). And during all this, his face dramatizes a whole theatre of feelings—tenderness, anger, bliss, sorrow.

Rameau's climactic pantomimic (and vocal) lunacy occurs in the midst of a critical analysis of musical—specifically, operatic—trends. Suddenly, gripped by an enthusiasm virtually indistinguishable from madness, he acts out with perfect, if jumbled, artistry the roles of a whole orchestra and of an entire acting and singing troupe. This picture of Rameau the possessed reveals a man who preposterously mesmerizes himself into another world, one that is both demented and miraculous. An ordinary homeless rogue and hungry cynic could hardly afford the luxury of such self-forgetfulness; but the Nephew obviously cannot adhere to the rules of realistic rascality. His extraordinary talents and vagaries make him a figure of Rabelaisian fantasticality, as Diderot himself realizes while meditating on the hoax of legal and religious gravity.

Unfortunately, this fantasticality cannot overcome poverty. Yet the needy Nephew once had a brilliant plan to conquer his pennilessness. He began to show off his wife at certain musical gatherings; and, hoping to make a fortune from her sexual conquests, he encouraged her to captivate important admirers. Who indeed could resist her—a creature so birdlike, brave, beautiful, and talented, and with such a luscious rump? (Rameau pantomimes her coquettish walk to show Diderot what a darling she was.) But she died young: "Alas! I lost her, the poor thing," Rameau murmurs. Diderot reports that "he began to sob and choke as he said: 'No, no, I shall never get over it. Ever since, I've taken minor orders and wear a skullcap.' " "From grief?" Diderot asks sympathetically. "If you like," Rameau replies. "But really in order to carry my soup plate upon my head" (p. 89). Whereupon this caddish rupturer of sentiment blithely marches off to the opera. Authentic tears ending in nonsensical nonchalance, true pathos burying itself in burlesque jokes—such is the play of psychic farce in Rameau the clown.

Rameau's witty sanity surfaces often enough to insure his recovery from his obsessions. His self-bifurcation is therefore not a symptom of sickness but an indication of almost mythological resourcefulness. This does not mean that psychic farce may not be fused with pathology, as in Dostoevsky's early novel *The Double*. But unlike Rameau's nephew, Golyadkin, the protagonist of *The Double*, has no unusual talents and no special merits. Nor does he play the buffoon consciously, either in order to cope with (or profit by) his humiliations or because he is endowed with comic vivacity. Golyadkin becomes a buffoon unwittingly (in this he resembles Chekhov's lecturer), because anxiety thoroughly, and ludicrously, disorders his mind—to such an extent that his entire existence becomes farcically paranoid in its self-contradictions. Rameau may be tossed onto a rubbish heap, but he can rebound with a nimble vaudevillian madness that will more than match his sense of grievance. Golyadkin, on the other hand, can only sink deeper and deeper into an abyss of panic and derangement. But psychic farce does not ordinarily involve a collapse of the mind; for if it is to slay sham consistency of character, bogus uniformity of mind and feeling, and overregularized, overrevered reason, it cannot fall into the enemy camp by exhibiting its dislocations as the product of disease or mental incapacity.

The initially not so lucky titular character in Kingsley Amis' *Lucky Jim* far more aptly exemplifies psychic farce (in the sense that he manages a happy avoidance of certifiable mental imbalance) than Golyadkin does. Jim Dixon is panicky (panic, though less emphatically than in Golyadkin's case, is one of his trademarks), but he preserves his equilibrium and compensates for his many secessions from integrity by conjuring up anarchic fantasies of outrage which involve ferocious sadism, unspeakable obscenity, and scatological murder. Instead of enduring civilized repression, Jim in his fantasies deliriously tastes the liberation and power provided by sheer beastliness.

Nor are fantasies his only sanity preservers. Jim's facial mimicry, together with his bodily contortions, also sustains his many transformations from polite worm to brutal savage; the more uncivilized those grimaces and contortions are, the more effectively his psychic tensions leak away. Dixon's crazy-peasant face, for example, is an excellent therapeutic symbol of his revulsion from the refined, arty façade the Welches have subjected him to (though that very same face also betrays the prelapsarian ignorance Dixon uninspiringly feels at home with). Whatever else they do, moreover, Dixon's faces point up the permanent farcical adolescence located in the substratum of his psyche. Actually Amis' early observation about Jim's habit of nourishing "outrage as a screen for . . . apprehension"[19] has

---

[19] Kingsley Amis, *Lucky Jim* (New York: Viking, 1958), p. 61.

suggested that his hero's anarchic impulses may never transcend acts of merely juvenile vandalism and revolt. But the point is that Jim's juvenility is his saving grace—and even his salvation.

At the very end of the novel, after telling Christine (who will be going to London with him, *con amore*) that he has beaten Welch's art-minded, snobbish son, Bertrand, out of a job as Gore-Urquhart's boredom-detection secretary, the two young people laugh noisily. For a moment Dixon cannot think what face to put on in order to depict his joy: "He thought what a pity it was that all his faces were designed to express rage or loathing. Now that something had happened which really deserved a face, he'd none to celebrate it with. As a kind of token, he made his Sex Life in Ancient Rome face" (p. 255). His exultant love for Christine, spurred by his release from the chains of academe and by his victory over Bertrand, is thus displayed in a burlesque of a Hollywood orgiastic seizure. There is a funny but suitable suggestion here that, for Jim, love will be forever immature—like his indispensable indulgence in psychic farce.

4

A third kind of farce, by no means sealed off from erotic farce or psychic farce, is chiefly social in nature. It slants its explosive buffoonery not so much toward erotic respectability or psychic normality as toward the artificiality and absurdity of social entities: class stratifications, intimidating institutions, legislated values, and so on. Social farce says to hell with society—and therefore also to a good deal of history. Society is imaged as organized bunk or as a chimera draining the life out of natural man; and history is figured as a series of abominable grotesqueries. Unlike conventional social satire, which seeks to purify the idols and idioms of the tribe, social farce aims to pulverize the very idea of idols and idioms.

Consider, for example, Alfred Jarry's *Ubu Roi*, a notorious ancestor of the contemporary literature of the absurd. Clearly, King Ubu emblematizes both the incubus of society and the diabolism of history by farcically exemplifying the predatory and lunatic patterns of each. And as decent citizens we can only detest his infamy. But insofar as we are wanton children and ingrained immoralists, we joy in Ubu's vast disintegration of controls; for Ubu is also the beast from the id. This means that when the delinquencies of an individual in a particular social farce blatantly symbolize the scandals of society, those delinquencies may at the same time provide a welcome fantasy of liberation.

Fat, pear-shaped Ubu is "polymorphously perverse" in a way that goes beyond the Freudian signification of the phrase. Twin caricatures of Ubu drawn by Jarry himself reveal a bloated creature who is masturbating his huge phallus while shamelessly disclosing an enormous vagina.[20] The first word Ubu utters—"Shittr!" (I.i)—almost matches the drawings. No manly oath, the word registers a childish rejection of the whole adult toilet-training system of civilization. From this first word on, indeed, excrement litters the dialogue. And sometimes food: at the beginning of the play, Ubu's spouse prepares a menu for her husband's partisans that consists, in part, of "ice pudding, salad, fruit, dessert, boiled beef, jerusalem artichokes" and—"cauliflower à la shittre" (I.iii). To further season the meal (which he at first tries to devour all by himself), Ubu throws a lavatory brush onto the dining table and orders his men to taste it. Lending themselves cravenly to this insane nonsense, "several taste it and are poisoned" (I.iii). Boorish Ubu has positively no regard for etiquette, hygiene, or the welfare of mankind.

If his coprophagous tastes appear rather startling, Ubu's anal-sadistic political ambitions are no less shocking. Ubu and his wife are wining and dining political partisans, in the first place, because Mère Ubu, a sort of farcically scatological Lady Macbeth, has provoked Père Ubu, former king of Aragon and at present the king of Poland's trusted officer (Poland is a metaphor for the absurd), to seize royal power for himself.

[20] These drawings precede the text of Alfred Jarry's *Ubu Roi* in *Four Modern French Comedies*, intro. Wallace Fowlie (New York: Capricorn, 1960), p. 27.

She lures him into this act of betrayal by appealing to his inordinate childishness: "If I were you, what I'd want to do with my arse would be to install it on a throne. You could increase your fortune indefinitely, have sausages whenever you liked, and ride through the streets in a carriage." When Père Ubu proves somewhat recalcitrant—"Gadzookers, by my green candle, I prefer to be as poor as a skinny, honest rat than as rich as a vicious, fat cat" (I.i)—his carminative wife mutters, "Fart, shittr, it's hard to get him moving, but fart, shittr, I reckon I've shaken him all the same" (I.i). And in fact Père Ubu has been shaken all the way down to his flabby foundations. Soon he aims to be the fattest, most vicious cat around. The result is that *Ubu Roi* becomes the chronicle of a mad, grisly, savagely burlesque Shakespearean political plot.

Ubu's brutal assumption of power inaugurates a reign of clownish terror, activated by the fat fool's murderous lust for gold and property. Indeed, "phynance" (orthography, the child's bane, is freely tortured by Ubu) becomes one of the leitmotifs of the play; we see or hear of a phynancial horse, a phynancial helmet, a phynancial song. This contamination by finance is really one long scatological scream for wealth. Ubu, in fact, develops a whole arsenal of sinister slapstick contraptions to extort money or exterminate wealthy nobles—for example, trap doors, pig-pinching devices, and disembraining machines.

In this fantastic comic play of greed, cruelty, treachery, and murder, Jarry seems to be driving home the point that the origins of modern disgust lie in political and economic lust. But in viewing the monumental stupidity and colossal callousness of Ubu, it is difficult, as I have suggested, to separate the perversions of civilization from the seductive willfulness of the id. In the following fragment of dialogue, for example, the insanity of international conflict is a mere parenthesis in the forbidden delectation of childish bestiality and chaos:

Mère Ubu.   Adieu, Père Ubu. Be sure and kill the Czar.
Père Ubu.   You bet. Wringing of the nose and teeth, extraction of

the tongue, and driving of the little bit of wood into the earens. [III.viii]

Nevertheless, Ubu's dungy, violent, cretinous, hoggish impulses translate sufficiently into society's diverse brutalities, both at the bourgeois and the aristocratic levels. In the goofy postscript to the farce—the merry, insouciant, lunatic "Song of the Disembraining"—one notes a special animus against the middle class. An impure animus, for the "Song of the Disembraining" is not a transparent indictment of a single social group. It does point up the filthy practices of bourgeois society; but it also emphasizes the absurdity of the common man's protest against the Establishment. The song is sung by an insensitive cabinetmaker who pays homage to Père Ubu, honored here (untypically) not as infantile irrationality's own fat darling, but as a great annihilator-equalizer. The singer recounts the details of his family's past Sunday outings as they promenaded in all their finery to the disembraining machine on the rue de l'Echaudé, where they watched trembling landlords and other middle-class exploiters being chewed up. The popcorn for this festival was provided by showers of brain matter: "Soon we were white with brain, my loving wife and I. / The brats were eating it up, and were as merry as hell."[21] Unfortunately, the cabinetmaker's wife once made the mistake of encouraging her husband to throw a heap of dung at one of the victims of the machine. The dung splattered over the executioner's chest, with the result that the cabinetmaker himself became the next client for extermination, and was duly slain. (This proof of his mortality does not prevent him from composing "The Song of the Disembraining" after his death. But far weirder developments are entertained by the "science" of pataphysics, which, as developed by Jarry's character Dr. Faustroll, extends "as far beyond metaphysics as the latter extends beyond physics," and can find solutions to the improbable or the imaginary because it consists of "laws governing exceptions.")[22] Thus the social

[21] *Ubu Roi*, p. 92.
[22] Alfred Jarry, *Exploits and Opinions of Doctor Faustroll, Pataphysician*, in *Selected Works of Alfred Jarry*, ed. Roger Shattuck and

farce in the song dissolves into a generalized, if piquant, madness. Or, seen in another light, the social farce is perfected by this final glimpse of society's frivolously lunatic use of power.

Ubu Roi violently reduces social phenomena to incorrigible and nefarious nonsense. Yet lunatic social comedy can be quite nonchalant in its techniques. Thus all levels of society in Evelyn Waugh's *Decline and Fall* are coolly presented as belonging to an antic graveyard of reason, virtue, and aspiration. The scene in which a black named Mr. Sebastian Cholmondely (nicknamed Chokey) becomes the dominant figure at a Llannaba gathering of parents and visitors following the school's dishonestly arranged sporting competitions indicates how Waugh pushes social satire (with its suggestion of the remediably ridiculous) toward social farce (with its suggestion that society is possessed of incurable folly).[23] First of all, biases against the black man proliferate. Stuffy Colonel Sidebotham, for example, is annoyed because he "saw enough of Fuzzy-Wuzzy in the Soudan—devilish good enemy and devilish bad friend."[24] Middle-class Mrs. Clutterbuck is not happy either; she thinks that "it's an insult bringing a nigger here, . . . an insult to our own women." Her husband points out, furthermore, that black men have "uncontrollable passions" (p. 291).

Simon Watson Taylor (New York: Grove, 1965), p. 192. An entire issue of the *Evergreen Review*, 4 (May–June 1960), ed. Shattuck and Taylor, is devoted to pataphysics. See also Shattuck's discussion of Jarry's absurdism, in *The Banquet Years* (New York: Harcourt, Brace, 1958), pp. 146–194, and Ihab Hassan's "From Pataphysics to Surrealism," in *The Dismemberment of Orpheus* (New York: Oxford University Press, 1971), pp. 48–79.

[23] Frederick J. Stopp, in *Evelyn Waugh: Portrait of an Artist* (Boston: Little, Brown, 1958), writes that "Mr. Waugh's earlier comic extravaganzas are to traditional, objective satire as existentialism is to academic philosophy—the bottom has dropped out of the world picture. There is no correction, but only rejection" (p. 194). Stopp defines Waugh's early novels as mixtures of "farce, comedy of character and satire" (p. 64), but emphasizes the "fundamentally fantastic nature" of Waugh's writings (p. 67). He observes, indeed, that in Waugh's first book (*Decline and Fall*) the novelist is "already a master of what has been described as 'the higher lunacy' " (p. 65).

[24] Evelyn Waugh, *Decline and Fall*, in *"A Handful of Dust"* and *"Decline and Fall"* (New York: Dell, 1959), pp. 291–292.

Similar racial clichés sprout up elsewhere in this scene; and they too are caricatural counters in a game of social mindlessness.

The game is rendered totally farcical when the black man is burlesqued just as flagrantly as the whites. In the circle of absurdity Waugh sets up, Chokey becomes the star performer. This unreal jazz musician, who is Lady Beste-Chetwynde's current paramour (and whom she has been shepherding about on a presumably educative tour of Great Britain), is a puppet of vaudeville attitudes about race and culture. Consider his well-rehearsed folkloric-Shylockian defense of the black man: the "poor coloured man has a soul same as you have. Don't he breathe the same as you? Don't he eat and drink? Don't he love Shakespeare and cathedrals and the paintings of the old masters same as you? Isn't he just asking for your love and help to raise him from the servitude into which your forefathers plunged him? Oh, say, white folks, why don't you stretch out a helping hand to the poor coloured man, that's as good as you are, if you'll only let him be?" (pp. 293–294). Waugh has perpetrated here a double racial massacre which leaves little for traditional social satire to salvage.

Though *Decline and Fall* remains consistently light-weight, social farce at its most extreme can be infernal beyond anything Waugh has written, even in his most insouciantly macabre comedies. This is certainly true, for example, of Günter Grass's *The Tin Drum*, in which fantasticality is both a legacy of history and a characteristic of Grass's protagonist, Oskar, the self-willed midget. Little Oskar is the queerest child in Germany, for he was born with the miraculous power of a complete mental development. He is childish enough, however, to find security and even a sense of wonder in certain middle-class stores (generally owned by morally flabby burghers) which are lovingly detailed by him—especially Sigismund Markus' toy store, which supplies him with a good many of his drums. No matter where he gets them, Oskar's drums are always magic instruments. They are the tools with which he wondrously conjures up autobiographical and historical memories. Even more remarkable than Oskar's drumming is his voice, whose scream, whether audible or silent, is capable of destroying glass both near and far—at times not very innocently.

Oskar is, in fact, often an immoralist (quite appealingly so). But what is Oskar's immorality in comparison with the social evils and historical aberrations he records? Oskar has not avowed any satiric intentions in writing his memoirs: dispassion is apparently to be his style of commentary. Nevertheless, his presumably detached observations—on, say, German "psychic emigration" (inner exile) during the Nazi period—are frequently indistinguishable from carefully controlled mockery. When Oskar, as an adolescent, hid under rostrums and wrecked Nazi rallies and marches by drumming totally distracting rhythms, thus converting totalitarian programs into disorderly extravaganzas, he had, he insists, no political mission; he was not being a "resistance fighter."[25] He acted simply as a protestant musician whose aesthetic tastes were offended by Nazi art and ceremony (he disrupted the meetings of the Boy Scouts and Jehovah's Witnesses for the same reason). The fact remains that Oskar, by playing merry waltzes and hectic Charlestons, did cause Nazi dignitaries to lose command and Nazi discipline to erode. His noncommittal posture is therefore simply one of Grass's techniques of dissolvent comedy.

Oskar's attitudes may, on the whole, be transmitted obliquely, but they have a devastating effect. As he scans the course of his private life in the context of contemporary history, he cannot help being, for all his supposed neutrality, an ironic documentarian of grotesque happenings. Oskar's private life is itself thoroughly and funnily bizarre (familially, erotically, musically). But public life, which Oskar focuses on keenly, if for the most part casually, is a frightful social and historical farce. Consider in this connection the story of Herbert Truczinski, Oskar's good friend. Truczinski is not as odd as Leo Schugger, without whose crazy appearance at funerals one is

[25] Günter Grass, *The Tin Drum* (New York: Crest, 1964), p. 448.

not properly dead; and he is not as strange as Raskolnikov the artist, who stares fanatically at his model Ulla's genitals while hoarsely muttering phrases about crime and punishment; nor is he as eccentric as Zeidler the landlord, who expresses his fury at his wife by periodically hurling liqueur glasses at a cast-iron stove door, after which he carefully sweeps up the pieces. No, Herbert is not phantomatic like Schugger, not obsessed with guilt like Raskolnikov, not nasty-tempered like Zeidler. Herbert Truczinski is in fact a peacemaker. And that is why his life is a catastrophe.

As a waiter, Truczinski is accustomed to serving an international clientele which is not only a "linguistic volcano" (p. 168) but a political inferno as well. When the inferno erupts, as it often does, Herbert helpfully intervenes. The result of his pacificatory efforts is that he is frequently brought home in an ambulance, for his beneficence is rewarded only by a series of treacherous stabs in the back. That scarred and welted back becomes, among other things, a multicolored symbolic portrait of European grievances and hatreds. These are inescapable. As a guard, later on, in the Maritime Museum in Danzig, a city which, like Truczinski's back, is a locus of European evils, Herbert tries to rape the Green Kitten, Niobe, a notoriously sinister ship's figurehead, and is found hanging from her façade with an erection he has not been able to anchor and with a double-edged axe ensconced both in her wood and his flesh. This farcical fiasco is Herbert's climactic involvement in ludicrous and frenzied European passions—an involvement in which he is bested by a green and naked sorceress who is virtually the immobilized progeny of the Black Witch (the novel's pervasive, half-antic, chilling emblem of demonic madness).

The most grotesque European lunacy in *The Tin Drum* is of course the rise and fall of Nazi Germany. One of Oskar's chapters, ironically entitled "Faith, Hope, Love," envisions Nazi inhumanity as though it were a darkly burlesque fairy tale. This chapter, which has constant recourse to the innocent fairy-tale gambit "once upon a time," is composed, for the most part, of mocking and maddening incremental variations on a horror story (the chapter is therefore also a ballad of bestiality). Condensed and stripped of its repetitive structural elements, the story goes this way: Once upon a time a musician and SA man named Meyn, who kept four cats and drank a great deal of gin, was screamingly recognized as an evil omen by Leo Schugger at the burial service for Meyn's friend Herbert Truczinski. Meyn found himself, on his return from the cemetery, without gin in his smelly, cat-infested apartment; the consequence was that he reached for a poker and clouted the cats to death. Or so he thought. But Laubschad the watchmaker, a member of the SPCA, saw Meyn deposit a dripping, half-filled potato sack in a garbage can whose lid began to rise as the undead cats beneath it squirmed about. Laubschad reported this case of cruelty, and Meyn was expelled from the SA for "conduct unbecoming a storm trooper" (p. 192).

Oskar now contrasts Meyn's dismissal from the SA for cruelty to animals with the official recognition of his "conspicuous bravery" (p. 192) on Crystal Night, when he helped burn down a synagogue, and on the following morning, when he helped destroy Jewish stores. Oskar well recalls that day; Sigismund Markus committed suicide in his toy store while certain firemen destroyed his window, ransacked his shop, and "played" with his toys; some of the firemen had even "taken their pants down and had deposited brown sausages" (p. 193) on the toys. Oskar was there. And as he was leaving this strange scene, after salvaging a few drums, he came across a group of ugly pious women dispensing religious tracts. This memory occasions Oskar's reference to the three white elephants in the Epistle to the Corinthians: faith, hope, and charity. Oskar does not offer an inclusive indictment here. He does not formulate large equations of outrage; for example, he does not equate banishing toys with banishing all happiness, or killing Jews with killing mankind, or peddling Christianity with peddling submission to evil. But he registers his disgust clearly enough. It is therefore not true that Oskar depicts the Nazis "without argument, demonstration, protest or any display of enlightened anti-Fascist sentiment."[26] But even if it were, Oskar's thematic grotesqueries and ironic juxtapositions would be criticism enough.

Consider Oskar's later recounting of an episode in which a number of French nuns are cruelly and idiotically butchered by the Nazis. He arranges a long section of his narrative in strict dramatic form (Oskar becomes merely one of a number of actors here) and sets the scene by showing us Bebra's midget troupe making merry at, and on, an Atlantic pillbox called Dora Seven. A certain Corporal Lankes uses this pillbox, along with others, as raw material for his artistic ornamentations, which he hopes future archeologists will recognize as works of genius. Lankes has given his aesthetic creations a title: "Barbaric, Mystical, Bored." "You have given our century its name,"[27] Bebra declares, rather expansively.

The barbaric aspect of the century is soon exemplified by Lieutenant Herzog, who madly insists that certain figures on the beach (in actuality, these are five kindergarten-teaching nuns from Lisieux, who have been seeking crabs and shellfish and are now sporting about with their umbrellas) are probably camouflaged agents and are therefore to be shot down at once. (At this point, Oskar the stage manager introduces a backdrop of running nuns.) The impending assassination gives Bebra's troupe a slight shiver of spiritual discomfort; but they are chiefly affected by a childlike apprehension of loud military noises, which they will inadequately muffle by turning on a phonograph record. Because he is acting under orders (he is hardly an angel in any case), Lankes finally mows the nuns down with a machine gun. Immediately afterward, the nuns reappear on another backdrop, flying heavenward. By transforming unbearable horror into farce, Grass has lightened, but by no means lost, the sense of moral damnation he has been

[26] W. Gordon Cunliffe, *Günter Grass* (New York: Twayne, 1969), p. 15. Cunliffe overemphasizes the view, which is commonly held, that Oskar is the "infantile destructive principle" (p. 60). But however misbegotten he may be, Oskar is not a superimp of the perverse.

[27] *The Tin Drum*, p. 325.

focusing on. Oskar depicts himself as quite unheroic in this scene; he feels no shame or even dismay as he sees the nuns slaughtered. Instead, he composes a satiric poem portending the fat German future—a future which will be nibbled at only minimally by a sense of collective guilt. The poem is about the trend "toward the bourgeois-smug" (p. 326), which will be activated once the hardships of the war are over.

The metamorphosis of the massacre of the nuns into a blithe farcical ballet makes for a startling mixture of frivolity and monstrosity (a mixture which by no means threatens to anesthetize our sensibility). Oskar's glimpses into the state of the German soul in peacetime reveal nothing comparable in shock effect. But they do disclose much fever, much opportunism, and much sterility. This last aspect of the German character is symbolized in Schmuh's Onion Cellar, an unadorned nightclub designed to thaw out and loosen up the frigidified emotions and stymied tongues of dispirited people. Redemption is achieved by a collective chopping of onions on boards until tears start flowing, at which point people begin crying crazily and are prompted to confess to their neighbors, without restraint, a whole tissue of griefs and self-accusations (only some of which stem from Nazi ignominy or national guilt). Thus, onion-irrigated, orgiastic encounter groups get back to the facts of feeling. Without the onions, shame and alienation would remain bottled up and hence become destructive and maddening. Without the onions (and an audience), a sense of humanity and brotherhood would not flood the moneyed and mechanized scarecrows in Schmuh's cellar.

The whole onion saga is obviously a species of comic insanity. Moreover, the confessions released in the cellar compound Grass's burlesque of Germany's buried humanity; for the most interesting ones portray farcically subhuman situations. Take, for example, Miss Pioch and Mr. Vollmer, two strangers in a streetcar who fell in love with each other when Mr. Vollmer stepped on Miss Pioch's right foot with crushing power. When Miss Pioch lost her black and blue toenail (the fruit of their collision), Vollmer's love cooled. A solution was found: he trampled her left big toe, and found his love fully regained. Then the left toenail went, and Miss Pioch rebelled against Vollmer's plan to start again on the right one. "If your love for me is really so overpowering," she told him, "it ought to outlast a toenail" (p. 510). It didn't. Afterward, Miss Pioch surrendered her toenails, right and left, until they became permanently maimed—with the result that Vollmer's love totally ceased. But after crying together in Schmuh's Onion Cellar sometime later, they were so emotionally moved that they got married. This amusingly bizarre story of Miss Pioch and Mr. Vollmer (it is by no means an isolated narrative) suggests that if wartime Germany was grotesque, postwar Germany, in its milder way, is a potpourri of the continuing absurd.

In the final pages of the novel, Oskar is thirty and wondering whether he is obligated to go out into the world and gather disciples, who this time, presumably, will be unlike the Dusters, the adolescent gang of thieves whose Jesus-wizard he was until betrayal disbanded the group. Oskar has intermittently fancied himself a kind of Jesus infant ever since, early in the novel, he put drumsticks into the hands of little Jesus' statue in the Church of the Sacred Heart and virtually dared the "preposterous naked kid" (p. 135) to drum out a miracle. The miracle finally comes—half a novel later. Jesus not only drums Oskar's autobiographical kind of music but asks him thrice, as the latter takes to his heels (in revulsion, not awe) whether Oskar loves Him. "You bastard," Oskar shouts, "I hate you, you and all your hocus-pocus." This outcry does not prevent Jesus from giving Oskar a highly anachronistic mission: "Raising his forefinger like a lady schoolteacher, he gave me an assignment: 'Thou art Oskar, the rock, and on this rock I will build my Church. Follow thou me!'" (p. 346).

Oskar's urge to discredit and surpass Jesus is anticly blasphemous; but his reaction is hardly psychopathic. We have noted that in the "Faith, Hope, Love" chapter Oskar sees Christianity as overvalued and impotent. And toward the end of the novel, Christianity yields to the power of the Black Witch (who can easily assume the mask both of Nazi diabolism and bourgeois prosperity and can even use Goethean discipline to suit her purposes). Were Oskar to become a subversive neo-Christ, his powers could hardly be more sinister than those of a society in which the stench of cadavers in concentration camps was disinfected by benevolent men driven half-mad by their sufferings—men like Oskar's Jewish friend Fajngold, who with his cans of Lysol once had the job of fumigating concentration camps, but who, after his release, pathetically and funnily disinfected imaginary worlds.

5

In 1959, Rosette Lamont applied to Ionesco's *The Chairs* and Beckett's *Endgame* the label "metaphysical farce." In the same year Ruby Cohn called Beckett's decompositional jokes examples of "cosmological comedy," though Kafka is the writer she singled out as the master of such comedy in modern literature.[28] Of these two phraseological attempts to describe the contemporary vaudeville of the void, "metaphysical farce" seems to suggest more neatly that for Kafka, Ionesco, and Beckett, among others, it is possible to clown in a philosophic abyss.

Lamont's thesis about metaphysical farce is that Ionesco and Beckett have created nihilistic plays of ideas in which the language of futility, mated to primitive physical comedy, becomes the last illusory game in which man can indulge on earth. The message of metaphysical farce is simple: "No one listens. No one understands. God is dead, or paralyzed and blind. Love is a forgotten word among men tied to each other through need. The world outside is a wasteland." Yet naked, grotesque man is still comic protoplasm, twitching about in "a desperate and senseless game, an Endgame, to pass the time between being and nonbeing."[29] In *The Chairs* and *Endgame*,

[28] See Rosette Lamont's "The Metaphysical Farce: Beckett and Ionesco," *French Review*, 33 (Feb. 1959), 319–328; and Ruby Cohn's "The Comedy of Samuel Beckett: 'Something Old, Something New,'" *Yale French Studies*, 23 (Summer 1959), pp. 11–17.

[29] "The Metaphysical Farce," p. 319.

specifically, "we find the last survivors from a world cataclysm," for whom conversation is only "a time filler, a kind of temporary tranquillizer in a world without meaning" (p. 324).

The main problem of metaphysical farce is that it has to find convincing ways of channeling a zany universe's killing confidence game into recognizable human experience. This is not easy. There are certain earthly materials that metaphysical farce can work with well enough—symbolically, that is: a bare room may connote cosmic nothingness, a paralytic bureaucracy may hint at divine palsy, a queer funeral may conjure up a galactic morgue, and so on. But though metaphysical farce is limited in its furniture, it does provide (ideally) the same kind of psychic release that is procured in the enjoyment of a funnily adulterous bed, a laughably disheveled mind, or a preposterously disjointed social circumstance. Metaphysical farce does not enact a defeat so long as it can half-buoyantly say, in one way or another, to hell with the universe.

Thus Kafka, the "master of cosmological comedy," manages, at least in part, a burlesque rejection of the metaphysically grotesque. Consider *The Trial*, a novel in which the murky sense of the insoluble which hangs over the arrest of Joseph K. (there are, it is true, indications of some unassessable guilt in the protagonist)[30] infiltrates an entire universe—to the extent of establishing absurdity and alienation as the core of transcendental power. This evilly silly supernaturalism is recorded, as far as the novel's farcical rhythms are concerned, in descendental antics and lunatic revelations. An example of the latter occurs when K. learns, not only that the contents of an incriminating charge against an accused man remain forever (and crazily) inaccessible both to the accused and his lawyer, but

[30] The idea that Joseph K.'s arrest signifies he can no longer obscure the fact that he has always been an accused man on trial is aptly analyzed by Martin Greenberg in *The Terror of Art: Kafka and Modern Literature* (New York: Basic Books, 1968), pp. 113–153. In his discussion of the infamous clownery of the court, Greenberg leans heavily on a solipsistic interpretation which makes the court "K.'s own conscience, which because it is alienated from him appears to him as something external, set over against him" (pp. 132–133).

that the accused's lawyer also has to waste an immense amount of time actually guessing what the accusation may be—only to receive, in almost all cases, annoying hints that he has guessed wrong. The protagonist of *The Trial* is in this case fully tuned in to madness, which elsewhere is conveyed in more blatant forms, via pure slapstick. Thus the humiliation inflicted on defense lawyers by the deranged omnipotence of the courts is symbolized in miniature by the physical appearance of the cramped defense lawyers' room in the attic of the law court offices, a room where an unmended hole in the floor permits clients in the corridor below the occasional view of the dangling leg of a lawyer.

That dangling leg is ridiculous; but it is less ludicrous than the fray lawyer Huld tells about, which occurred between an old, typically irritable official (officials, Huld points out, are likely to be childish and ignorant of human nature) who was studying a difficult case and a host of lawyers who were seeking to confer with him and who had decided to gain admittance to his office by tiring him out. Since the official "hid himself behind [his entrance door] and flung down the stairs every lawyer who tried to enter . . . one lawyer after another was sent rushing upstairs to offer the greatest possible show of passive resistance and let himself be thrown down again into the arms of his colleagues. That lasted for about an hour,"[31] at which point the official gave up the game.

Few functionaries of the absurd in *The Trial* escape this kind of idiotic buffoonery. It contaminates even the chaplain in the cathedral, who first speaks to Joseph K. from a torturous side pulpit whose discomfort seems less religiously purgative than gratuitously punitive. The priest's stoop may recall the hunchbacked girl in the painter Titorelli's circle of lecherous adolescents; it may also remind us of all the confined positions and airless places that so obviously symbolize the grotesque in this novel. There is an especially farcical instance of physical contortions in the "First Interrogation" chapter: Joseph K. finds

[31] Franz Kafka, *The Trial*, trans. Willa and Edwin Muir; rev. trans. E. M. Butler (New York: Schocken, 1970), pp. 120–121.

himself in a dim, dusty, suffocating meeting hall "which just below the roof was surrounded by a gallery, . . . quite packed, where the people were able to stand only in a bent posture with their heads and backs knocking against the ceiling" (p. 37). These balcony figures are less distinguished than those in the orchestra seats, so to speak, but some have an eye to comfort, having "brought cushions with them, which they put between their heads and the ceiling, to keep their heads from getting bruised" (p. 39). The ludicrous gallery structure is part of the shabby, smelly, coffined milieu of the law, whose apparent impecuniousness is associated with the tenements of the un-rebellious poor. Still, it is not poverty we think of as we en-visage the crouching spectators above in the meeting hall, with their cushions fixed between their heads and the ceiling. The buttocks are the usual beneficiaries of cushions at entertain-ments where some discomfort is expected; and the displace-ment of such cushions in this scene does little credit to the heads they crown.

The leader of the proceedings in this nightmare scene of farcical deformation is a fat, wheezing magistrate whose dog-eared notebook laughably misinforms him that K. is a house painter, whereas in actuality he is the chief clerk at a bank. The notebook resembles two other well-worn volumes Joseph K. intently inspects when the courtroom is deserted. These, evi-dently, are erotic works rather than lawbooks; in one of them, moreover, an indecent picture of a man and a woman, both naked, is incompetently drawn. We are led to conclude that not even first-rate obscenities can be expected of the courts. Joseph K. himself is no stranger to the relationship between sex and the absurd, for it is rampant in *The Trial*. But what could be more damagingly farcical in the purely metaphysical context of *The Trial* than the pornography of justice?

The mention of pornography in metaphysical farce may re-mind us that once upon a time there existed the clearest of secular connections between sex and antic comedy—for example in Chaucer's perfect, unmistakable farce, "The Miller's Tale." In metaphysical farce, as likely as not, outrageous sexuality is transformed into a scandalous buggering of man by the cosmos. In "The Miller's Tale," Nicholas and Alison, having engaged in naughty fornication, easily persuade their neighbors that old John the carpenter, who has just crashed to the floor in a wooden tub as a result of fear of a predicted flood, is the unhinged victim of a Noah complex. In Ionesco's *The Chairs*, on the other hand, an immense flood has actually taken place. What is in Chaucer a practical joke, successfully conceived as an aid to adulterous sex, is in *The Chairs* a universal catastrophe in which mankind has been decidedly sodomized. Among the few survivors of the catastrophe are two virtual centenarians who make the imbecility of John the carpenter appear to be the essence of mental illumination. These two have brief seconds of sanity and long moments of bizarre befuddlement. In the games they play, the Old Woman constantly mothers her husband, while the Old Man incessantly magnifies his infantilism. Though the Old Woman regularly has the Old Man sift through fragmentary recollections which hint that a great historical devastation has taken place during their lifetime, doubtless leaving them in their present state of incoherence, we learn little that can be considered as fact.

In any case, the gigglingly demonic cosmic hoax that is apparently responsible for their situation is channeled mainly through a farcical annihilation of the criteria of sanity. Most of the metaphysical farce in *The Chairs* is filtered through psychic (and physical) japery—often in the form of linguistic delirium. But the translation of an absurd universe into a wacky desecration of mentality obviously has its shortcomings. After a while, the fact that Ionesco postulates a wrecked world with invisible but somehow verifiable people in it becomes less farcical than the realization that his two oldsters are addled enough to be perfectly capable of inventing both an invisible and an absolutely unverifiable population.

Beckett's *Endgame* communicates a more convincing (but distinctly less funny) brand of metaphysical farce than *The Chairs*. Beckett's Hamm and Clov are not primarily comic madmen. In fact, their rationality is not so much annihilated as twisted to very strange purposes—purposes that are, in their own way, just as far as those of *The Chairs* from the world of Chaucerian farce. Instead of three Chaucerian hanging tubs, Beckett's play offers a wheel chair on castors and a couple of ash cans domiciling two aged parents (Hamm's) who are both infantile and underfed. Instead of Chaucerian sexual frolics, there are varieties of corporeal paralysis and psychic despair (with several pungent pinches of obscenity and scatology). Instead of Chaucerian anal kisses and thunderous farts and incendiarized buttocks, the play presents minor monkeyshines acted out in an atmosphere of queer cantankerousness. Instead of a jolly quest for coupling, there is a posture of sterile isolation. Instead of a private hoax, the play proffers a circumambient sick joke. Instead of energetic, guiltless tricksters playing diversified games, two devitalized figures engage in a single, terminal contest.

Both Hamm and Clov are capable of mustering up antic gestures and words, but they do not appear to make good buffoons. They seem, instead, to damage the whole historical drift of farcical clowning. How could decaying survivors malfunctioning in a lost interstice of an almost obliterated world sparkle with traditional zaniness? Both tyrant (Hamm) and servant (Clov) do little more than feed with semijocular bitterness on their daily diminishing existence. Nevertheless, their way of acting out the hideous comedy of decomposition emancipates them (and us), to some extent at any rate, from the power of the absurd. Moreover, their farce of dying is occasionally invigorated by truly burlesque conjunctions of idea, image, and fact. When Clov, for instance, discovers a flea on his body while Hamm is philosophizing on the possible birth, or rebirth, of meaning between them, Hamm, perturbed, cries out, "But humanity might start from there all over again! Catch him, for the love of God!"[32] The joke becomes scatological, not merely Darwinian and metaphysical, for as Clov loosens his trousers to powder the flea to death, Hamm simultaneously enjoys a pee.

[32] Samuel Beckett, *Endgame* (New York: Grove, 1958), p. 33.

A moment later, the combined gratification of the death of the flea and the flow of the pee evokes from Hamm a rare paradoxical outburst of enthusiasm for renewing the search for life —that is, for dignified, mammalian life.

Hamm often alternates between high levels of thought and childishly dotty exhibitionism and sadism. The latter element is well exemplified in his waiting for Clov to complete a three-legged (as yet unsexed) toy dog and anticipating its imploring posture (the dog will only topple over helplessly, though). Yet Hamm is not merely infantile-sadistic. He is also a part-time rebel and world condemner. When Clov reminds him that the whole universe stinks of corpses, Hamm, who defines God as a bastard who does not exist, angrily retorts, "To hell with the universe" (p. 46).

To hell with himself, too, he sardonically implies; but it is not easy to finish with life—and not altogether desirable. Certain vaudeville turns delay the finale and ease the pain of its imminence, and there are other means of retarding doom— especially Hamm's recurrent refurbishings of a self-incriminating, self-justifying, monstrous Christmas Eve story. This most important of his theatrical games inventively prolongs and palliates the fading hours. Even when Hamm learns from Clov, who is preparing to desert the blind, crippled dictator, that there are no more medical painkillers left—a piece of information which elicits the scream, "What'll I do!" (p. 72)—the endgame still promises not to end. Nevertheless, Clov does finally vanish (there may be a sign of life in the outside world), and Hamm, before burying himself beneath his bloody handkerchief, mixes a last bit of irreverence (a kind of dim, distant supplement to "The Miller's Tale")—"Peace to our . . . arses" (p. 82)—with a final peck at poetry, stage effects, and stoicism. The general somberness of the last scene reminds us that the farcical moments in the play have been somewhat strained.

Clearly, metaphysical farce runs a great risk in attempting to create an amalgam of immedicable woes and transfiguring play; for clowning with the materials of nothingness is easily choked by bitterness, tedium, or despair. Metaphysical farce is also liable to become anemic because of a lack of adequate symbols and metaphors to translate the transcendent absurd into sublunary terms. In Beckett's case, in fact, metaphysical farce is best conveyed in the precarious minds of his novelistic protagonists—minds that seem to be limitless theatres of rumination featuring both the nuances and the hammer blows of madness and absurdity. But even here metaphysical farce tends to get swallowed up, mainly by psychic farce. Take the titular character in Beckett's *Molloy*, for instance. In many ways he is a vivacious buffoon of benightedness, a spirited clown of decay. But in the most obvious sense, he is only drifting bones and a disordered consciousness lost in a dismantled world. Like most of Beckett's characters, he cannot finish dying; he keeps staving off putrefaction with incredibly muddled tenacity. But in the incompletion of Molloy's decadence we can find a host of both deliberate and unwilled macabre jokes which, on the one hand, rub in the lunatic futility of taking breath in this world and, on the other, constitute some kind of victory over absurdity and death itself.

The swirl of Molloy's mental confusions and self-contradictions is not always farcical. On the contrary, there is much sober, poetic, and pathetic chaos within him. But when the astonishing attrition in his head (exuded, paradoxically, in splendid linguistic playfulness) is concentrated on the immemorial targets of farce—family pieties, say—the desecrations of antic comedy reach an extraordinary aberrancy. Consider the relationship between smelly Molloy, "neither man nor beast,"[33] and his fecally and urinarily incontinent, jabberingly mad mother:

I got into communication with her by knocking on her skull. One knock meant yes, two no, three I don't know, four money, five goodbye. I was hard put to ram this code into her ruined and frantic understanding, but I did it, in the end. That she should confuse yes, no, I don't know and goodbye, was all the same to me, I confused them myself. But that she should associate the four knocks

[33] Samuel Beckett, *"Molloy,"* in *"Molloy," "Malone Dies," and "The Unnamable"* (New York: Grove, 1959), p. 20.

with anything but money was something to be avoided at all costs. During the period of training, therefore, at the same time as I administered the four knocks on her skull, I stuck a bank-note under her nose or in her mouth.   [pp. 18–19]

Molloy's infrequent conflicts with hazy, fragmentarily figured society are almost as lunatic as his connection with his mother (disconnection, actually: mentally chaotic and physically paretic as he is, Molloy searches for her, in vain, through the first half of the novel). For example, after Molloy the crippled cyclist is hauled before the law merely for resting on his bicycle in a manner required by his infirmity (his crutches prove his case), but not as public order and decency will allow, he cannot even identify himself for quite some time. The only papers he carries are bits of newspaper that serve him for defecatory purposes (in reality, though, he is not used to wiping himself very much); and his own surname generally escapes him. Not that he wishes to be recalcitrant. He has "the exasperated good-will of the overanxious"; and if he behaves like a bum and a pig— his habits include "the finger in the nose, the scratching of the balls, digital emunction and the peripatetic piss" (p. 28)— that is largely because he has never been taught the essence of deportment. Molloy simply cannot control certain inner resistances to good manners. For instance, he farts, ordinarily, three hundred and fifteen times in nineteen hours; but this maniacally statisticalized phenomenon he considers too trivial to need much mentioning.

Molloy, prone to accidents, lapsed memory, and disgraceful conduct, knows he is quite unlovely, though: sick leg, old body, squeezed-out, dangling testicles—"decaying circus clowns" (p. 43)—and so on. He is a permanent dirty joke— when he considers himself alive. At times, as he goes from muck to muck, he can envision himself as a butterfly of sorts, and even as an exemplar of ataraxy. But his sense of misery easily dominates the image of the butterfly and the idea of ataraxy. Wretchedness, in fact, whether spun along by poetry or mummified by absent-mindedness or ventilated in zesty, random foolery, is Molloy's specialty. What has he enjoyed in this life? Has he ever known true love, for example? A certain Ruth-Edith once introduced him to love's labor:

> I toiled and moiled until I discharged or gave up trying or was begged by her to stop. A mug's game in my opinion and tiring on top of that, in the long run. But I lent myself to it with a good enough grace, knowing it was love, for she had told me so. She bent over the couch, because of her rheumatism, and in I went from behind. It was the only position she could bear, because of her lumbago. It seemed all right to me, for I had seen dogs, and I was astonished when she confided that you could go about it differently. I wonder what she meant exactly. . . . Perhaps she too was a man, yet another of them. But in that case surely our testicles would have collided, while we writhed. Perhaps she held hers tight in her hand, on purpose to avoid it. [pp. 72–73]

No, Molly's inner world has not been much enriched by this entropic version of Millerian sexuality. And the outer world, although it provides some sweet moments, remains spectrally bruising. Thus Molloy's penultimate exterior landscape, the blue-gloomy forest, is especially disappointing. Resorting to the expedient of crawling painfully on the forest floor because it is even more torturing to proceed otherwise, Molloy questions his ceaseless agony, then suddenly (and seriocomically, as though he were destined to be the last echo of romantic irony) stops: "Before I go on," he comments, "a word about the forest murmurs" (p. 118). But—supreme blow—there aren't any celebrated forest murmurs; all he can hear is a mortifying gong from time to time.

Molloy, the ultimate incarnation of the tragic clown, ends the first part of Beckett's novel by suggesting that succor is coming his way. But occasional succor cannot counterbalance the absurdity of a scurvy planet. Though the farce in *Molloy* is heavily psychic (Molloy is full of whimsically mad dichotomies and inconsistencies of experience, imagination, and judgment), we sense metaphysical grotesquerie—the dark trollish buffoonery of the transcendental—in the background. Both the psychic and metaphysical qualities of Beckett's farce stimulate our cathartic, repudiative laughter.[34] But it is a terribly uneasy laughter all the same, for we sense that comedy, confronting a void that tantalizingly and painfully refuses to be transformed into a cosmos, is playing a frightening archprank by drifting to the verge of its own destruction. Yet when comedy, on that very verge, can play with sepulchral laughter directed against itself as well as against the nature of things, virtually a blooming miracle occurs.

This does not mean that the laughter of comedy necessarily signifies salvation. It has even been claimed, quite to the contrary, that laughter and comedy bear only the imprint of damnation. Is the truth on either side? Certainly the whole question of the relationship between irrational comedy and the demonic-divine is important enough to be worth investigating—especially in connection with Baudelaire's splendid essay "The Essence of Laughter." An analysis of this essay will also provide a basis for considering two ultimate, matchless exemplars of the spirit of farce: Harlequin, bequeathed by the commedia dell'arte, and Panurge, the principal buffoon in Rabelais's *Gargantua and Pantagruel.*

[34] David Krause, in "The Principle of Comic Disintegration," *James Joyce Quarterly*, 8 (Fall 1970), relates Beckett's funereal clowning to the comedy of Joyce and O'Casey, claiming that all three "survived because they were masters of the mythology of comic anarchy, that uniquely though not exclusively Irish form of knockabout comedy, the superbly vulgar tradition of music-hall clowning which deflates or desecrates, according to the provocation, those standards of success and esteem which the political and clerical princes of society are determined to sanctify" (p. 4).

5

From Demonic Laughter
to Magic Buffoonery

In his essay "On Cheerfulness in Religion" (*The Spectator*, Number 494, September 26, 1712), Addison politely scorns Puritan vestiges of sacred solemnity. Such vestiges cannot have been abundant among fashionable people, however, for in an earlier paper, "On Vicious Modesty" (*The Spectator*, Number 458, August 15, 1712), Addison claims that the men of mode, persistently aping Restoration escapists from Puritan hypocrisy, have been so influential among the well-bred, causing a reversion to libertinism in religious matters, that they have in some measure worn out the impress of Christianity in England. Nevertheless, in Number 494 Addison invites his readers to discount the alliance between the sacred and the solemn and to recognize the inevitability of mirth in the soul of the truly religious, and therefore truly cheerful, man. A saint need no longer wear a face of sorrowful sanctity in order to be fully accredited, nor need the ordinary churchgoer stuff his countenance with the message that religion is meaningful only as it resembles bitter medicine. Anyone having the airs of a Sombrius (one who sees piety as gravity and even grief) is ridiculous, for this kind of fellow "looks on a sudden fit of laughter as a breach of his baptismal vow. An innocent jest startles him like a blasphemy."[1] Cheerfulness and joy, Addison insists, are the nec-

[1] *Selected Essays from "The Tatler" and "The Spectator,"* ed. Warren L. Fleischauer (Chicago: Regnery, 1956), p. 169.

essary attributes of God's votaries. He winds up his remarks on this subject by paying homage to man's unique faculty of laughter, which he elevates to a spiritual region somewhere near the precincts of God himself.

Although the concept of a Divine Being who both inspires perpetual good humor and is himself (especially in the form of the Sacred Person) a believer in laughter is vastly beyond the limits of Addison's speculative assumptions, by now the idea of holy laughter has deeply infiltrated religious thinking.[2] The notion of the laughter of the Savior, specifically, is well on the way to becoming common. That Christ was motivated in his task of conversion and cure, not only by sublime love, but also by a brilliant exasperation expressed in oblique comic modes has been argued, for example, by Elton Trueblood, in *The Humor of Christ*. Trueblood complains that biblical scholars, zealously maintaining the image of an intensely sober Christ (an image buttressed by all the solemn associations surrounding the Crucifixion), have blinded themselves to New Testament playfulness and the Savior's provable propensity to joke.[3]

There is, however, a great, if flawed, counterargument to any theory that places salvational sportiveness at the heart of the divine. This argument is developed by Baudelaire in his essay "The Essence of Laughter,"[4] where he not only purges the heavens of gaiety but hands over to Satan and satanized humanity the only genuine (and abominable) franchise for

[2] Some of the essays in *Holy Laughter: Essays on Religion in the Comic Perspective*, ed. M. Conrad Hyers (New York: Seabury, 1969), would have astonished Addison. For example, in "The Comic Profanation of the Sacred," Hyers suggests that the loss of a comic perspective is equivalent to the pride occasioned by the Fall, and that comedy is essentially a "reminder of paradise lost" (p. 15). (This, as we shall see, is Baudelaire turned inside out.)

[3] Elton Trueblood, *The Humor of Christ* (New York: Harper and Row, 1964), p. 15. In "Christ the Harlequin," in *The Feast of Fools* (Cambridge, Mass.: Harvard University Press, 1969), Harvey Cox sees Christ the clown as an indispensable "personification of festivity and fantasy" (p. 139), mingling play, satire, hope, and ironic equivocation.

[4] For a number of probable influences on Baudelaire, see James S. Patty, "Baudelaire and Bossuet on Laughter," *PMLA*, 80 (Sept. 1965), 459–461.

laughter. This maneuver is interesting, since the devil, though he is associated in a number of literary works with derisive laughter (one thinks especially of Goethe's Mephistopheles),[5] rarely gets his due in theories of comedy. Meredith, for instance, snuffs him out, while Bergson leaves him in the shadows; and Freud secretes him deep within the id. Baudelaire stands alone among the great theorists in unabashedly supporting the claim that laughter springs from hell—a premise that would make the devil the father of comedy.

Baudelaire's vantage point is essentially theological: human laughter is the product of the Fall; one has only to glimpse the hideous convulsions laughter produces in the human face and frame to realize that it is rooted in a profound spiritual degradation. Why else does the wise man who is imbued with divinely ordered peace and goodness turn away in trembling malaise from the reverberations of laughter? He turns away because he senses in this strange phenomenon a kind of moral leprosy, a stigma of perdition. Spiritual purity also shuns laughter in the perfectly placid Earthly Paradise (since laughter and tears are the children of suffering), and especially in the laughterless life of Christ and the flawless sobriety of the world's sacred books. But since 1855, the date of Baudelaire's essay, the image of a Christ devoid of laughter (or a Bible that is wholly solemn) has been scrapped, as we have seen; and comparable religious figures, such as Buddha, have been granted their own measure of smiling enlightenment.[6]

[5] In Thomas Mann's *Doctor Faustus: The Life of the German Composer Adrian Leverkühn as Told by a Friend* (New York: Modern Library, 1966), Serenus Zeitblom refers, apropos of Adrian Leverkühn's somewhat orgiastic sense of the comic, to a story told him by Adrian: "It was from St. Augustine's *De civitate Dei* and was to the effect that Ham, son of Noah and father of Zoroaster the magian, had been the only man who laughed when he was born—which could only have happened by the help of the Devil" (p. 85).

[6] Martha Wolfenstein suggests that only the omnipotent can dispense with "humor"; that is why "the ancient Greek gods, who enjoyed only limited powers, made Olympus ring with their laughter" (*Children's Humor*, pp. 12–13). Baudelaire of course does not mention the laughter of the Greek gods. We may recall, incidentally, that in the first chapter of *Heroes and Hero-Worship*, Carlyle, searching for grave, brave deities, downgraded the half-sportive Olympians and endorsed the earnest Norse.

Baudelaire presumably takes up a more solid position when he selects, as a paradigmatic figure who will clinch the parallelism between innocence of soul and the absence of laughter, a character who is neither a god nor a sage. He chooses an angelic girl, whom he lifts right out of the pages of an eighteenth-century novel, *Paul et Virginie* (by Bernardin de Saint-Pierre), and deposits, through an act of speculative license, in the very heart of mephitic European civilization—Paris. He sets Virginie down in front of a typically cruel caricature in a Parisian shop window and then, extrapolating her reaction from her lovely attitudes on a primitive island in the East Indies, shows her to be appalled by the demonic power of the artist's comic exhibition:

> To us, [the caricature] would seem alluring, so overflowing is it with gall and rancor, the product of a bored and shrewd civilization. We will suppose it to be a farcical boxing scene, some British enormity, a thing of caked blood seasoned with a few monstrous goddams. Or, if your imagination runs that way, we will assume our virginal Virginie to be confronted by a charming and enticing impurity, a Gavarni of the period, and one of the best in its kind, an insulting satire at the expense of royal follies. . . . What she is looking at is something completely outside the range of her comprehension. She has but the vaguest inkling of what the thing means, of what purpose it serves. I would, however, draw your attention to a sudden folding of the wings, to the shudder of a spirit veiling its face and longing to turn away. The angel has felt herself to be in the presence of something evil. . . . An immaculate angel faced for the first time by a caricature, is filled with feelings of fear and suffering.[7]

Baudelaire can hardly be faulted in his choice of an immaculate angel. But Virginie is a paradisal creature who does possess some knowledge of evil. On her tropical island home she witnesses scenes of cruelty inflicted by slave owners; and in her

[7] *"The Essence of Laughter" and Other Essays, Journals, and Letters,* pp. 114–115. Baudelaire is not entirely consistent in his verdict on the morbid animus of the caricaturist. In "Some French Caricaturists" (in *The Mirror of Art,* ed. and trans. Jonathan Mayne [Garden City, N.Y.: Doubleday, Anchor, 1956]), Baudelaire stresses Daumier's capacity for capturing the sinister and farcical monstrosities of Paris (p. 167), yet soon afterward remarks that Daumier's gift of caricature is "quite without bile or rancor" (p. 170).

short period of time in France, she is tangentially introduced to Paris-tainted modes of existence. So she would not have fainted away at the sight of a caricature. Moreover, Virginie's virtue is not without its ridiculous side. Her death, which is the consequence of that virtue, has with the passage of time become transposed to an unintended key, has become in fact somewhat risible. Virginie dies, amidst storm and shipwreck, for one reason only: she is reluctant to disrobe. Actually, it is a marvel that Virginie, whose modesty is almost as incredible as it is inviolable, still seems, at the point of extinction, to be at least as much a stricken angel as a mortally silly prude.[8] Nevertheless, there is no forgetting the burlesque element in Virginie's demise. Which is another reason why she is less useful to Baudelaire than he imagines her to be.

Another literary character, utterly the reverse of Virginie in temperament, serves Baudelaire's aims rather better: the incomparably accursed protagonist of *Melmoth the Wanderer*, the creation of Charles Robert Maturin, the Dostoevsky of the Gothic novel. Maturin's wanderer superlatively exemplifies Baudelaire's notion that man's damnable pride, mingled with his propensity to madness, peals out in his laughter. It is Melmoth's destiny to be unremittingly cognizant of the malediction (the future consignment of his soul to hell) which haunts the extraordinary powers he once purchased of the devil. (Melmoth had been possessed by the Faustian malady, the intoxication of intellectual glory, "the mortal sin . . . of boundless aspiration after forbidden knowledge.")[9] The very motive of his wandering is the chance that he may remove this curse by capturing the unsullied soul of a tormented man or woman so

[8] Anthony Winner, editor of *Great European Short Novels* (New York: Harper and Row, 1968), is less charitable toward Virginie. He accentuates the "ludicrous propriety of her death, a triumph of the punctilious delicacy dictated by the code of sentiment." And he adds that "the exemplary bathos of her martyrdom to this code obscures the detail that her refusal to abate one jot of modesty is, under the circumstances, hardly natural" (I, 160).

[9] Charles Robert Maturin, *Melmoth the Wanderer*, intro. William F. Axton (Lincoln: University of Nebraska Press, 1961), p. 380.

caught up in a desperate extremity that he or she will be willing to escape from it by inheriting both Melmoth's power and his damnation. But Melmoth never succeeds in making his intended victims forfeit their salvation. He fails, above all, with Immalee, who belongs, with Virginie, among the angels.

Immalee, a flower maiden (virtually a fairy child) who has been orphaned on a luxuriant island in the Indian Sea (she is later reunited with her family in Spain, where she bears the name Isidora), is alone able to extract from Melmoth evidences of a buried sensibility. She elicits from him a self-conscious wounded laughter, radically different from the diabolic mockery with which he usually probes and horrifies the souls of others. This duality in Melmoth's sardonic temperament enables Baudelaire both to underscore and to qualify laughter's infernal genealogy:

What greater, what more powerful figure, compared with the poor ruck of humanity, could there be than the bored and pallid Melmoth? Yet there is in him something weak, something abject, something warring against God and against the Light. He laughs and laughs, ceaselessly comparing himself with the poor human worms who form the bulk of mankind. *He* is strong. *He* is intelligent. *He* is the man for whom part of the laws that rule humanity exist no longer! His laughter is the perpetual explosion of his anger and his agony. He is . . . the necessary resultant of his double and self-contradictory nature, infinitely great when set in the scale with Man, infinitely vile and base in his relation with Absolute Truth and Absolute Justice.[10]

When Melmoth releases his customary blood-chilling, demoniac laughter, he is clearly demonstrating, as Baudelaire suggests, his overt contempt for mankind. (Mankind deserves it, by the way. Melmoth is a brilliant lecturer on the cruelty and suffering that dominate this world; and except for a few genuine Christians, like those who reject his terrible bargain, he seems fully justified in evaluating the human spectacle with gloomy ferocity or malign mirth.) Nevertheless, Melmoth's burning irony does yield to intimations of compassion in the

[10] *The Essence of Laughter*, p. 117.

presence of the beautifully devoted Immalee: "For a moment, he experienced a sensation like that of his master when he visited paradise,—pity for the flowers he resolved to wither forever."[11] In fact, throughout an astonishingly prolonged (though discontinuous) relationship, Immalee recurrently awakens within this "demon of superhuman misanthropy" (p. 233) a searingly bitter realization of his dehumanized soul. At such times his laughter (which he will be quick to disdain as a weakness) is no longer merely a vindictive assault upon venal humanity or a dark commitment to hell; it expresses, in part, a tormenting memory of a lost spiritual glory. "This union of inward despair and outward levity is not unnatural," Maturin observes. "Smiles are the legitimate offspring of happiness, but laughter is often the misbegotten child of madness" (p. 237).

The compassionate element in Melmoth's bifurcated nature induces him, though only intermittently, to disabuse Immalee of her unquestioning love for him, and even to teach her that he is an engine of hatred and an object of hatefulness. But her perfect guilelessness, which casts upon Melmoth's weird statements and frightening acts a benign, reassuring glow, inevitably revives "that half-ironical, half-diabolical glance Immalee could not understand" (p. 218). Because she is immune to diabolism, Immalee will never actually surrender her soul to Melmoth. At the beginning of their strange alliance on her Indian isle, she had been challenged by him to become his everlasting bride of darkness. Immalee had preferred heavenly light as her nuptial symbol, and her choice had, in effect, temporarily routed Melmoth. When she does finally grasp the true nature and destiny of her lover, she again rejects him. And Melmoth himself eventually sinks shrieking, not laughing, into an ocean of fire.

The Gothic reprobate's fusion of laughter and despair has its profane interest, but it is the theological dimension of Melmoth's laughter that particularly concerns Baudelaire. This laughter, which betokens a blend of satanic superiority over

[11] *Melmoth the Wanderer*, p. 218.

man and a profound convinction of turpitude before the Absolute, can hardly be universalized; Melmoth is obviously one of
a kind. Baudelaire therefore attempts to construct a bridge between the unique miscreant's laughter and that of the ordinary
man, which, he suggests, "is at once a sign of infinite grandeur
and infinite wretchedness: of infinite wretchedness by comparison with the absolute Being who exists as an idea in Man's
mind; of infinite grandeur by comparison with the animals. It
is from the perpetual shock produced by these two infinites
that laughter proceeds."[12]

This transposition of the dual nature of Melmoth's laughter
onto Everyman's is nevertheless inadequate. For one thing,
Baudelaire makes no effort to close the gap between the throes
of the great Gothic sinner and the miseries of common humanity. For another, the "infinite grandeur" portion of Baudelaire's
statement, with its stress on man's superiority over animals, is
hardly a valid conclusion for an analysis that begins by emphasizing man's satanic laughter at the expense of his fellow
men. Helpfully, Baudelaire soon amplifies his dictum. Within
the category of animals he manages to include "the numerous
pariahs of the intelligence" (p. 118)—a phrase which presumably pertains to fools as well as imbeciles. And he secularizes
his aphorism a good deal by subsequently changing "absolute
Being" to a more tractable phrase, "the wise." Yet Baudelaire's
accent on man's spiritual duality, on the confluence of heaven
and hell within the human psyche, remains central to his argument. If man were a unity, Baudelaire observes, he would be a
creature of joy—which is what a child is, or should be—not an
exponent of acrid, joyless laughter. A child's wholesome, unitary joy is expressed in smiles or innocent laughter—the equivalent of the wagging tail of a dog or the purring of a cat (p.
120). But the perverse laughter of the adult is proof of a sick,
divided psyche.

The subject of the child's joy is the major transition between
the two halves of Baudelaire's essay. The second half is preoc-

---

[12] *The Essence of Laughter*, p. 117.

cupied with "the comic" in literature. Baudelaire divides "the comic" into the "significantly comic," which is more or less synonymous with satire, and the "absolutely comic," which, as can be seen from Baudelaire's own illustrations, is divisible into a Hoffmannesque type and a commedia dell'arte type (there is no impassable gulf between them; E. T. A. Hoffmann's "Princess Brambilla," for example, was inspired by Callot's engravings of fantastic commedia characters). The basic distinction between the significantly comic and the absolutely comic is that the former caters to common sense, morality, and social utility, while the latter, embodying the spirit of the grotesque, defies utilitarian common sense and shuns the moralization of laughter. Also, the significantly comic generates a fairly moderate or delayed laughter, while the absolutely comic produces an immediate hilarity "that has in it something profound, axiomatic and primitive, which more closely relates it to innocence and absolute joy than does the laughter occasioned by the comedy of manners" (p. 121).

Initially, Baudelaire permits neither of these two modes of the comic to be sealed off from its redoubtable parentage. Each is given a source in diabolic arrogance: the laughter of the significantly comic is rooted in the sense of superiority over other men, while that of the absolutely comic is anchored in the sense of superiority over nature. But the whole matter of the satanic core of the comic soon vanishes from Baudelaire's discussion, particularly as he waxes enthusiastic over the fabulous irrationalities of the absolutely comic, a category which he virtually defines as comedy for comedy's sake. He reports that England, Germany, Italy, and Spain are all predisposed to cultivate the absolutely comic; recognizable variations depend on differences in intellectual and spiritual climate. Germany makes the grotesque dreamy and profound; Spain adjusts it to the cruel and the somber; Italy touches it with gay insouciance, England with wild ferocity. The great European exception is France, which, as the pre-eminent representative of clarity and purpose, pursues in isolation its cult of the significantly comic. Even

Rabelais, "the great French master of the grotesque," Baudelaire states, "mingles in his wildest fantasies . . . an element
of the useful and the rational" (p. 123). But a mixture of
moral utility and extravagant fantasy also characterizes the
tales of E. T. A. Hoffmann, the king of the absolutely comic—
the writer most capable, in Baudelaire's opinion, of dreaming
up delightfully preternatural comic inventions.

Baudelaire's essay alludes to four Hoffmann tales: "Daucus
Carota," "Peregrinus Tyss" ("Master Flea"), "The Golden
Pot," and "The Princess Brambilla". The second and third are
merely mentioned; the fourth is highly commended and mar-
ginally glanced at; but the first is given more coherent study
(pared down to two paragraphs) as an emblem of the absolutely comic. This tale, usually called "Die Königsbraut" ("The
King's Bride"), is delightfully whimsical in its play with the
fantastic. The whimsicality is clearly brought out in Baudelaire's summary of a crucial segment of the tale—a segment
which is concerned with the disillusionment of Fräulein Anna
as she spies on her kingly little topheavy lover and his gor-
geously appareled armies, only to discover, to her chagrin, that
they are all muckily sleeping in their authentic and ignoble
identities as carrots, onions, turnips, and so on. Even in
Baudelaire's brief account, the fecund fancifulness of Hoffmann's imagination is unmistakable. Carrots and kings, love's
idleness lost on a vegetable fraud, elaborations of the occult—it
is all deliciously intriguing.

Equally pertinent to the tale is a fundamental attitude which
Baudelaire himself has declared to be the essence of the genuinely grotesque: a "prodigious dose of poetical good-humor"
(p. 123). This phrase presents a semantic difficulty of no mean
order. Baudelaire instances poetic good humor in Molière's
daffy interludes in *Le Malade imaginaire* and *Le Bourgeois
Gentilhomme* and in Callot's carnival figures—so "bonne
humeur" clearly possesses, for Baudelaire, a somewhat exuberant, antic charge. But the English connotation of "poetical
good-humor," which would suggest to Anglo-American readers

a wedding of benevolent spirits and imaginative amusement, is as germane to Hoffman's "absolutely comic" as the fantasticality he regularly cooks up.

Hoffmann's comic tales are packed with fey, esoteric, zany anomalies. At the same time his good humor, in the English sense, is truly prodigious. One consequence of this merger of comic energies is that the reader may be seized by the impression that Hoffmann is something of a Sterne who has happened upon fantastic and farcical supranatural material and has managed to convert it into the shape of benign eccentricity. Certainly Hoffmann's good-natured playfulness domesticates large quantities of mad nonsense in "The King's Bride."

The father of the bride, the dippy Herr Dapsul von Zabelthau, has his mind fixated on the stars. His daughter Fräulein Anna lacks his intellect and is therefore less neglectful of the circumstances of daily life. She is the buxom mistress of the kitchen garden: friendly agriculture is her passion, as aloof astrology is her father's; she digs the earth while he inspects the sky. Her digging leads to a perilous adventure with a gnome, a diminutive suitor called Baron Porphyrio von Ockerodastes. When Herr Dapsul, who has foolishly begun to glory in his association with so noble an elemental aristocrat, learns that the baron is actually a king, Daucus Carota, he is revulsed; for the baneful truth is that Daucus Carota lords it over the most inferior order of gnomes, the vegetable tenders (the most exalted gnomes are caretakers of diamonds). Moreover, like all gnome kings, this one will prove to be maliciously vindictive.

Anna herself initially views her suitor as a little monster, a repulsive goblin who has ruined her vegetable garden by settling his enormous retinue on it. But after the gnome reveals to her that, instead of devastating her dear earth in order to quarter his cortege, he has created under a massive tent the most resplendent of all possible vegetable gardens, and after he discloses his real identity and makes her the dazzling offer of a queenship, not only over the garden, but over the whole world's vegetables, she sees him as quite a handsome fellow. The poor girl therefore urgently needs her father's disenchanting disclosure of the truth; besides, she is becoming uglified by a gradual metamorphosis into a carrot. Acting on her father's instructions, Anna uses a pair of scissors to cut open a seam in the king's silken palace. What she witnesses (Baudelaire makes his major reference to this part of the tale) is not a gala garden spectacle but a deep puddle of nauseating mud alive with horrible wriggling creatures. The sight of the unfrocked armies of the king—a rank mass of vegetable nightmares—is so loathsome to Anna that, after almost fainting, she flees.

But her flight and Herr Dapsul's paternal protectiveness are useless against the king's wiles. Papa's cabalistic counterstratagems are foiled time and again. In the end, the resolution of the Zabelthau family's difficulties depends, as Herr Dapsul has foreseen, on a lunatic act committed by Anna's poet-lover, Amandus von Nebelstern. Amandus, accompanying himself on a guitar in the presence of Anna and the king, sings some of the songs he has been composing at the university. But his voice, like his poetry, is so excruciating that "Daucus Carota twisted and turned on Fräulein Ännchen's lap and groaned and whimpered more and more bitterly, as though he were suffering from a terrible colic."[13] Finally, Daucus Carota utters a loud screech and sinks into the earth. Herr Dapsul, released from a spell that has recently made him a toadstool, congratulates Amandus without being cognizant of the literary affront he is offering as he equates Amandus' verses with potent intestinal poisons. Fräulein Anna, quite accidentally, behaves even more like a critic; instantly ready to set to work again in her liberated vegetable garden, she inadvertently strikes Amandus hard on the head with her spade, thus reactivating his common sense and curing him of the malady of atrocious poetizing. And they live happily ever after.

The reunited lovers are hardly as memorable and certainly not as funny as the two archcontestants for esoteric dominance: cracked Herr Dapsul and demonic Daucus Carota. Of these

[13] E. T. A. Hoffmann, "The King's Bride," in *The Tales of Hoffmann*, trans. Michael Bullock (New York: Ungar, 1963), pp. 208–209.

two, the latter is the more remarkably comic; for the king cannot be considered simply a miniature version of what Herr Dapsul is—a whimsical humor character who is often pushed into the realm of burlesque. In creating Daucus Carota and his edible myrmidons, Hoffmann has installed within his tale magic, mirth-provoking presences that elude the grip of merely "significant" commentary or merely humorous labeling.

The thorny problem of "superiority to nature" in Baudelaire's notion of the absolutely comic is not easily resolved. Is our laughter evoked by a sense of superiority to vegetable nature, as well as to elemental nature spirits, no matter how mythical "nature" may be in this connection? The question is not insignificant; but in the long run it is likely to seem merely an ancillary instrument with which to plumb the comic wonderment of Hoffmann's tale. It suffices to point out that the comedy of the gnomes is set in motion by a charmingly daffy irrationality that is really the equivalent of brilliantly organized nonsense. The root sustenance of the tale is farce; and farce seeks, not superiority over nature (whatever that means), but superiority over obligatory sense and banal sanity. Hoffmann's grotesque portrait of that terrifying pint-sized buffoon, Daucus Carota, a nasty gnome with an enormous head and minuscule legs, presents a madly whimsical fracturing of normality.

Despite his fantastic farce, Hoffmann has told this queerest of tales with the sweetest of dispositions. Although the fundamental energy of the tale is farcical, its encompassing spirit bubbles with another important ingredient of the absolutely comic: prodigious good humor (in the English sense). This eccentric, indulgent, benign temper is not mentioned by Baudelaire in his discussion of "The King's Bride." In fact, in neglecting the whimsical humor traits in both father and daughter, he distorts Hoffmann's characterization. Baudelaire portrays agricultural Anna, in passing, only as an "unhappy young woman obsessed by dreams of greatness," while her dotty father is referred to only as "a prudent man, well versed in magic";[14] one

---

[14] *The Essence of Laughter*, p. 128.

would therefore scarcely be able to gather from Baudelaire's essay that Hoffmann has created funnily, innocuously odd human characters in "The King's Bride," and that Hoffmann's humorous impulse is intimately linked to the amazingly mad elements of the absolutely comic.

In addition to Hoffmann's tales, Baudelaire uses an English pantomime to exemplify the grotesque—a pantomime (which he witnessed in Paris) featuring both turbulent fantasy and immoralist monkeyshines. It is evident that the basic difference between Hoffmann's comic tales and the English pantomime is that the latter provides certain cathartic pleasures of primitive farce, whereas there is no similar instinctual release in Hoffmann. In the tales there is much whimsical hostility and much gorgeous nonsense; but there are no sexual, scatological, or nihilistic capers. In delineating the role of Pierrot in the English pantomime, Baudelaire is clearly willing to incorporate such capers—and indeed all the Freudian ingredients of farce: aggression, obscenity, scatology, cynicism, nonsense, and lunacy —into the rhythm of the absolutely comic. But not for long: the common denominator he finally establishes for the furious exuberance of the English pantomime and the rich fantasy of Hoffmann's tales turns out to be a kind of dizzy enchantment, which is far from being the equivalent of instinctual exhilaration.

The major figures in the pantomime that once intoxicated Baudelaire with gaiety derive ultimately from the commedia dell'arte. Pierrot became singularly French, however. That is why Baudelaire comments that Pierrot has suffered a remarkable sea change as a result of being transported to England from France.[15] Formerly a creature of "moonlit pallor and silent mystery," he has been metamorphosed by the English taste for comic violence into a hurricane of buffoonery.[16] But his in-

<hr />

[15] For suggestions about which pantomime Baudelaire witnessed, probably in the early 1840's, see *The Mirror of Art*, ed. Mayne, p. 147n. And for an extraordinarily detailed study of the harlequinade in early nineteenth-century England, see David Mayer III, *Harlequin in His Element: The English Pantomime, 1806–1836* (Cambridge, Mass.: Harvard University Press, 1969).

[16] *The Essence of Laughter*, p. 125.

creased vehemence only accentuates his usual rapacious flouting
of morality. To shift from Baudelairean to Freudian terms, we
may say that whether Pierrot is pale or flushed, he is a splendid
representative of the id—one who, gratifying his primitive
drives with shameless gusto, irresponsibly destroys decency and
decorum. Observe Pierrot as a monstrously greedy thief and an
outrageously sexual simian:

We were shown Pierrot encountering a woman engaged in washing
her doorstep. After first picking her pockets, he tried to stuff into
his own, the mop, the broom, and the pail—even the water. As to
the manner in which he showed his love for her, it can best be
imagined by those who have witnessed the nuptial exhibitionism of
the monkeys in a certain celebrated cage of the Paris Zoo. I should
explain that the part of the woman was played by a very tall, very
thin, man, whose outraged modesty found vent in loud screams.
This, truly, was the very quintessence of drunken buffoonery, at
once horrible and irresistible.   [pp. 125–126]

The abyss between Pierrot's animal lusts and the magic dissolution of logic in Hoffmann's comic tales is plainly revealed here.
Pierrot's antics destroy deep-seated ethical restraints. On the
other hand, Hoffmann, while using the grotesque to wreak
havoc on normality, is by no means embracing instinctual satyr-
dom.

There are, nevertheless, comparable moments of fantasticality in both the pantomime and the comic tales. Thus Daucus
Carota can hurl himself like a grenade out of a powerfully and
perilously closed saucepan; and Pierrot can walk away from a
guillotine which has just gorily severed his head from his shoulders: "Suddenly, the decapitated trunk, revived by the force of
the creature's irresistible thievish monomania, got to its feet,
and triumphantly made off with its head, which, like a ham or
a bottle of wine . . . it stuffed into its pocket" (p. 126). But
unlike the gnome-king, Pierrot, that unsavory, beautifully bes-
tial clown, outwits death (or at least the machinery of death)
with resources that seem more human than not.

How close is the pantomime to the comic tales, according to
Baudelaire? Quite close, simply because Pierrot's monstrous
buffoonery dims and then vanishes; the clown's freedom from

controls becomes part of a generalized "breath of the marvelous" (pp. 126–127) which is put in motion by a fairy's wand. And we may wonder whether that particular fairy, though fixed in the English harlequinade tradition, would not be peculiarly at home in the world of Hoffmann. But we may also wonder whether her dizzying commandment—thou shalt be released from the pull of gravity and custom—is not, for all its liberating sweep and the dazzling animation that ensues, tangential to Pierrot's feral seizures.

Though Baudelaire's memory of the pantomimic performance remains chiefly impregnated with "the marvelous"—with a Hoffmannesque, delightfully capricious magic—it is Pierrot's rude buffoonery that inspires Baudelaire to declare that pantomime is "the very spirit of the comic concentrated and released," and that the quintessential fun he has enjoyed has been a "monstrous display of the farcical" (p. 126). Since, moreover, Pierrot's pantomimic lunacy (this is the pure, unverbalized core of the absolutely comic, in Baudelaire's view) gambols in forbidden zones, sporting anarchically with authority and morality, its power of psychic emancipation transcends, as I have suggested, the liberties with order and sense permitted by Hoffmannesque anomalies.

Which brings us to the most important characteristic of the absolutely comic: its inherent reversal of Baudelaire's original proposition that laughter is evidence of man's damnation. Baudelaire prepares the way for this reversal in his early remark that laughter is, in part, proof of man's infinite sense of wretchedness before God. This rather strong hint that the human soul may yet make an arduous progress toward redemption is reinforced later in a brief comment to the effect that "with tears a man may wash away man's sufferings, and with laughter soften men's hearts and draw them to him. For the phenomena engendered by the Fall can become the means of salvation" (p. 113). Unfortunately, this promising declaration gets submerged by the attention Baudelaire gives to the dynamics of devilry. In fact, the idea of levity remains more or less stigmatized until the absolutely comic is introduced—at which point the hilarity of the grotesque opens up a miraculous avenue to the revivification of the body and the spirit: "It distended the lungs and renewed the blood in the ventricle" (p. 127), Baudelaire remarks of the "breath of the marvelous." The statement is physiological, but that its implications also convey a strong sense of psychic renovation is evident from Baudelaire's total view of the absolutely comic. We may even claim that Baudelaire, who started with the premise that laughter is diabolic, ends (despite a last-minute, attenuated reminder that the curse of the comic can never be entirely lifted) with a paean to comedy's regenerative powers.[17] In truth, Baudelaire virtually sanctifies the energies of farce.

2

The English pantomime Baudelaire witnessed in the middle of the nineteenth century derived, via the French theatre, from a robust Italian tradition of clowning which, in its English transplantation, developed a somewhat more decorous, if still violent, zaniness. The nineteenth-century harlequinade, whose basic characters were Harlequin, Columbine, Pantaloon, and Clown, was replete with colorful pageants, vertiginous fun, and burlesque fiascos; but its comic audacity hardly matched that of the sixteenth-century professional, improvisational commedia dell'arte (which flourished for a couple of centuries and reached widely throughout Europe). In fact, the commedia's greatest single legacy is its superbly stylized outrageous lunacy. Not that the commedia dell'arte restricted itself to comedy alone, or that it specialized, within the field of comedy itself, only in buffoonery. Still, a cursory glance at the titles of the fifty commedia scenarios published by Flaminio Scala in 1611 reveals that forty of the plays are essentially farces imbued—to use a phrase of Baudelaire's—with "the deathless and incorrigible

---

[17] Early in his essay, Baudelaire shows contempt for "charlatans of gravity" (p. 111) who immure queer drolleries within the sarcophagus of pedantry. And he postulates, if somewhat murkily, that intellectual power during the growth of civilization is tied to the development of comedy (p. 119).

spirit of mirth,"[18] whereas only ten belong to one or more non-comic genres: the pastoral, the tragic, and the operatic.

The commedia farces all thrive on hectic irrationality; grotesque nonsense, whirlwind aggression, bawdy tricks, and bizarre mystifications shatter the forms of sanity and the contours of reality. The farces are often extraordinarily congested with the problems and machinations of young lovers whose brains are sometimes scrambled and whose hearts are sometimes inanely fickle. The finales of all the comedies celebrate amorous unions or reunions (which are based on wildly protean plot developments), but the festive, conciliatory, nuptial last scenes of the zanier farces are sops to romantic or moral conventions which have already been hilariously annihilated. The amorous intrigues in the comedies with a pronounced clownish, irreverent bias can therefore be regarded only in the flimsiest sense as ends in themselves; they are, for the most part, pegs on which to hang an assortment of farcical incidents. Crammed into the framework of sets of lovers seeking fulfillment (lovers who may be, as in Roman comedy, forgotten or forsaken paramours in disguise, or lost sons and daughters—singles or twins) is a world of fun triggered by epidemic lunacy and burgeoning with irrational whims, fantastic imbroglios, demented dialogue, lewd antics, delerious drubbings, and mad pranks.

Logic, dignity, and morality are to some extent destroyed by the lovers themselves, but two other kinds of characters outdo them in multiplying absurdities: the fools and the Fools. A great deal of silliness is registered in the conduct of such recurrent characters as Pantalone, the old fool of family authority and social position; Dr. Gratiano, the old fool of learning and pedantry; and Captain Spavento, the fool of military braggadocio. But a far more extravagant freedom from sense, rules, and respectability is exercised by the genuine Fools—the clever-foolish servants who may be technically underdogs of society but who are, more authentically, demons of play. The Scala scenarios feature two buffoons above all: the sly but not always

---

[18] *The Essence of Laughter*, p. 110.

unscathed Pedrolino and the somewhat less important, more bumbling, but occasionally brilliant Arlecchino. Pedrolino (who engendered Pierrot) outshines Arlecchino in these particular scenarios of 1611, but it is Arlecchino (Harlequin) who eventually attained the premier position among the clowns bequeathed to us by the commedia dell'arte.

Scraps from the Scala scenarios offer a representative range of Arlecchino's activities, propensities, and *lazzi* (funny business, both physical and verbal) before he reached the acme of comic glory. Sometimes frustrated, sometimes fulfilled, resilient Arlecchino exhibits his miscellaneous japery most frequently as a subordinate. Occasionally, he is his own man. Thus, in *Isabella the Astrologer*,[19] Arlecchino, a free agent—an entrepreneur, no less—sings the praises of the pimp's profession and flourishes an enormous sheet of paper on which is inscribed a long list of international courtesans in his employ. He is avid for more personnel, however, and even tries to draft strangers like Isabella and Rabbya Turca (Turkey is the commedia dell'arte's chief source material for exotic mystery, recoverable children, and converted heathens) into his whorehouse by main force, despite the fact that Isabella, playing the astrologer, reads his palm, examines his face, and tells him he is ripe for the galley and the gallows. (The women are saved when Arlecchino is frightened off by the roaring regent of Naples.)

In the role of servant, forced to be wily though often fated to be ambushed, Arlecchino has a greater chance to be in the thick of things—which is where he belongs, whether he is weeping hysterically, pandering piously, ululating anticly, collapsing ludicrously, or escaping ingeniously. Consider his job in *The Fake Magician*, a comedy which presents, among other things, two illicit, big-bellied pregnancies belonging, respectively, to

[19] The selections cited are to be found in *Scenarios of the Commedia dell'Arte: Flaminio Scala's "Il Teatro delle favole rappresentative,"* trans. Henry F. Salerno (New York: New York University Press, 1967). This translation, which is an important sourcebook, also has a brief foreword on the commedia dell'arte by Kenneth McKee, as well as an appendix by Salerno that traces sixteenth- and seventeenth-century repercussions of the commedia in the drama of England and France.

Pantalone's daughter Flaminia and Dr. Gratiano's daughter Isabella. To this disreputably piquant situation Captain Spavento
applies his customary military-amatory muddle: he wants to
send a love letter to Flaminia (whom Oratio, as the captain can
hardly be expected to know, has already fecundated); so he
tells Arlecchino, Dr. Gratiano's servant, that he will give him
fifty scudi to drop the letter through Flaminia's window. For
this nocturnal enterprise Arlecchino plans to get a lantern and
a ladder; he says he will pretend that he is catching birds if
ever he is questioned about his urge to elevate himself. He is
not especially adroit with his ladder, however, for he has drunk
too much of the wine newly bought by his master, Gratiano;
still, he does succeed in stumbling his way up to Flaminia's
window—only to fall off the ladder at the noisy arrival of the
police, who chase after him and the captain.

Arlecchino's difficulties are only at the commencement stage.
Pedrolino plies him with the medicine (he palms it off on
Arlecchino as wine) which a physician has sent to cure Flaminia's swollen condition. The consequence is that Arlecchino
vomits on some cheese which has just been purchased by
Gratiano, and indeed keeps vomiting as numerous characters
confer with him. This exhibition of corporeal grotesquerie is
soon matched by the *lazzi* of Gratiano and his festive companions, all of whom, drunk as apes, topple successively to the
ground directly in front of the dumbfounded Pantalone. Naturally it is up to Arlecchino to carry them indoors, one by one,
and this he does in all kinds of ridiculous ways. After having
filed away an army of drunken bodies, Arlecchino makes as if
to carry sober Pantalone's body indoors too; but the old man
hurtles up the street.

The Fake Magician lives up to its title in the last act. Pedrolino informs the two fathers, who are worrying about their
daughters' ballooning bodies, that he has found a magician
whose skill will thin their daughters' bellies down to normal.
(Stupid Gratiano, incidentally, is convinced that his own
daughter's state of enlargement is a temporary affliction having
nothing to do with sex; but he laughs maliciously while think-

ing about Pantalone's daughter and opines that she will never recover without marrying her lover.) Arlecchino is to play the magician, and is soon equipped with a Mercury rod, a winged cap, and winged boots. Acting out his role with relish, he plants the fathers in two magic circles which he traces on the stage, then conjures up spirits (these are the girls' camouflaged lovers, Oratio and Flavio) who give the old men a good fright. Arlecchino even calls on Mercury himself, the messenger of the gods, to appear on top of Gratiano's house. The servant Franceschina, suitably tricked out as the god, obliges; she warns Pantalone and Gratiano that if they don't permit their daughters to marry Oratio and Flavio—for such is the gods' design—the spirits will take them straight to hell. No further pressure is needed; and Arlecchino, after a few more magic flourishes, is himself rewarded with Franceschina.

Mercury, the god Arlecchino summons, is, among other things, master of magic, thievery, and trickery; as such, he seems the perfect deity for the clown-servant to give his allegiance to. In *The Italian Comedy*, Pierre Louis Duchartre goes so far as to hymn a Harlequin who is "without doubt of divine essence, if not, indeed, the god Mercury himself"; but in a less divinizing statement, Duchartre speaks of Harlequin's motley as signifying, in addition to poverty, " 'neither fish nor flesh,' which indicates the diverse and dubious resources of Mercury's protégés.' "[20] Chief among these diverse and dubious resources

[20] Pierre Louis Duchartre, *The Italian Comedy*, trans. Randolph T. Weaver (New York: Dover, 1966), p. 124. For an ecstatic assessment of Harlequin's protean magic of body, mood, and mask, see Vsevolod Meyerhold's "Farce," in *Theatre in the Twentieth Century*, ed. Robert W. Corrigan (New York: Grove, 1963), pp. 202–203. And for figurations of Harlequin in modern fiction, see Richard Pearce, *Stages of the Clown* (Carbondale: Southern Illinois University Press, 1970). Historical perspectives on Harlequin, incidentally, are scarcely uniform. As Allardyce Nicoll puts it in *The World of Harlequin* (Cambridge, Eng.: Cambridge University Press, 1965): "One historian emphasizes the early association of Harlequin with Renaissance courts and, sadly, traces his decline to the gradual vulgarization of his art at times when he was forced to appeal to less intelligent spectators; another supplies a Marxist interpretation, insisting that at the start Harlequin was created by the common people and owed his decrepitude to his entering ducal

are a hilarious body language and a mad, chameleonic spirit of jest.

The image of Harlequin with all his various, warring selves has been superbly captured in Leon Katz's full-scale amplification, entitled *The Three Cuckolds*,[21] of the commedia scenario *Li tre becchi*. Katz's Arlecchino is the highly verbal cousin of Baudelaire's pantomimic English Pierrot, whose silent barbaric yawps offered so marvelous a release from psychic captivity. These two buffoons, engaging in an orgiastic dance of the id, embody the gospel of unadulterated zaniness, that rejuvenescent tide which washes away the sense of sin and the sin of sense.

Arlecchino is galvanized by food, sex, and trickery; but it becomes clear soon enough that the one urge from whose impromptu commands he can never dissent is the love of pranks. As he explains to Pantalone's wife, Flaminia (who, after promising him "meat" in exchange for duping her husband and helping her lover Coviello into her house, has denied Arlecchino both of his two possible banquets), he is incapable of disregarding alluring promises that inspire his clowning—even

---

and princely palaces" (pp. 2–3). It seems clear, in any case, that the commedia's farcical dementia is not basically an insurrection against the Establishment. Certain socially dominant characters do, however, find themselves mocked in the commedia. (Thus the creation of the frequently grotesque Captain Spavento was hardly meant, originally, to honor the Spanish occupiers of the Italian peninsula.) Fortunately, the eminence of individual actors in the commedia could obtain for them immunity from reprisal for their mockery, though the dangers of topical satire forced certain commedia troupes to move too frequently for comfort. See Giacomo Oreglia, *The Commedia dell'Arte*, trans. Lovett F. Edwards (New York: Hill and Wang, 1968) for brief notes on the development of Captain Spavento (pp. 101–103), the satiric liberties taken by Tiberio Fiorelli, known as Scaramouche (pp. 112–114), and the fate of the acting companies (pp. 128–130).

[21] Leon Katz's *The Three Cuckolds* is to be found, along with such well-known pieces as Machiavelli's *The Mandrake* and Goldoni's *The Servant of Two Masters*, in *The Classic Theatre*, ed. Eric Bentley, Vol. I: *Six Italian Plays* (Garden City, N.Y.: Doubleday, Anchor, 1958). The scenario *Li tre becchi* is in K. M. Lea's *Italian Popular Comedy, 1560–1620, with Special Reference to the English Stage* (Oxford: Clarendon Press, 1934), II, 580–584.

promises made by those who have already deceived him. Arlec-chino may generalize sagely about the poison of irrationality, but when temptation appears anew, he rejects sagacity and im-petuously enthrones the wisdom of absurdity.

At the end of the play, Flaminia is genuinely ready to offer Arlecchino a share in a sumptuous collective repast. But even then, Arlecchino balks at the idea of fulfillment, realizing that it would mean the death of his buffoonery. "What would be-come of Arlecchino," he asks Flaminia, "with so much meat and wine inside him? Arlecchino has many follies, dear lady, but he is not so foolish as to digest his injuries and drown his wit. . . . From my empty stomach I get my whole wisdom, and from my folly, my whole prosperity."[22] A principle of perpetual clown motion is at work here. Since Arlecchino's buffoonery thrives on deprivation rather than repletion, he can preserve his capacity for gulling the asinine, especially the cornuted crea-tures of this world, only by savoring the defeat that promotes his powers. This paradox may seem pathetic, stupid, or patho-logical to the utilitarian, rational mind—and to Arlecchino's own mind, on occasion. But this buffoon's salvation lies pre-cisely in such a paradox: zaniness is all.

Arlecchino's madness—his deification of buffoonery—is not unique in *The Three Cuckolds*, for he is caught up in a net-work of three marital infidelities that are inherently insane; and these infidelities are in turn based on three marriages that are intrinsically lunatic, for the husbands are old and decaying—albeit noisily so—while the wives are young and burgeoning. Neither the ancient lecherous goats nor their robust wayward wives are plagued by intimations of morality. Coviello is the husband of Cintia but yearns for the love of Flaminia; Panta-lone is married to Flaminia but craves the embraces of Fran-ceschina; Zanni is the spouse of Franceschina but slobbers over the image of Cintia. Whatever dictated these three January-and-May unions? And however did the subsequent promiscuous hodgepodge get started? What prompted the marriages, it

[22] *The Three Cuckolds*, II.xxi.

turns out, was simply a transitory marital fashion that made weddings between oldsters and youngsters all the rage.

These crazy marriages are counterpointed by demented, inconceivable adulteries. The three Methuselahs crow fiercely about their virility, but we have good reason to doubt that they possess any potency at all. According to the following dialogue, we might think that Pantalone, at least, must be providing some kind of pleasure for his mistress Franceschina:

Franceschina.   Pantalone, my sweet lover and my impotent husband's cuckolder, how are you?
Pantalone.   Not so loud, good Franceschina—
Franceschina (still shouting).   When can we be in bed again together? Can you be rid of your harlot wife tonight and taste the joys of an honest woman's love, or is your painted slut so malicious that she will tie you like a dog to the foot of her bed to keep you virtuous and in sight while she romps all night with lewd actors and mountebanks before your very eyes?
Pantalone.   Good Franceschina, I know how evil evil appears in your eyes.
Franceschina.   Bawdry is my abomination.   [I.ix]

Discretion in the use of her vocal chords (not to mention her power of reason) is also Franceschina's abomination. To be sure, her husband Zanni is practically blind and deaf, as well as the dumbest thing around. But even if Zanni were fully alive and genitally well and had perfectly gray brain matter, Franceschina's manner would doubtless remain the same. At any rate, when she appeals to her "impotent husband's cuckolder," we may deduce that the epithet "impotent" applies as much to the cuckolder as to the husband. A glaring illogicality? But *The Three Cuckolds* reverberates from the first scene to the last with the impact of shattered reason. Impotent cuckold makers and satisfied unsatisfiable wives are merely components of a general madness.

The farcical demerit of biological impotence is conjoined in *The Three Cuckolds* with the risible disgrace of mental sterility. Consider, for example, the imbecility revealed in the fatherhood hoax that is perpetrated on Zanni. This sapless fool is made to think that his potency (his palsy, in truth) can be converted into an inseminating force if only he is willing to rely on Dr. Arlecchino's obstetrical science, which has already, the doctor mendaciously reports, made Pantalone, who is an odious object of comparison for Zanni, a father. So great is Zanni's competitive thirst for paternity that this shriveled, one-foot-in-the-grave creature, who sometimes thinks that his wife, for some inexplicable reason, does not lust for his body, joyfully accepts Arlecchino's plan, which requires digging a son out of the very earth. A spade, a rope, and a basket are needed for this terrestrial parturition, as is Franceschina's speedy connivance; for Arlecchino intends ultimately to enter the basket, hoping to give and receive erotic blessings in Franceschina's unorthodox arms. So Franceschina digs while Arlecchino supervises and Zanni, with fussy eagerness, awaits the miracle that is to come to pass. Soon Zanni frantically strains to help the miracle along by jumping into the hole and digging like a madman. But the only signs of life that emerge from the hole come from the out-raged Devil.

The Devil's justifiable grouchiness is received by Zanni as though it were manna from heaven. And when the Devil abu-sively dares Zanni to pull him out ("Come here and try, you old corpse"), Zanni responds with delight: "What spirit! What a voice! Give me your hand, little angel." He does get the hand, and then an arm—in fact, an endless arm which finally gets detached from the Devil's body. Zanni shrieks at this dismem-berment, then moaningly wonders how his son will manage with only one arm. The Devil, fed up with Zanni's sentimental wailing, throws out a whole cluster of arms—and legs. Zanni's alarm now reaches a crescendo. "Franceschina," he screams at his wife, "don't stand there gaping. Help me deliver our son be-fore he throws away *all* his precious parts!" When his wife dis-misses him as a lunatic, the lunatic rushes over to clasp the head of his incredibly gifted and multiform baby boy, in order that both father and child may exert themselves in rhythmic, though motherless, travail. A lot of sailorly heave-hoing stretches the Devil's neck up out of the ground, and a final tug proves catastrophic: "*This time the Devil's head emerges five feet out of the hole and emits smoke through his mouth and ears. Zanni,* *taking in the sight, faints dead away. The Devil's head, in a* *flash, shoots down into the hole and disappears"* (I.xiv). Which does not prevent Zanni from subsequently swallowing the delusion of having been present at the birth of an exceedingly tall son.

Zanni's cretinous mistreatment of the obvious—his freakish delinquency of perception—is farcical enough. But it is considerably enhanced by the irreverence and fantasticality that accrue from the Devil's joky gymnastic appearance, which makes immediate casualties of logic, piety, and nature. The Devil, moreover, is such a first-rate buffoon, so great a master of the burlesque-grotesque, that Arlecchino is reduced to ancillary clownhood.

But only temporarily. Arlecchino generally supplies enough zaniness to satisfy all the desiderata of clown comedy. His most memorable lunatic trait, one quickly recognizes, is his genius for dramatizing the dualities of psychic farce. Arlecchino is honorable and knavish, sophisticated and naïve, ingenious and duncelike, buoyant and pitiable, quiescent and uncontrollable, masculine and feminine, discarnate and fleshly, self-exalting and self-scoffing, self-preserving and self-destructive. In the first and last scenes of the play, and quite often in between, he stands before us as a split creature, shivering soliloquies into duologues and dissolving plain attitudes into ardent-ironic ambivalences. For example, early in the play we observe a bit of lunatic self-division that is related to Arlecchino's sexual fortunes. We see him intent on reclaiming apparently familiar sexual sensations (presumably, sometime in the past Arlecchino successfully seized upon the delights of an adulterous rendezvous or a chance erotic encounter; his buffoon's psychology of self-denial cannot, after all, absolutely fence him off from orgasmic pleasure). He is even tempted to make two killings (Cintia and Flaminia) in one night. But as soon as his decision is made, psychic dissociation sets in, and he begins to sneer at the figure he cuts: "Look at you, Arlecchino, bragging of loving two in a single night! Which of them would love you?

Would any? You lying, stinking, starving, cheating, whining, shrinking little exclamation point! I saw you at the fair, remember, when you made love to the farmer's wife, and the old sow she was selling fell on her back in her litter and laughed herself to death." This self-dismissal is quickly countered as Arlecchino proudly rises to his full height and answers himself awesomely: "Shut your eyes, shut your eyes and turn around this way. And when you open them, may you be struck dumb at once by the radiance of my visible passion, my easily read ardor, and my audibly heroic manly mould!" But when his skeptical self opens his eyes, he jeers barbarically at his supposed manly self. At this point Arlecchino, deeply wounded in his self-esteem, whirls about and slaps himself hard in the face, addressing to himself a single word: "Beast!" (I.ii).

An antic-frantic disposition, indeed. Yet this comic maniac, shanghaied from reason (self-kidnapped, actually) though pledged to cunning, this inadvertent sow killer and dichotomous slapper of his own face, this enthusiastic worshiper and terribly denigratory critic of himself, can exorcise his antithetical sensibilities in an instant and bask in absolute psychic reunification. Arlecchino's clownish chemistry does not act in accordance with any predictable cycles, moreover; his only reliable characteristic is his cultivation of farcical chaos.

Arlecchino's hilarious destructiveness in *The Three Cuckolds* separates him from such Fools as Shakespeare's, who, for all their wit and lively clowning, are not given to insatiable, nihilistic buffoonery. It is difficult to imagine Arlecchino as a character in *Twelfth Night*, for example. Yet Allardyce Nicoll, in *The World of Harlequin*, does not see much difference between the spirit of Shakespeare's clowns and that of the commedia dell'arte's. The commedia scenarios, he suggests, usually provide merriment controlled by a "general atmosphere" that "breathes the air of pleasant romance, not too far removed from that of such a play as *Twelfth Night*."[23] In other words, the

[23] *The World of Harlequin*, p. 10.

prevalence of romantic intrigues in the commedia proves that Harlequin's iconoclasm is not all-important, and also that cuckoldry is not a primary source of theme developments. Nevertheless, *The Three Cuckolds* is a legitimate distillation of the daring of commedia farce. Katz's recreation of the spirit of Harlequin, however Freudianized, is securely anchored in the clown's traditional motives and antics; and these diverge significantly from the mentality and modes of mischief of characters like Sir Toby Belch and Feste in *Twelfth Night*.

Feste is basically a humorous clown who seems to share Sir Toby Belch's pagan cakes-and-ale psychology; but he is not instinctively committed to outrageous saturnalianism (which is Arlecchino's constant comic reflex). If his comic spirit does not, like Arlecchino's, destroy dullness at any cost, that is because it is tempered by a wise though skittish tolerance, itself the product of his sensitivity to human patchiness and misfortune. Feste can be satiric toward his betters with relative impunity and indeed with profit, for clever mockery enables him to pocket coins. But his realization of Everyman's exceedingly rainy existence has alloyed his gaiety (inconspicuously, on the whole) with elements of sadness and charity, which are not, it must be added, readily available for the likes of such affected asses as Malvolio.

Feste keeps his sense of disenchantment in the background of his being, for in the forefront his sport derives from a sense of security, from a feeling that the world is well superintended after all. And "when the normal is secure," as C. L. Barber observes in *Shakespeare's Festive Comedy*, "playful aberration is benign."[24] Such benign playfulness, divorced from a radical taste for subversion, is at the very center of Feste's revelries. As far as Arlecchino is concerned, on the other hand, to revel is to tear apart outrageously and irredeemably whatever is normal and expectable. Feste's wit and nonsense stop far short of such all-out farcical effrontery.

[24] *Shakespeare's Festive Comedy*, p. 245.

Because Arlecchino is a farcical buffoon, not a humorous clown, he neither respects norms nor salves wounds. And he abides by the suggestions of others only when they accord with the nothing-sacred pleasure principle. Whereas, in Barber's words, "the fooling with madness" in *Twelfth Night* "is an enjoyment of the control which knows what is mad and what is not" (p. 261), the fooling with madness in *The Three Cuckolds* is an enjoyment of irrationality for its own wild, exuberant, heedless sake. No comic character in Shakespeare, not even Falstaff, although he "makes a career of misrule" (p. 251), embodies quite that spirit of zaniness.

Nicoll's frequent analogizing, in *The World of Harlequin*, between Shakespearean romantic comedy and the majority of the commedia scenarios is certainly helpful; but he suggests that the two spheres of comedy differ in degree, rather than in kind; the lovers in the scenarios may be more irrational than Shakespeare's, and the comedians crueler and more frankly animalistic,[25] but otherwise the spirit of fun is much the same in both kinds of comedy. Moreover, unlike those who see the commedia's development toward farce as a successful consolidation of its most typical drives, Nicoll regards this development as the degeneration (especially under Neapolitan influence) of a multifaceted comedy. He is of the opinion that the commedia, though "basically a theatre of laughter" (p. 144), has too often been tagged as pre-eminently a clown's theatre; that is why he has taken pains to give full value to the large part played in the commedia by amorous complications.

Though Nicoll declares that the soul of the commedia is "a continual aspiration towards expressing a certain kind of comic spirit" (p. 158), he does not, oddly enough, actually define that spirit. But it is not really necessary for him to do so, for we have seen that he considers the commedia temper to be essentially that of Shakespearean romantic comedy, galvanized into a more fitful tempo, made more labyrinthine in its circum-

[25] *The World of Harlequin*, p. 148.

stances and crazier in its characterizations, and stimulated more blatantly by injections of vulgarity, fantasticality, and buffoonery. In this definition, farce is a secondary, though highly important, phenomenon. But even if Nicoll's evaluation were beyond contention, a Freudian age, and a comically nihilistic one to boot, must seek its own level of interpretation in re-creating the commedia; and it will inevitably be tempted to highlight those irreverent, mad energies that disclose affinities with its own irrational appetites.

3

The only competitor of the commedia dell'arte, or of Hoffmann, in Baudelaire's essay "The Essence of Laughter" is Rabelais, whom Baudelaire views, but only in passing, as the greatest exemplar of the absolutely comic in France. Baudelaire's point is that no matter how extraordinary a comic fantasist Rabelais is, he always manages, in good French style, to infuse into his fabulous fictions a strong proportion of the significantly comic. Nevertheless, Rabelais's fantasticality is situated at the very heart of farce (which does not mean that it exhibits all the drives of farce). It is fitting, therefore, to continue the present anatomy of comic irrationality by considering certain zany aspects of *Gargantua and Pantagruel*.

Rabelais's use of two hermeneutic metaphors in his prologue to the first book of *Gargantua and Pantagruel* makes for a very special mixture of the significantly comic and the absolutely comic. The first metaphor is concerned with the little boxes called sileni (after Silenus, mentor of the god Bacchus), which were "painted over with merry and frivolous figures . . . designed to give pleasure and to excite folks to laughter. . . . But inside these boxes were kept fine drugs . . . as well as medicinal stones and other precious things."[26] (Rabelais notes that Alcibiades called his preceptor, Socrates, a Silenus precisely

[26] François Rabelais, *Gargantua and Pantagruel*, in *The Portable Rabelais*, ed. and trans. Samuel Putnam (New York: Viking, 1946), pp. 47–48.

because the philosopher, whose external appearance was comical and grotesque, proved to be internally a repository of incomparable sobriety and divine wisdom.) Rabelais cheerfully appropriates the Silenus duality of outer frivolity and inner worth by asking the foolish loafers who read him—"most illustrious Drinkers and . . . most precious Syphilitics" (p. 47)—not to equate sign with substance, not to judge that jesting titles, for example, must be preludes to joky contents.

His surface prankishness, Rabelais teasingly maintains, is merely a device to lure the reader into opening the box that is his book, so that he may benefit from the valuable drugs (moral, intellectual, spiritual, and so forth) concealed within. Since the formula that his book is a treasure trove of wisdom masquerading as nonsense is somewhat simple, Rabelais adds that if the reader does find comic as well as sober substance within his book, he is not to be adversely transfixed by the author's apparent lightheartedness but ought, rather, to interpret in a higher sense whatever jests he may find. Though one cannot tell at this point just how tightly Rabelais's tongue is wedged in his cheek, the box metaphor does imply that the function of Rabelaisian comedy is both Socratic and therapeutic, both instructive and curative. (In his later prologues Rabelais, doctor of gaiety and scientist of mirth, insists chiefly on the therapeutic aspects of his comedy.)

Rabelais introduces his second metaphor with a provocatively irreverent thump on the reader's skull: "Didn't you ever do any bottle-opening? Son of a bitch! Then try to recall the countenance you had upon such occasion. Or have you never seen a dog falling upon a marrow bone?" (p. 49). The point of the latter question is that the dog sucks diligently on the bone in order to get at the marrow. Rabelais rousingly suggests that the dog's crunching of the bone corresponds ideally to the intelligent reader's careful perusal of his comic work: both will reach what the bone and the book ultimately supply —"substantific marrow" (p. 50). The organic metaphor of the bone is actually more germane to the assimilative act of reading than the mechanical metaphor of the box. Nevertheless, Rabelais is expectably (and bracingly) facetious in playing with the implications of this metaphor too. He declares that the substantific marrow of his book is crammed with Pythagorean symbols that will make the reader "prudent and valorous" by disclosing all sorts of "high sacraments and horrific mysteries" in the fields of religion, politics, and economics. But the next moment he scotches this assurance, or rather makes it ironically charlatanistic, by pointing out that his fellow artist, Homer, knew nothing of symbols and that his fine epics were spoiled by the allegorical interpretations of later, parasitical commentators. A confession immediately follows, in which Rabelais swings from overinflation to understatement: like Homer, he never gave a thought to abstruse considerations in writing his chronicles; in fact, he ate and drank his way through his literary compositions. What better time, he asks, than mealtime to treat of exalted matters and profound sciences? His book has not, he insists, been born of academic labor and midnight oil. No, his writings are the offspring of wine and festive fellowship. "For me," Rabelais asserts, "there is only honor and glory in being looked upon as a good fellow and a good companion; and in this name, I am welcome in any good company of Pantagruelists" (p. 50).

Pantagruelism, in this passage, suggests an ideal sanity of individual and collective good cheer capable of merrily expunging artificiality and frustration. Clearly, a Pantagruelistic gaiety of spirit accounts for much of Rabelais's whimsy in the Prologue; it accounts for his unbuttoned mockery of himself and his readers, for example, and for his spoofery of scholarship and profundity—and also for his jocoserious toying with dogs, bones, and substantific marrow. (If one focuses mainly on the Christian-Neoplatonic elements in Rabelais, one gets a different view: Pantagruelistic laughter becomes a pipeline to divine truth; food and wine become metaphors for inspiration provided by the Holy Spirit—and by the Muses; Bacchus becomes Christ; and the box and the marrow become the whole

Evangel.)[27] And the same Pantagruelistic spirit suggests that Rabelais's levity is as packed with marrow as his sobriety.

That Rabelaisian gaiety provides its own kind of nourishment is an insight which is at times mystifyingly passed over. Samuel Putnam, for example, quotes with approval Jean Plattard's opinion that Rabelais's " 'substantific marrow' is to be found . . . in those chapters in which Rabelais openly lays bare his ideas on education, war, monks, superstition, and the ideal of the free life."[28] One must admit that these chapters are finely illuminating, but Plattard's view (which incidentally is based on the metaphor of the box rather than on that of the bone) reduces Rabelaisian comedy to a kind of carrot, decoying the reader along antic paths that lead sooner or later to "serious" enlightenment. Rabelais's nutritive comedy hardly merits this disservice. The verve of a genius of farce, Baudelaire's essay suggests, leads to our revitalization. Surely this is substantific marrow enough. In any case, playful Pantagruelism is not mindless vivacity; it does not expel gravity in order to extend an invitation to imbecilic merriment. When Montaigne observes, in his essay "Of Solitude," that gaiety and health are the best parts of humanity,[29] he is not stipulating that intelligence should be sacrificed to ebullience. Similarly, the gay irresponsibility of Pantagruelism, despite its vinous interests, does not sacrifice mind to festive riot. Instead, it proffers both psychic liberation and intellectual enrichment.

---

[27] Florence M. Weinberg summarizes the interesting but restrictive argument for Rabelais's "Bacchic Christianity" in *The Wine and the Will* (Detroit: Wayne State University Press, 1972). See especially pp. 32–53. For a nicely balanced discussion of the demonic and angelic voices in Rabelais, see Thomas M. Greene, *Rabelais: A Study in Comic Courage* (Englewood Cliffs, N.J.: Prentice-Hall, 1970). Greene points out that Rabelais embraces the wild "lunacy that underlies our rational constructions" and that Panurge "is precisely the incarnation of the universal perversity in things" (p. 10). Yet there is also in Rabelais "an opposing intuition of moral and religious seriousness" (p. 11).

[28] Quoted in *The Portable Rabelais*, p. 216.

[29] Michel de Montaigne, "Of Solitude," in *The Complete Essays of Montaigne*, trans. Donald M. Frame (Garden City, N.Y.: Doubleday, Anchor, 1960), I, 250.

Curative comedy, which allows us to purge ourselves of sickly inhibitions, is generously on display in the early portion of Book First, in which Gargantua is exhibited as the unruly child par excellence. The little giant's extravaganzas, to be specific, are primarily fecal (or urinary), phallic, and nonsensical. First of all, Gargantua is possessed of formidable genital equipment. His six-feet-long codpiece is described as a succulent, verdant, flourishing cornucopia—a splendid warranty of interior treasures which become highly active between Gargantua's third and fifth year of life. In the following phallic rhapsody, one can see that Rabelais's fantasticality is distinctly more Freudian than Hoffmannesque:

Do you know what, my lads? I hope you drink so much you tumble over arse-backwards, if this little lecher wasn't always feeling his nurses, upside down, backside frontwards. Giddy-up, old girl! For he had already commenced to give his codpiece a little exercise; and each day, his nurses would adorn it with pretty bouquets, pretty ribbons, and pretty tassels; and they would spend their time making it come up between their hands, like a suppository; they would burst out laughing, when it began to prick up its little ears, as though this were the best joke in the world. One of them would call it my little spout, another my peg, another my coral-branch, another my stopper, my plug, my centerbit, my ramrod, my gimlet, my trinket, my rough-and-ready-stiff-and-steady, my prop, my little red sausage, my little booby-prize![30]

But though Gargantua's penis, cherubically inquisitive rather than criminally tumescent, is imaged here in a burst of playfulness, candor, and robust charm, elsewhere the ungovernable infant romps outrageously through the whole structure of adult tidiness and social taboos—and not least by way of performing excremental antics.

Scatological comedy is potentially a more powerful source of psychic release than sexual comedy, not merely because bowel control is anterior to, and more primitive than, genital restraint, but because fecal blunders are fouler (and therefore more objectionable) than genital nonconformities. At any rate,

[30] *The Portable Rabelais*, p. 80.

in exercising his natural functions rather indiscriminately, Gargantua gets wackily, incorrigibly enmired in filth. In fact, defecation, in contrast to phallic frolicking, almost proves his undoing—until his monumental evacuatory sloppiness leads to an unusual quasi-scientific revelation. At the end of his fifth year, literature's dirtiest child actually attempts exquisite anal grooming. In a new, revolutionary hygienic venture, he ingeniously tests varied rump wipers, using laboratory materials which must be unique in the history of the human posterior. For example:

> I wiped myself . . . with a kerchief, with a pillow, with a slipper, with a purse, with a basket—but, oh, what an unpleasant rump-wiper that was—and finally with a hat. . . . Then, I wiped myself with a hen, with a rooster, with a pullet, with a calf's skin, with a hare, with a pigeon, with a cormorant, with a lawyer's bag, with a chinband, with a hood, with a decoy bird. But in conclusion, I will state and maintain that there is no rump-wiper like a good downy goose, providing that you hold its head between your legs. And you may believe me, on my word of honor, that you will feel in your bunghole a miraculous pleasure. . . . And do not think that the beatitude of the heroes and demigods in the Elysian Fields comes from their asphodel or their ambrosia or their nectar. . . . In my humble opinion, it comes from the fact that they wipe their arses with the neck of a goose.   [pp. 89–90]

The boy's father, Grandgousier, detects in his son's efforts a brilliant pattern of scientific trial and error; and he has no religious or literary objection to Gargantua's definition of Elysian bliss as the beatitude of the behind.[31]

---

[31] Gargantua's scatological irreverence—for example, he insouciantly juxtaposes "mer Dé" (mother of God) with "merde" (shit) (p. 88)—is part of a popular and literary tradition of carnival release from the bonds of official and officious Christianity that Mikhail Bakhtin explores in *Rabelais and His World*, trans. Helene Iswolsky (Cambridge, Mass.: M.I.T. Press, 1968). Bakhtin declares that *Gargantua and Pantagruel* turns everything into gaiety and that it "is the most fearless book in world literature" (p. 39). The fearlessness is in the festiveness, in the laughter of replenishment, integration, and liberation that characterizes a saturnalian dedication to grotesque realism—that is, to the positive, chaotic appetites and joys of the body. Of particular interest in Bakhtin's argument is his overwhelming emphasis on the radical, democratizing,

Grandgousier is convinced that his son's anal adventures, smacking as they do of curiosity, enthusiasm, and daring, constitute a voyage into the unknown consummated by an invaluable discovery. But his son's excremental interests and powers become even more astonishing as the boy grows up. We discover that his urine (like wine, that dissolvent of psychic rigidity which Pantagruelists find indispensable for the happy glow of camaraderie) has innovative, liberalizing powers; for it not only washes away the barricades that hedge in the energies of the id but even engenders new myths—as when, after inundating curiosity-ridden Parisian ninnies with the vintage wine of his phallus, Gargantua is instrumental in bringing about the renaming of Paris. Hitherto called Lutetia (in honor of the white buttocks of its ladies), the city will henceforth bear a name that signifies the reaction of the urine-sodden citizens (survivors of the mass deluge) who found themselves "almost done for from laughing ('par rys')."[32]

Gargantua eventually derives from his remarkable humanistic education qualities of grace, perceptiveness, and temperate power that change the once snotty, rowdy infant into the most humane of philosopher-princes (though he has wonderful moments of regression). His character-transforming wisdom may be seen, for example, in his address to the vanquished side

---

utopian nature of medieval "folk humor." He considers Rabelais's vulgarities, which have assimilated such "folk humor," to be priceless, not only because they give expression to a re-creative hilarity, but because they symbolize a universal drive to liberate the human spirit from whatever terrifies it—including class privilege and religious dogma. Bakhtin uses the metaphor of "uncrowning" in this connection; and he applies it to both past and future. Thus the uncrowning utopianism of medieval laughter, he says, seeks "the return of happier times, abundance, and justice for all the people" (p. 99), much as the laughter of the Roman Saturnalia signifies a resumption of the Golden Age of Saturn. On the other hand, just as Marx sees comedy lighting up cultures in decline—Marx is cited as remarking that representatives of old authority and truth are "mere comedians of the world order whose real heroes have already died" (p. 213)—so Bakhtin views medieval festiveness as prospectively embodying "the people's hopes and strivings," and as ultimately expressing "the general gay funeral of a dying era" (p. 99).

[32] *The Portable Rabelais*, p. 155.

(the army of King Picrochole) in the cake peddlers' war; on this occasion he offers his father's enemies reasoned benevolence, not humiliating reminders of conqueror and conquered. He also makes certain that hostilities will not easily recommence, for he is aware that "a too spineless and relaxed complacency displayed in the pardoning of malefactors, does not but encourage the delinquents to commit mischief the more thoughtlessly the next time" (p. 193). (This speech is a perfect illustration of Rabelais's noncomic substantific marrow. It is not isolated, however; it has been preceded by a wildly comic substantific marrow consisting of dialogue that has registered an idiotic epidemic of Caesarism on the part of King Picrochole and his demented advisers. What Rabelais offers us, then, is a double-barreled assault on the madness of militarism.)

One of the saviors of Grandgousier's cause in the cake peddlers' war is Friar John Hackem, the ideal monk. Shortly before the end of the war, Grandgousier and Gargantua, together with the latter's comrades (Eudemon, Gymnastes, and Ponocrates) feast Friar John, whom they cherish on account of his utility, valor, and joviality. How could they do otherwise? Friar John is a living refutation of diseased, inert monkhood. Neither the conventional idea of sin nor the traditional concept of piety defiles his consciousness, which is the product of a joyous pagan-Christian love of life. His zany slaughter of a sizable part of Picrochole's army proves that he can release a marvelously healthy aggressiveness. And his sexual buoyancy, as well as his capacity for eating, drinking, and carousing, is equally energetic. Erotic improprieties run right through Friar John's lively, seemingly disjointed conversation. Thus a reference to his prominent nose elicits from him the explanation that his nurse had soft teats, so that his infant proboscis sank into buttery flesh when he suckled and hence could not help puffing out. "The hard teats of a nurse," on the other hand, "are responsible for pug-nosed children" (p. 183).

This brief history of his nose is followed, not erratically, by a blithely blasphemous reference to erection. Not that he needs to be blasphemous in recurring to this phenomenon. For example, at another merry moment during the feast, he asks a totally unanticipated question: "Wouldn't it be a funny death to die with an erection?" (p. 178). This playful query is appetitively associated with his next comment, which deals with the white meat of a capon. A moment later, his satisfaction with the hare's rump he is consuming prompts a not unrelated bit of speculation about why a young lady's thigh is always nice and cool. He offers three reasons (before calling for more wine and further festiveness): "*Primo*, because water trickles down it all the time; *secundo*, because it is a shady place, dark and obscure, where the sun never shines; and thirdly, because it is constantly fanned by all the breezes that blow through the northwind-hole, as well as by the shirt and, very frequently, by the old codpiece as well" (p. 178). Friar John is splendidly at home in the world of bawdry.

As a reward for his invaluable aid in the cake peddlers' war, Gargantua constructs for Friar John the abbey of Thelema, whose atmosphere presents a mixture of pagan vitality and Christianized refinement. Thelema is actually a seminary of pleasure, art, and sport for handsome, gifted, psychologically unhobbled young men and women. Especially significant is the fact that its utopian aspects provide what Rabelais's farce also supplies: release from pathological inhibitions. The abbey of Thelema offers this release, not through primitivism, but through humanism. The difference in modes is ultimately unimportant, for farcical liberation and utopian idealism turn out to be two sides of the same coin.

To ascribe total freedom to the Thelemites would nevertheless be misleading. The basic rule of the abbey, "Do What Thou Wouldst," contains a clear-cut emancipatory intent. Yet the narrator's assurance that the Thelemites' "whole life was spent, not in accordance with laws, statutes, or rules, but according to their own will and free judgment" (p. 214) is somewhat inaccurate. No individualistic projects, let alone private eccentricities, can bloom in the abbey of Thelema; its guiding spirit is so thoroughly marked by an exquisite conformity—

that of harmoniously grouped souls—that it is the very reverse of a budding anarchist's dream.

In any case, the abbey's young, beautiful, gay inhabitants can be counted on not to be disruptive, because "those who are free born and well born, well brought up, and used to decent society possess, by nature, a certain instinct and spur, which always impels them to virtuous deeds and restrains them from vice, an instinct which is the thing called honor" (p. 214). Imbued as they are with the sublime restraints of honor, and knowing nothing whatever of privation or tyranny at the abbey, the Thelemites can hardly be envisaged as having a taste for insurrection—or even for idiosyncrasy. Their activities, their games, their very clothing, depend on unanimity, which is described as "laudable emulation" (in reality, the young men gallantly defer to feminine inclinations). Their perfection of taste and education, furthermore, prohibits them from seeking even intermittently the pleasures of vulgarity. And whatever amorousness they develop never yields to clandestine affairs. Departure from the abbey does, however, lead to the privacies —and endless marvels, it would seem—of marriage.

Though Rabelais's model Abbey casts off repression elegantly, whereas his farce destroys repression primitively, the two movements have unequal thrusts. In general, farcical unrestraint in *Gargantua and Pantagruel* far outweighs fantasies of the ideal. In Book Second and Book Third, for example, the spirit of buffoonery is overwhelming. It is embodied especially in Panurge, the scapegrace friend of Pantagruel, Gargantua's son. Pantagruel, inspired by his father to eat fully of the heavenly manna of fine learning (but never at the cost of divorcing science from conscience), meets Panurge while studying in Paris. Because Panurge seems to be interestingly down on his luck, Pantagruel repeatedly, though unsuccessfully, interrogates him about his condition. To Pantagruel's questions, Panurge responds in a dazzling flurry of diverse languages (three of which are his own nonsense creations). This linguistic proclivity seems at first to betoken only a demented brilliance; but the common denominator of all his speeches is actually an urgent request that his hunger be satisfied, a request which Panurge finally clarifies in agreeable, coherent French. This extended specimen of Panurge's ingenious sportiveness is perfectly characteristic of the true clown: buffoonery comes first, even before need.

We quickly become acquainted with other aspects of Panurge's elastic imagination as he recounts a grotesquely preposterous tale of how he escaped being roasted to death by the fiendish Turks. And we soon realize that this phoenix-buffoon can hardly be described simply as a jolly knave or a fun-loving trickster, for such terms merely prettify him. The truth is that he betrays, especially in Book Second, a harrowingly larcenous imagination. His brain is a hive of plans for scandalous misdeeds—irreverent, scabrous, scatological, and anarchic shenanigans. But where Arlecchino, in *The Three Cuckolds*, is ready to sacrifice sex and food for the greater glory of antic trickery, Panurge, while still honoring prankishness as the master motive of his life, also insists on a glut of satisfactions for his other major appetites. He parades his sexual urges, for example. This is not surprising, for he has a codpiece apparently three feet square—a codpiece which he wields with the vigor of a whirling dervish. Also, he is clearly magnetized by feasts and banquets, at which he sits equipped with a bottomless stomach.

At the age of thirty-five, Panurge is a supreme incarnation of adolescent japery. When he is in the mood for finesse, however, he can assume an extraordinarily civil and debonair spirit. In fact, for someone whose forte is excruciatingly bad manners (the region of the id is his natural habitat, and the dislocation of manners and morals is his favorite activity), this ability to feign an exquisite sensibility is not the least fetching of his qualities. Consider Panurge's reaction to the great (but not greatly pure) Parisian lady to whom he presumptuously and insistently proposes fornication. The lady rejects his vulgar advances and warns him that his outrageous idiocy merits the amputation of his arms and legs. Panurge faces this threat bluntly and buoyantly: "Well," he remarks, "it would be all the same to me to have my arms and legs cut off, provided you and I had a bout of fun together, at the up-and-down game. For," he goes on, showing his long codpiece, "here's Master John Thursday, who will play you a jig that you'll feel in the very marrow of your bones. He's a sprightly fellow, and he is so good at finding all the cracks and quirks and special spots in the carnal trap that after him there is no need of a broom." Since this phallic braggadocio proves most unwelcome, Panurge decides to con the lady with the language of poetic love: "Your beauty is so transcendent," he softly tells her, ". . . so singular, and so celestial that I believe Nature has made you for her paragon, so that we may understand how much she can do if she chooses to employ her full powers and her entire wisdom."[33] And so on. But he gets absolutely nowhere.

The next day, as he kneels next to her at Mass, he impatiently reduces his poetic Petrarchizing (one of whose motifs is the alternating fever and chills of lovesickness) to plain prose: "Madam," he informs her, "I must tell you that I am so amorous of you that I can neither piss nor shit for love" (p. 240). Because the lady refuses to envelop him at once in her arms in order to ease him of his amorous constipation, another ploy, involving bribery and deceit, becomes necessary. Jingling a heap of false coins in his purse, Panurge offers to supply the lady with whatever precious stones or expensive materials she fancies, provided she returns his love. He attempts to clinch the bargain by pointing once more to his outsized codpiece: "Here's Master John Owl, who wants a nest" (p. 242). John Owl is again rejected; and Panurge plans revenge. The trick he plays on the lady is superlatively scurvy. He cuts up a bitch's genitals into tiny pieces (a natural prankster is inevitably and often unthinkingly cruel) and sprinkles them over the lady's gown while she is waiting in church to take part in the Corpus Christi procession. The consequence of this gay nastiness is a massive invasion of dogs: "Small and great, big and little, all came, lifting their legs, smelling her

[33] *The Histories of Gargantua and Pantagruel*, trans. J. M. Cohen (Baltimore: Penguin, 1955), p. 240.

and pissing all over her. It was the most dreadful thing in the world" (p. 243).

Panurge's malice is obviously in atrocious taste. The cruel murder and mincing of the bitch, the monstrous persecution and degradation of the lady (who is no saint; she would have yielded to a subtly corrupt millionaire) are unpardonable phenomena. Panurge's insolent, disproportionate, fatuous vindictiveness, provoking as it does a colossal quantity of nauseating canine urine, would even appear to extinguish the pleasures of farce. But this would be the case only if we inappropriately humanized the atmosphere of grotesque revelry in which Panurge engages in his annihilatory sport. Since he is presented to us as the stagemaster of droll, often revengeful games whose props and hurts are too fantastic to be assessed on a scale of normality, any effort to examine Panurge through the lens of realism, sentimentalism, or moral responsibility would simply dehydrate his clownery and make it subject to punitive action. Interestingly, no one in Rabelais's story who views the harassed lady is ethically outraged or even aesthetically disgusted by the dirty deal engineered by Panurge. Pantagruel himself, invited by his clown-comrade to see the most beautiful woman in Paris fend off a horde of dogs attempting to copulate with her, gladly accepts the invitation and, after getting an eyeful, finds the show both excellent and original. Other people who watch the spectacle admire the high-leaping dogs instead of commiserating with the shamed, discomfited lady.

Rabelais's last words on the subject of the Parisian lady's horridly embarrassing experience not only reinforce the innocence of the onlookers' gaiety but transform an apparently merciless bit of devilry into a productive phenomenon: "Once she was inside and the door closed behind her, all the dogs ran up from two miles around, and pissed so hard against the gate of the house, that they made a stream with their urine big enough for the ducks to swim in. And it is this stream which now passes by Saint Victor, in which Madame Gobelin dyes her scarlet, thanks to the specific virtue of those piss-hounds"

(p. 244). This positive outcome is the kind of thing Mikhail Bakhtin emphasizes in his study of Rabelais's carnival imagery: the bodily element of degradation (feces or urine) in popular-festive laughter, Bakhtin claims in *Rabelais and His World*, is also a procreative, regenerative force.[34] (Which does not mean that Rabelais's excremental episodes are not primarily the material for riotously debasing fun.)

Panurge's unbridled penis, like his unabashed brain (they are twin tributaries of his folly), is similarly regenerative as well as destructive. If its disintegrative effect seems of prime importance, that is because Panurge's vitality in Book Second is absolutely shattering. In Rabelais's extended summary of Panurge's past follies and glories, what shines out above all is the impulse to destroy decorum and devastate authority. Panurge continually feeds this impulse by contriving astonishingly wanton jokes.

But this diabolically sophomoric prankster also reveals an impressive catholicity of interests and talents. Thus he can range from carminative melodies to practical advice on the art of fortification. Uncle Toby would hardly approve of Panurge's reflections on the latter subject. Borrowing from the wisdom of Greece, Pantagruel suggests that a city's best defense is the virtue of its (male) inhabitants. Panurge's plan of defense, however, would depend on a reversal of antiquity's insights: he believes that the genitals of unvirtuous women (that is, women in general) can provide a substance for rebuilding the walls of Paris that would be cheaper than stone—and stronger, especially when reinforced with monastic phalluses; for the women's syphilis would weaken even cannon balls, while the men's consecrated penises would resist even lightning.

Building materials such as these bespeak a fantastically low degree of chivalry in Panurge.[35] Yet he cannot be pinned down

[34] *Rabelais and His World*, pp. 23–31.

[35] Bakhtin claims that "the cheapness of Paris women is merely a secondary theme, and . . . even here there is no moral condemnation. The leading theme is fecundity, as the greatest and safest array of strength" (*Rabelais and His World*, p. 313). Not even the women's dissolvent syphilis budges Bakhtin from his ruling theme of regeneration, for syphilis is "the merry disease" (p. 330).

simply as an uncouth antifeminist. The disgusting hags he makes sport of in his fable of the humane lion (a creature unversed in human female anatomy) who summons a fox to keep the flies off a gaping "wound" between an old woman's legs are the very creatures he charitably, even gallantly (in a left-handed way), rescued at an earlier moment of his life when he was preoccupied with spending money far more ingeniously and compulsively than he acquired it. In fact, he relates how he once exhausted half his fortune in arranging marriages for the purpose of restoring sensual salvation to toothless, ugly, superannuated women; but the mirthmaker-trickster in Panurge must also have been active in this salvaging operation, which doubtless provided a burlesque view of scarecrow females pitching convulsively into sex for the last time.

Panurge is so intimately acquainted with female lapses from virtue that his intellectual odyssey in Book Third, organized for the purpose of research into the question of cuckoldry (can it be avoided, or is it inevitable?), seems at first glance to involve a foregone conclusion. Panurge's personality in Book Third is flexible enough, however, not only to accommodate almost any new experience or idea, but to complicate and enhance old ones enthusiastically. This flexibility may be disconcerting, but roguery and buffoonery (which naturally batten on variousness) make Panurge's character sufficiently consistent.[36] In Book Third, it must be admitted, the roguery is often subdued, and the buffoonery is considerably mentalized.

What specifically stirs up a host of variations on the endless theme of marriage and cuckoldry in Book Third is Panurge's aberrant angling for tranquility and safety. He has cast off his militaristic breeches, including his codpiece, his "holy anchor, his last resort in all the shipwrecks of adversity,"[37] and has adopted the toga of peace—of civic and financial

[36] W. M. Frohock, in "Panurge as Comic Character," *Yale French Studies*, 33 (Summer 1959), says that Panurge's consistency lies solely in his inheritance of stage-farce slapstick and sophistry: "The various mutations, from Villonesque trickster to quailing coward, would represent nothing that had not been represented on the comic stage" (p. 77).

[37] *The Histories of Gargantua and Pantagruel*, p. 306.

responsibility. Fortunately, there is nothing normal or respectable about the way he translates a horde of signals prophesying conjugal doom. The specimens of cuckoldry lore that are conveyed to Panurge are, in any case, so often dispensed by queer ducks that Rabelais's farce in Book Third is frequently balanced between the recommendations of cracked consultants and Panurge's clownish commentaries on them. Consider, to take a single example, the benighted Herr Trippa, an extraordinary occultist who offers to prove in a thousand prophetical ways— by pyromancy, hydromancy, ichthyomancy, and so on and so forth—the ineluctable threat of cuckoldry (as well as beatings, the pox, and robbery) that will await Panurge (but that has not, presumably, affected wise men like himself) if he gets married. None of this is awe-inspiring to Panurge, for he has inside information about Herr Trippa's own marital affairs: "I do know," Panurge reveals, "that while he was talking to the great king one day about celestial and transcendental matters, the Court lacqueys were screwing his wife to their heart's content" (p. 356). The kind of farcical combination presented by Herr Trippa's idiocy and Panurge's scabrously irreverent talk is what makes the marriage survey in Book Third the successful circus it is.

It is not always a circus, however, for Panurge is often thrust into a context which requires of him numerous considerations of moral maturity and matrimonial obligation. What develops is a strange equipoise: Panurge's free-wheeling, antic spirit is very much alive, but it is balanced by an interest, encyclopedically developed, in a cluster of stabilizing values associated with marriage—especially reason, "honor," and self-preservation. At times, the farce in Book Third is almost perfectly counterbalanced by responsible sensibility and rational argumentation. When, for example, early in Book Third, Panurge's decision to seek a lawful relationship is accompanied by a declaration about the value of marital and filial love and legitimacy (p. 312), his words would appear to presage the funeral of a clown. Yet as Book Third evolves, Panurge's playfulness remains irrepressible, since the marriage question gives him many opportunities to make fun of that faulty paradise while often assuming its defense.

At key points that defense simply crumbles. Panurge's comic spirit is especially detrimental to marriage when it acts as the correlative of his penile exuberance. For, in spite of his paeans to sex within marriage, the magic of his penis has tremendous antimarital and extramarital implications. Note how, in the very middle of his quest, he reaffirms his faith in his indefatigable member: "I beg you to believe—and it's the cold sober truth," he assures Friar John, "that my pioneer of nature, the sacred Ithyphallus, Mister Thingumajig of Tiddly-push is the 'primo del mondo.'" This detail is rather interesting to Friar John, whose lighthearted religiosity involves continual exercise of his own John-Thomas. Friar John, indeed, believes that one of the great commandments is that a man shall not be caught with full ballocks on the Judgment Day. If this preoccupation seems to involve too testicular a mode of preparing to meet one's maker, consider the incident in which the power of Christ himself yields instantly to Panurge's pagan phallus: "Once when I came into the spectators' enclosure, as they were acting the passion-play at Saint-Maixent, I suddenly saw everyone, players and audience alike, overcome by [my penis'] occult properties. They were seized with such a terrific temptation that there wasn't an angel or a man, or a devil, male or female, that didn't want to play the two-backed beast" (p. 364). And in fact everyone, from St. Michael to Lucifer, made ready to do so. When the holiest of Christian suasions can disintegrate so quickly in Panurge's phallic presence, it is not likely that the lesser sanctity of matrimony will prove more resistant. In any event, one can hardly imagine Panurge, however bacchically he may one day exult in the idea of marriage, inviting the absurd catastrophe of horns and thus becoming the perfect butt of farce instead of its exemplary practitioner.

There are other Fools in Book Third; but Panurge's special anarchic charm is not to be found among them. There is, for example, the well-known Fool Triboulet, who is supposed to have prophetic powers by virtue of his natural madness. It is Pantagruel who presents the argument for Triboulet's kind of fatidic endowment: the man ordinarily reputed to be wise— the shrewd materialist—is likely to be a fool in the perspective of the gods, whereas his opposite number—the man usually cited as a fool—is apt to be prized by the gods and hence to receive divine inspiration. The same argument, in Christian thinking, focuses on the Fool of God, or the Fool in Christ— that holy, hilarious, natural innocent whose mind, though darkened with respect to secular circumstances, is peculiarly accessible to the word and love of God.

Actually the most interesting case Pantagruel cites in emphasizing a saintly Fool's brand of wisdom (which puts mere intelligence to shame) deals, not with Triboulet, but with Seigny John, a famous Fool of Paris. But Pantagruel's story about him has, in fact, nothing to do with divination; it has, rather, a lot to do with the uncannily fine, witty judgment of a professional Fool. It happened once that "a porter was standing in front of a roast-meat stall eating his bread in the steam from the meat, and finding it, thus flavoured, very tasty. The cook let this pass, but finally, after the porter had gobbled his last crust, he seized him by the collar and demanded payment for the steam from his roast. The porter answered that he had done no damage to his meat, had taken nothing of his, and was not his debtor in any way. The steam in question was escaping outside, and so, in any case, was being lost. No one in Paris had ever heard of the smoke from a roast being sold in the streets" (p. 391). The quarrel was prevented from becoming bloody only because the two disputants agreed to accept Seigny John's verdict as to who was in the right. Seigny John prepared his adjudication by ordering the porter to give him a piece of silver, whose authenticity he then tested in various ways—to the despair of the porter and the satisfaction of the cook. After making the coin ring several times, Seigny John announced his decision: "The court declares that the porter who ate his bread in the steam of a roast has civilly paid the cook with the chink of his money" (p. 392). A truly Solomonic judgment.

Triboulet has no chance to render an admirably equitable decision of this sort. He is not, after all, asked to settle an altercation but to deliver himself of the truth (which turns out to be ugly) regarding cuckoldry. But it would be difficult, in any case, to conceive of Triboulet as a wise arbiter, for this natural Fool is much queerer than the professional Fool, Seigny John. Of course oddity is Triboulet's badge of divine merit. But in warning Panurge about cuckoldry, Triboulet exhibits antics that are particularly baffling in their infantilism. The recalcitrant Fool within Panurge himself is infinitely more captivating.

Panurge admits that he, like everyone, is foolish: "[I do not wish] shamelessly to exempt myself from allegiance to the realm of folly. I am its vassal, and I belong to it; that I confess. . . . All are fools. . . . And I should be a raging fool if, being a fool, I did not consider myself one" (pp. 414–415). This declaration, Walter Kaiser remarks in *Praisers of Folly*—an illuminating study of Erasmus' Stultitia, Rabelais's Panurge (as presented solely in Book Third), and Shakespeare's Falstaff—is "too easy a way out. . . . He has not reformed, he has not been humbled, he has not accepted his own ignorance, he has not deferred to the will of God: he remains the silly fool he always was."[38] Panurge may be an irresistible, lovable, joyous, and relatively wise optimist, Kaiser remarks (not quite consistently), but his refusal to accept transcendent folly causes the collapse of his best qualities and brings about a regression from an incomplete to a hopeless foolishness (p. 178).

Kaiser offers his critique without any admixture of details from Book Second, which he considers superfluous to his analysis. His description of Panurge's antics in Book Second is in fact confined to a solitary phrase, "roguish amusement." And his account of Panurge's development between Book Second and Book Third is restricted to the unsatisfying observation that since experience has brought about changes, Panurge abandons "the wit of the rogue for the ignorance of the fool" (p. 105). But experience is not all-powerful in the life of a

---

[38] Walter Kaiser, *Praisers of Folly* (Cambridge, Mass.: Harvard University Press, 1963), p. 176.

buffoon; moreover, what Panurge abandons is the mayhem of
the rogue, not his wit. He is still a brilliantly subversive jester;
but in Book Third he has become a much less freakish clown.

In any case, one would hardly know from Kaiser's description that Panurge remains a powerhouse of farce in Book
Third, even though his mad buffoonery is now more verbal
than kinetic. Kaiser neglects this continuing aspect of Panurge's
personality because he chooses to concentrate on Panurge's presumptive spiritual failure to bridge the gap between wise and
foolish folly. (Thus Panurge's scabrous demolition of Herr
Trippa—it is a small farcical glory, one among many in Book
Third—never surfaces in Kaiser's scholarly drawing of paral-
lels between Rabelais's magician and the historical Cornelius
Agrippa.) It must be affirmed, however, that the center of
levity in Panurge, despite the anxieties he gives voice to as the
idea of marriage becomes increasingly negative, continues to
be situated in nihilistic gaiety. And there is a tremendous
amount of comic material in Book Third to stimulate that
gaiety. With much justification, Kaiser sees the search for
truth (which he makes a salvational issue) as the basic theme
of Book Third. But the highly important subjects of marriage,
cuckoldry, and prophecy, all of which are riddled with farce
(though they are also treated intermittently with perfect "seriousness"), do not, as a result, receive their autonomous comic
due.

The truth about Panurge is that he belongs as little on the
threshold of transcendent folly as he belongs, say, in one of
Céline's nausea-crammed nightmare farces. That is why there
is no point in harping on Panurge's failure to resemble Triboulet, or Pantagruel, or even Bridoye. Kaiser considers the irrational Bridoye (the dice-throwing judge in Book Third) to
be a wise Fool because his decision-rendering dice are touched
by the wisdom of God. He holds witless Triboulet to be a wise
Fool because God's grace permeates his inarticulateness. And
he calls the learned Pantagruel (less convincingly) a wise Fool
because he too can be a simple child of God. Panurge, on the
other hand, is condemned by Kaiser as a foolish fool—a failed

Socrates and a delinquent brother of Erasmus' Stultitia, "whose message was summed up in her portrait of the Fool in Christ" (p. 148).

But if one expects Panurge to become a Fool in Christ, one might as well ask the same of the blithely shameless Arlecchino in *The Three Cuckolds* or of the Pierrot whose hurricane buffoonery so reinvigorated Baudelaire. All three are farceurs, reckless clowns, impudent buffoons whose secular antics, both verbal and physical, may be hazily related to Divine Foolery by a common irrationality, but whose drastic irresponsibility essentially demolishes the sacred and the taboo.

The fascination of a possible bond between the clown and the divine spirit is admittedly hard to resist. Even in Enid Welsford's unsurpassed study, *The Fool: His Social and Literary History*, the spiritual freedom of the Fool is ultimately made out to be an analogue of heavenly emancipation, for the Fool is held to deliver us from the imprisoning facts of earth.[39] Penultimately, and even more provocatively, Welsford sees the irrational freedom of the Fool as the key to the very meaning of comedy. The Fool, she remarks in her final chapter, "is a great untrusser of our slaveries, and comedy is the expression of the spirit of the Fool."[40] We may recall that Erich Segal, in his study of Plautus, defined comedy as a release from the burden of morality and mortality, and that in order to do so,

[39] Thomas Mann's Felix Krull might seem, initially, to support Welsford's hypothesis. Watching incredible circus clowns at work, he senses that they are not quite part of humanity. "Are these ageless, half-grown sons of absurdity . . . human at all?" he wonders. "No, they are not," he concludes; "they are exceptions, side-splitting monsters of preposterousness, glittering, world-renouncing monks of unreason, cavorting hybrids, part human and part insane art" (*Confessions of Felix Krull, Confidence Man* [New York: Vintage, 1969], p. 185). But Felix Krull's intuition is more aesthetic than religious. The clowns he observes are unique artists, not harbingers of heaven. Kierkegaard, incidentally, gives irony and humor (rather than farce) important roles to play in man's advance toward faith. See his *Concluding Unscientific Postscript*, trans. David F. Swenson and Walter Lowrie (Princeton, N.J.: Princeton University Press, 1944), p. 448.
[40] Enid Welsford, *The Fool: His Social and Literary History* (Garden City, N.Y.: Doubleday, Anchor, 1961), p. 324.

he was obliged to downgrade Meredith's emphasis on thoughtful laughter. But Welsford's view of Meredith is even harsher. She terms the Comic Spirit a Momus-Grundy, all too ready to censor aberrant specimens of humanity back into the fold of social conformity (p. 324).

Yet one must not enthrone irrationality at the heart of comedy, even after scrutinizing at length the vital role played by non-Meredithian impulses in the literature of lightness. For comedy is a composite construction. It may serve, for example, as a proving ground for the testing and clarification of ideas and forms of conduct. Such clarification is the achievement of satire, which vindicates the mind's capacity to defeat misapprehension and delusion. But comedy may also function as a sanctuary where the rigors of reality yield to, or where the joys of life fulfill, the illogical requirements of the heart. In this sanctuary, humor thrives. Again, comedy may serve as a tower of irony, from which life is safely envisioned as irremediably absurd, not corrigibly ridiculous (as in satire) or healingly resourceful (as in humor). Finally, comedy may function as a disorderly arena in which restraint, rationalism, and responsibility are swept aside by the anarchic winds of farce.

In short, neither acute rationality nor renegade irrationality is king in comedy. Nevertheless, the variousness of comic impulses is in greater danger of being constricted by those who speak for the mind of comedy than by those who celebrate comedy's liberation from mind. That is because critics like Enid Welsford are in the minority, whereas critics like James K. Feibleman, whose book, *In Praise of Comedy*, overintellectualizes comedy, are still in the majority. According to Feibleman, comedy is an affirmative, revolutionary art which assaults the limitations of actuality because they are not in accord with an ideal logical order. In other words, comedy is fundamentally an agent of historical progress. "The business of comedy," says Feibleman, "is to dramatize and thus make more vivid the fact that contradictions in actuality must prove insupportable. It thus admonishes against the easy acceptance of interim limitations and calls for the persistent advance toward the logical order and the final elimination of limitations."[41]

This restatement of the familiar idea that comedy thrives on the mocking detection of error, especially in the form of social inadequacy, confines comedy to a unilinear, crusading program. But Feibleman is aware that comedy cannot, in fact, be exclusively critical. What comedy "is not strong enough to replace," he admits, "it renders endurable" (p. 9). A sense of humor therefore also plays a role in comedy. But indulgent humor, which he discusses rather briefly, is not considered by Feibleman to be high comedy; it is not on a par with the significantly comic—with satire's corrective transmission of ideas and values (like Bergson, Meredith, Buchanan, and a host of other theorists, Feibleman extols satire above all, without actually spelling out the term). Humor, he claims, is essentially a psychological concession to the insuperable, a way of being "reconciled to defeat" (p. 189). It is not, therefore, in the vanguard of comic energies.

Satire, whose slogan is "Attack," is in that vanguard, thrusting upon actuality its aggressively ameliorative force. On the other hand, according to Feibleman, humor, whose motto is "Accept," merely fills up the slack when the spirit of reform is compelled to weaken. Feibleman never complains that humor is an insult to comedy's intellectual urgencies; at times, he even seems to suggest, though never quite lucidly, that humorous acceptance is somehow indistinguishable from satire's triumph over obstacles. Still, humor emerges mainly as a potentially dangerous sympathy for present or past (more or less retrograde) realities. Farce does not emerge at all as an independent entity, for Feibleman does not accept as valid the possibility that gaiety in comedy (true comedy) may be recklessly anti-reformatory.

The present work is concerned, not with comedy's ability to function as an eradicator of error, but with its ability to utilize and even glorify irrational freedom. I have stressed, not satire,

[41] James K. Feibleman, *In Praise of Comedy: A Study in Its Theory and Practice* (New York: Horizon, 1970), p. 178.

but farce, which like satire sabotages limitations, but not in the service of a logical ideal. The victories of farce do not honor the accomplishments of human reason; instead, they register vital revolts against reason's heavily regulative hand—and against all other onerous requirements of civilization.

For those who view comedy chiefly as an adjunct of critical insight or rational progress, farce will doubtless always signify low aspirations. Even defenders of farce are often reluctant to claim that it is an art form which rightly disrupts civilized dignity, responsibility, and guilt. For example, in a page or two of *The Summing Up*, Somerset Maugham, inspired not only by his practical experience in the theatre but also by an Erasmian awareness of the priceless seasoning with which folly enriches life, deprecates the relegation of farce to comedy's cellar. Unfortunately, he salvages farce only by defining it as indispensable intestinal entertainment. After classifying comedy as an artificial thing, incapable of representing life as the "tragic business"[42] it really is, Maugham makes a distinction between two kinds of comic escape from life's tragedy: "pure comedy" and "farce." Pure comedy makes its appeal to the "collective mind" of the audience. But since the collective mind cannot endure three acts of intellectual amusement without fatigue, farce must be called upon for relief. This it can provide because farce "appeals to a more robust organ," the "collective belly." And the laughter of the collective belly can always be counted on to dispel cerebral tension whenever comic purity threatens to become enervating.

Maugham further avows that farce is a true embodiment of comic vigor. "The great writers of comedy, Shakespeare, Molière, and Bernard Shaw, have never," he declares, "jibbed at the farcical. It is the lifeblood that makes the body of comedy viable" (p. 145). Without the blood nourishment of farce, the body of comedy falls lifeless. But what happens now to

[42] Somerset Maugham, *The Summing Up* (New York: Doubleday, 1938), p. 144.

Maugham's earlier aphorism indicating that farce focuses on the belly, while pure comedy concerns the mind? Is farce belly or blood? Is it the alleviation of mentality or the very flow of life? Since the belly-mind metaphor receives somewhat more of his attention, we must conclude that Maugham has succeeded only minimally in undermining the long-standing hackneyed contrast between low comedy (the visceral vulgarity of farce) and high comedy (the refinement of mental gaiety).

Maugham's most interesting point is nevertheless valid: the great comic writers often take naturally to the spirit of Harlequin, though their adaptations of the art of the clown vary considerably, as we have seen. Thus the three geniuses of comedy Maugham refers to—Shakespeare, Molière, and Shaw—may be prone to buffoonery, but they hardly dance the same antic hay. Shaw, for example, enlists the Fool principally as an aide-de-camp to a witty critic; the result is that symptoms of clowning in the Shavian canon testify mainly to intellectual vivacity. But even Molière, who of the three comic writers best fulfills the farceur's aim of jettisoning all forms of ulcerating restraint, customarily yokes the wild Fool of farce to a laughing legislator chastising a ludicrous world. In Molière's case, it is clear, farce and satire are born companions. And why not? They have extraordinary affinities for each other.

Yet we can easily discriminate between them. Consider a scene from one of Molière's early comedies, *The Flying Doctor.* In this play Gorgibus, a bourgeois father, respectable but brainless, is intent on arranging a marriage (all profit, no love) for his daughter Lucile, who finds the idea of such a marriage hateful. Lucile and Valère, the young lovers of the piece, hoodwink the father, then solicit Gorgibus' blessing once they are married. The fellow chiefly responsible for the success of the lovers' tactics is Sganarelle, Valère's valet, who is also a rascal and a clown.

The action of the comedy consists mainly of Sganarelle's busy antics as doctor, double, and acrobat. His first role, that of doctor, emerges from the stratagem plotted by Gorgibus' daughter and her cousin Sabine: Lucile will pretend to be ill, a phony doctor will recommend fresh air, and Gorgibus will open up his garden pavilion for his daughter, thus unwittingly setting the scene for an elopement. Sganarelle, who is supposed by his master to be thick-headed, and who is himself initially doubtful about his talent as a trickster on so professional a level, loses all hesitation about playing the medico as he pockets Valère's inducement (one hundred francs) to do so. Buoyed up by prosperity, Sganarelle presents himself as a miracle-working physician to Gorgibus. "In my opinion," he authoritatively observes, "all others are quacks. I have peculiar talents. I have secrets. Salamalec and shalom aleichem. Nil nisi bonus? Si, Signor. Nein, mein Herr. Para siempre."[43] The proof of his superiority having been internationally established, he is ready for urine analysis. Sganarelle is handed a beaker full of Lucile's urine, and he drinks it down!

Gorgibus (gaping).   You swallowed it?
Sganarelle.   Not immediately. I let it wash about in my mouth first. An ordinary doctor would merely look at it, but I am extraordinary. As the liquid touches my taste buds, I can tell both the cause of the illness and its probable development. But this was a meagre specimen. I need another bladderful.
Sabine.   She had enough trouble getting that much out.
Sganarelle.   I never heard of such reluctance. Tell her she must urinate freely, copiously. As much as she can manage.
Sabine.   I'll try.   [p. 34]

The urine is actually white wine; but the audience knows this, not Sganarelle. The latter is clearly incompetent to judge the difference between the taste of wine and the savor of the effluence of a maidenly bladder. Licking his beaker, Sganarelle actually says in an aside, "If every invalid pissed like this I'd stay a doctor for the rest of my life" (p. 35). Satire against inept physicians? Without a doubt. But the satire is virtually drowned in what is perhaps Molière's most delightfully dis-

---

[43] *The Flying Doctor*, in *One-Act Comedies of Molière*, trans. Albert Bermel (New York: World, 1964), p. 32.

inhibitory dose of scatological zaniness. How can we help relishing farce if its practitioners annihilate standard behavior and conventional attitudes with this kind of irreverent verve? And how can we help absorbing the irrationality of farce as a life-saving carnival of folly?

Index

239

COMEDY

Designed by R. E. Rosenbaum.
Composed by Kingsport Press, Inc.,
in 10 point linotype Monticello, 2 points leaded,
with display lines in monotype Bell.
Printed letterpress from type by Kingsport Press
on Warren's 1854 Text, 60 lb. basis
with the Cornell University Press watermark.
Bound by Kingsport Press
in Holliston Book Cloth
and stamped in All Purpose foil.